D1244587

Investing in Protection

Since the early 1990s the world has seen an explosion of preferential trade agreements (PTAs) between North and South. Mark Manger argues that current North–South PTAs are not primarily about liberalizing exports as is usually assumed. Rather, they are driven by the needs of foreign direct investment. The interests of multinational firms in investing in developing countries converge with the desires of the host countries to attract foreign capital. Yet to be politically feasible in the developed country, North–South PTAs must discriminate against third countries. PTAs thus create a competitive dynamic between countries, as excluded firms lobby their governments to restore access to important investment locations, leading to yet more preferential agreements. Based on extensive research in Europe, Japan, and the Americas and interviews with decision-makers in governments and the private sector, this book offers a new perspective on the roles of the state and corporations in international trade.

MARK S. MANGER is Lecturer in the Department of International Relations at the London School of Economics. His work has been published in the *Review of International Political Economy* and *World Development*.

Investing in Protection

The Politics of Preferential Trade Agreements
between North and South

MARK S. MANGER

CAMBRIDGE
UNIVERSITY PRESS

CAMBRIDGE UNIVERSITY PRESS
Cambridge, New York, Melbourne, Madrid, Cape Town, Singapore, São Paulo, Delhi

Cambridge University Press
The Edinburgh Building, Cambridge CB2 8RU, UK

Published in the United States of America by Cambridge University Press, New York

www.cambridge.org
Information on this title: www.cambridge.org/9780521748704

First published 2009

Printed in the United Kingdom at the University Press, Cambridge

A catalogue record for this publication is available from the British Library

ISBN 978-0-521-76504-6 hardback
ISBN 978-0-521-74870-4 paperback

Contents

Figures

Tables

Acknowledgments

In the course of writing this book I have incurred numerous debts to colleagues, friends, and family in many countries. First and foremost, I owe profound thanks to Max Cameron, whose scholarship, breadth of intellectual interests, passion for his work, and, most importantly, personal integrity has made him a role model for me. Max nurtured this project from the very beginning and has been a true mentor through the years. Yves Tiberghien has been an inspiration for me as a student of political economy in a multitude of ways. His vast knowledge of Japan and his unwavering support have been crucial for this project. He opened many doors to me, and has never hesitated to offer help and guidance. Without these two individuals, I would not be where I am now, professionally and personally. Werner Antweiler's insights and encouragement were crucial in shaping my economic thinking and reworking of several key arguments. He also never hesitated to answer my questions on econometric matters, no matter how inane they were. Much of the quantitative work related to this book I could only pursue thanks to him. Mark Zacher has always been a guide in professional matters, and convinced me to persist in my endeavors when I was about to quit.

Brian Job and Paul Evans were decisive in bringing me to the University of British Columbia in the first place, and have helped in many ways (some of which they may not even be aware of). Angela O'Mahony and Ben Nyblade whipped my job talk into shape when I went on the market, and offered crucial advice in other instances. At the UBC political science department I would like to thank Fred Cutler, Kathy Harrison, Diane Mauzy, Lisa Sundstrom, Richard Price, Don Blake, John Wood, Alan Jacobs and Antje Ellerman, Kal Holsti, Barbara Arneil, Laura Janara, Phil Resnick, Ken Carty, Peter Dauvergne, Petula Müller, Dory Urbano, and Josephine Calazan (quite possibly the most efficient administrative team I have ever experienced in any institution), and crucially, Richard Johnston, whose stewardship fundamentally transformed my experience, and who is never short of words to promote us UBC graduates. Julian Dierkes provided much encouragement and, together with David Edgington, secured a quiet place to work at the Centre for Japanese Research that allowed much more productive writing. I would also like to thank my office mates Yoshida Kaori, Seki Nobu, Julie MacArthur, and Jeff Alexander for enjoyable times. My fellow students and friends Rita Dhamoon, Scott Matthews, Mark Pickup, Andrew Lui, Mary Velpel, and Miki Fabry lent many a helping hand and taught me as much as my formal teachers. Matt Gillis deserves special mention for turning some of my ideas into images that were more impressive than the ideas themselves. Much work was also done at the desk in my room at St. John's College (UBC), a uniquely cosmopolitan place for sure. All of us at SJC owe much gratitude to the college's founders and their ongoing support.

In Japan, I have to be particularly grateful to Nakagawa Junji for offering various insights from the perspective of international law, for introducing me to a number of key contacts, and for intellectually stimulating discussions and feedback over countless cups of black coffee in this office. Greg Noble hosted me and took much time out of his schedule to read my work and helped me restate the argument at crucial times. I would also like to thank Nakamura Tamio for his support at the Institute of Social Science.

This book owes a lot to the time and advice offered by Konno Hidehiro, Suzuki Yoichi, and Ishigaki Tomoaki. It is ironic that a study working with the assumption of self-interested bureaucrats could only be completed with the help of three individuals who embody the precise opposite: true and selfless commitment to public service. My friend Ishigaki Tomoaki has provided me with much knowledge about the workings of the Japanese foreign policy apparatus, key contacts, and stimulating discussions for which I am very grateful.

Much of the field research in Japan for this study was financed by a fellowship at the German Institute of Japanese Studies (DIJ) and under-taken from this base. I would like to thank my colleagues Oliver Loidl, Julia Walkling, Mattias Zachmann, Eva Kaminski, Alexander Kimoto, and Michael Wachutka, as well as Josefine Moorman, Andrea Germer, Harald Dolles, René Haak, Irmela Hijiya-Kirschnereit, Matthias Koch, Andreas Moerke, Harald Conrad, Sven Saaler, Claus Harmer, Marga Dinkel, Asano Keiko, Sugimoto Eiko, Ursula Flache, and Horikoshi

Yoko. In Brussels, I am grateful to my friends Patrick Klein and Laura Sanz Levia for help and lodging. In addition, I would like to thank my interview partners in Brussels, Tokyo, Santiago de Chile, Ottawa, Mexico City, and London, whom I have assured of confidentiality. Your help is most greatly appreciated. Part of the research for this book was financed by an *Établissement de nouveaux professeurs-chercheurs* grant of the Fonds québécois de la recherche sur la société et la culture (FQRSC).

Several colleagues read all or part of the manuscript and have provided comments that sharpened the argument: Christina Davis, Jeff Frieden, Kerry Chase, Carol Wise, Yoichi Suzuki, Mark Brawley, Brian Rathbun, and Mireya Solís. Saori Katada offered useful feedback on several occasions. At Harvard, the Japanese politics study group participants Bill Grimes, Tom Berger, Amy Catalinac, and Hayashi Hajime gave much advice and encouragement. Obviously, the remaining errors and omissions are all my own.

This manuscript would have been difficult to overhaul in its entirety without the wonderful environment provided by the Program on U.S.–Japan Relations at Harvard. My gratitude goes to my office mates Sherry Martin and Okagaki Tomoko, who suffered and laughed with me through many months, to Shin Fujihira, Lianna Kushi, Bill Nehring, Nakamura Reiko, Fujii Eiichi, Kobayashi Naoki, Oki Kazuhisa, Eguchi Arika, Motozawa Ichiro, Oyama Mizue, Ishimura Kozo, Inoue Sayuri, Sugisaki Mikio, Onuki Shigeki, Koyano Taro, Ted Gilman, and, most crucially, Susan Pharr. At McGill, I would like to thank my colleagues Arash Abizadeh, Mark Brawley, Jason Ferrell, Phil Oxhorn, Steve Saideman, Erik Kuhonta, Juliet Johnson, Ben Forest, Catherine Lu and Lorenz Lüthi, Stuart Soroka, Christa Scholtz, Rick Schultz, and Khalid Medani for making the place quite special. My particular gratitude goes to T. V. Paul for his support of a junior colleague and to Armand de Mestral for his advice and espousal of interdisciplinary research. Also at McGill, Maciej Szepaniak, Matthieu Beauchemin, and Oana Ciobanu provided excellent research assistance. At Cambridge University Press, I would like to thank Carrie Parkinson, Christina Sarigiannidou, and especially my editor John Haslam for shepherding the book through the editorial and production processes. Philippa Youngman's copy-editing greatly improved every sentence she found wanting.

A number of friends have accompanied me throughout the sometimes strenuous times of work and deserve special mention. Andrew Lui has never failed to support me and been a sparring partner in many discussions and pool games. Scott Matthews and Mark Pickup were always willing to discuss any aspect of political science, especially late at night or in the wee hours of the morning. Pablo Heidrich has taught me much about political economy over many glasses of wine. Nicole Baerg did the same over even greater numbers of pints. Greg Bateman, Ed Jule, James Peacock, James Clarke, and the team of F. C. Matador and our captain Takeda Norio turned my time in Japan into a unique experience. Without a spot to sleep on the tatami mats in the James' 2DK, a crucial period of field research would have been impossible.

Finally, I owe much to my parents for instilling me with intellectual curiosity, for love and support, to my mother for persistence in intellectual and other pursuits, and to my father for a sense of politics and the political. Most importantly, I thank my wife Ivette for her love, companionship, and support throughout the years. This book is for her.

Abbreviations

ACEA	Association des Constructeurs Européens d'Automobiles
ACP	African, Caribbean, and Pacific Group
AFL-CIO	American Federation of Labor and Congress of Industrial Organizations
AICO	ASEAN Industrial Cooperation
APEC	Asia Pacific Economic Cooperation
ASEAN	Association of Southeast Asian Nations
BBVA	Banco Bilbao Viscaya Argentaria
BIT	bilateral investment treaty
BSCH	Banco Santander Central Hispano
Canacero	Comisión de Comercio Exterior de la Cámara Nacional de Acero (Mexico)
Canacintra	Cámara Nacional de la Industria de Transformación (Mexico)
CEFIC	European Chemical Industry Council
CLEPA	European Association of Automotive Suppliers
COECE	Coordinadora de Organismos Empresariales de Comercio Exterior
COREPER	Committee of Permanent Representatives of the EU
CSI	Coalition of Service Industries
CUSFTA	Canada–United States Free Trade Agreement
DL 600	Decree Law 600 (Chile)
EP	European Parliament
EPZ	export processing zone
ESF	European Services Forum
EU	European Union
EVSL	early voluntary sector liberalization
FDI	foreign direct investment
FTA	free trade agreement
FTAA	Free Trade Area of the Americas

GATS	General Agreement on Trade in Services
GATT	General Agreement on Tariffs and Trade
IMF	International Monetary Fund
JA Group	Japan Agricultural Cooperatives Group
JAMA	Japan Automobile Manufacturers Association
JETRO	Japan External Trade Organization
JMCTI	Japan Machinery Center for Trade and Investment
JOI	Japan Institute for Overseas Investment
LDP	Liberal Democratic Party (Japan)
MAFF	Ministry of Agriculture, Forests and Fisheries (Japan)
METI	Ministry of Economy, Trade and Industry (Japan)
MFN	most-favored-nation
MITI	Ministry of International Trade and Industry (Japan)
MNC	multinational corporation
MOFA	Ministry of Foreign Affairs (Japan)
NAFTA	North American Free Trade Agreement
OECD	Organisation for Economic Co-operation and Development
PITEX	Programa de Importación Temporal para Producir Artículos de Exportación (Mexico)
PROSEC	Programa de Promoción Sectoral (Mexico)
PTA	preferential trade agreement
ROO	rule of origin
SECOFI	Secretaría de Comercio y Fomento Industrial (Mexico)
TPA	trade promotion authority
UNCTAD	United Nations Conference on Trade and Development
UNCTC	United Nations Conference on Transnational Corporations
USITC	United States International Trade Commission
USTR	United States Trade Representative
WTO	World Trade Organization

Japanese names and conventions

Throughout the text, Japanese personal names appear in the order common in Japan, with the family name first. I have omitted macrons for words commonly used in the English language, such as Tokyo and Osaka. All translations, unless otherwise noted, are mine.

1 | Introduction

I n late September 2006, a short letter arrived at the Secretariat of the World Trade Organization in Geneva that formally announced the entry into force of the United States–Bahrain Free Trade Agreement, bringing the number of notified trade accords to 200. With every preferential trade agreement (PTA) – an arrangement that liberalizes trade between member states only – the principles of multilateralism and non-discrimination in international trade as embodied by the World Trade Organization (WTO) lose more relevance. When the letter was received, already more than half of global commerce was conducted under the rules of one PTA or another.

How different the world of international trade diplomacy looked only twelve years earlier. After almost eight years of negotiations, ministers of 109 countries shook hands in Marrakesh on April 15, 1994, on the occasion of the signature of the most ambitious multilateral trade agreement in history. The final deal brought agriculture into the domain of the General Agreement on Tariffs and Trade (GATT) and created the General Agreement on Trade in Services (GATS), a GATT counterpart for services, by then making up a third of global commerce. Most importantly, it established the World Trade Organization itself, a formal international institution with its own staff and seat in Geneva (Barton *et al.* 2006: 93).

The mood was euphoric. US Vice-President Al Gore, who had flown in to address the meeting, called the deal "truly momentous." Peter Sutherland, the Irish Director General of the General Agreement on Tariffs and Trade, said that he was tempted to dance a jig on the table to express his joy.[1] Multilateral liberalization appeared to be firmly established. During the 1980s and early 1990s, many developing countries had embraced an open trade policy and applied for GATT membership.

---

[1] This depiction of events draws on an article in the *New York Times*, April 16, 1994.

They were joined by central and east European states that had emerged from communist rule. Even China was in negotiations for accession. Yet, today, multilateral trade negotiations under the auspices of the WTO seem to be little more than a sideshow. Since the early 1990s the world has seen an explosion of preferential trade agreements. Notably, the majority are North–South agreements that bring together economies of vastly different sizes and levels of development.

The rapid proliferation of North–South PTAs is striking since, compared with even minor tariff reductions on a multilateral basis, they do not create much trade. The commitments to lower barriers they embody are dwarfed by the unilateral steps taken by many emerging market countries. Thanks to successive GATT negotiation rounds, most-favored-nation (MFN) tariffs[2] are at historically low levels. Trade economists are divided over whether PTAs improve welfare (compare *inter alia* Freund 2000; McLaren 2002), but almost unanimously judge them a second-best solution to multilateral and unilateral liberalization.

But arguments against PTAs are not just theoretical. The multitude of agreements creates a patchwork of different rules that burden exporters with paperwork and bureaucracy, leading the chairman of Li & Fung, Hong Kong's largest trading company, to pronounce in the *Financial Times* that "multilateralism creates value, bilateralism destroys value."[3] If the complex rules are hard to follow for major trading firms, then they are simply too costly to comply with for most companies from developing countries. One study shows that only half of the imports into the European Union (EU) from least-developed countries make use of the full tariff preferences available. The other half is covered by MFN tariffs, since exporters would rather pay the higher duty than deal with the documentation requirements (Brenton 2003).

Especially for developed countries, individual PTAs with developing economies offer very limited export prospects. Even Mexico, a country with a population of over 100 million, registered annual vehicle sales of only 500,000 in 2005 – about the size of the auto market of Los Angeles. Many PTAs specifically exclude those goods in which developing countries have a comparative advantage. Conventional exports

---

[2] MFN tariffs are the duties countries charge on a non-discriminatory, unconditional basis. Art. 1 of the GATT requires its signatories to grant market access equal to "the most favored nation" unless, of course, they sign a preferential agreement.

[3] *Financial Times*, November 3, 2005.

are an unlikely explanation for the popularity of North–South PTAs. Why, then, the sudden proliferation of these preferential trade agreements? Why do major economic powers sign agreements with partners that bring little market size and overall welfare benefits?

This book argues that foreign direct investment (FDI) by multinational firms and the attendant trade are key driving forces of North–South PTAs. FDI flowing from developed to developing countries changes the incentives for governments in both, motivating them to pursue bilateral and regional options because they satisfy the political demands of multinational firms. As these firms invest in developing countries to produce goods for developed markets, they call for the reduction of barriers at home and abroad because it facilitates vertical integration, or the specialization of production according to technological capacity and labor cost. Firms produce high-end goods in the North and low-end products that require cheaper labor in the South, and ship these goods to the other partner.

Yet many multinational firms no longer see the WTO as the best way to meet their trade liberalization needs. Unlike multilateral deals, preferential agreements for trade and investment offer a special benefit: They can be used to raise the barriers for competitors from non-member states. Without such barriers, North–South liberalization would attract "beachheads" of FDI from outsiders, turning the developing country into a back door to the market of the northern partner. To make North–South liberalization politically feasible, governments therefore erect new barriers as they tear down others.

Raising barriers requires the use of discriminatory tools. Since nearly all recent PTAs are free trade agreements (FTAs)[4] in which the members set their own external tariffs, they require rules to determine the origin of goods. In the absence of such rules, goods would simply be imported via the partner country with the lower tariffs. These rules of origin (ROOs) can be designed to the disadvantage of outsiders and to provide protection for insiders. A related mechanism is at work in the service sector, which attracts a large share of FDI. Market and regulatory structures penalize late entry and provide incentives for preferential liberalization.

---

[4] Throughout the book, I refer to preferential agreements in general as PTAs, and to FTAs only in specific cases where the legal text uses the term. This applies to the FTAs between Japan and Mexico, Chile and the United States, the EU and Japan, and Japan–Thailand and Japan–Malaysia.

North–South PTAs thus trigger an endogenous dynamic unanticipated by earlier proponents of preferential trade agreements: other countries conclude defensive agreements with the host country out of fear of being shut out of markets and production locations. North–South PTAs are therefore not just a beauty contest among developing countries over who is the most open to foreign trade and hence to be rewarded trade agreements with rich partners, as the former US Trade Representative (USTR) Robert Zoellick suggested when he coined the term "competitive liberalization." It is a contest between major economic powers to gain access to emerging markets and important production locations, to impede such access for competitors, and to restore it when others have moved first.

This book offers a political economy account of the endogenous competition driving much of the proliferation of North–South PTAs. The approach assumes that governments decide their policies in response to pressures from organized societal groups. Although political variables may shape the decision to pursue PTAs, I emphasize the economic incentives that cause their proliferation, since even a PTA concluded for non-economic reasons is likely to have redistributive effects within and between countries. At the centre of the argument is a model of trade policy formation at the domestic and systemic level. Domestic sources of trade policy, in particular the interests of multinational firms, lead to policy outcomes at the international level. Since these interests not only influence the decisions to seek trade agreements, but also the design of PTAs, they have (at times unintended) consequences that reverberate abroad. Multinational firms in other countries in turn seek to influence the trade policy choices of their home government.

Through several case studies the following chapters explain how this process results in a spiraling model of more and more PTAs. The in-depth case studies cover the North American Free Trade Agreement (NAFTA) and the two defensive agreements with Mexico signed by Japan and the EU. I then apply the framework to several cases of North–South PTAs concluded in recent years: Japan's FTAs with Thailand and Malaysia, and the FTAs with Chile signed by the United States, the EU, and Japan.

Unequal partners: the proliferation of North–South PTAs

If trade liberalization is defined as the lowering of tariff barriers, the GATT should be considered a spectacular success. Negotiations have cut down manufactured goods tariffs on MFN basis from an average of over 50 percent to between 5 and 10 percent. Most manufactured imports into the industrialized countries face near-zero or no tariffs. In the light of this achievement, the sheer number of North–South PTAs signed in recent years is particularly striking. A closer look at the institutional features of the global trade regime and the character of recent PTAs shows that today's agreements coincide with profound changes in the world economy. Developing countries have reintegrated with the global economy, causing changes in the character of investment in these "emerging markets" and affecting the multilateral trade regime in turn. As such, this trend does not herald a return to the protectionist blocs of the 1930s. The scope of recent PTAs, covering new issues beyond trade in goods, their character as partnerships between countries of unequal levels of development, and their often "extra-regional" geography set them apart from past trade arrangements.

The experience of the interwar years, when retaliatory tariffs led to the creation of protectionist blocs, provided the initial impetus for the United States to support the creation of the GATT. Based on the constitutive norm of non-discrimination as expressed in MFN tariffs, Article XXIV of the GATT stipulates that regional integration measures have to conform to three standards. First, they should cover substantially all trade. Second, they should liberalize trade between the members within a reasonable time frame. Third, they must not raise the barriers against third parties above the initial MFN level at which tariffs are "bound" by GATT members. However, many developing counties apply much lower tariffs than their bound rates, leaving room for increases in tariff rates. Moreover, no similar clause exists with regard to non-tariff barriers such as rules of origin or the regulation of FDI. Although PTAs have to be "nested," or made compliant with the overarching GATT/WTO regime,[5] the weak disciplines of Article XXIV give states considerable freedom in creating discriminatory measures.

Because of the leeway given by the GATT, PTAs vary in their coverage of trade and in the inclusion of the flows of the factors capital and labor. A considerable number of agreements fall under the "enabling clause" of the GATT that allows developing countries to sign agreements among themselves with generous time frames for tariff reduction, often

---

[5] See Aggarwal (1998) and Aggarwal and Urata (2006) for an analysis of the "nesting" of multiple international regimes.

resulting in little or no actual liberalization. Many recent PTAs have this declaratory character. Other agreements only reaffirm existing tariff-free trade between states that previously belonged to the same political entity, as in the 1992 FTA signed by Slovakia and the Czech Republic, or agreements between former Soviet republics. Finally, some agreements are superseded by later PTAs, while others are suspended for political reasons.[6]

Counting only the PTAs in force and joint GATS Article V (trade in services) and GATT Article XXIV (trade in goods) agreements such as NAFTA as a single institutional package, we arrive at a cumulative figure of about 170 PTAs in 2008. Taking a minimum difference of US$15,000 in per capita gross domestic product (GDP) in purchasing power parity terms as threshold to count a country as "developed," about 100 are "North–South PTAs" – here used as a shorthand, although some "Southern" countries such as Macedonia and Armenia (partners of the EU and Switzerland, respectively) would be better characterized as economies in transition. This figure is much smaller than is to be expected based on the number of countries involved, since the EU has a common external trade policy and the European Free Trade Area (EFTA) member states[7] usually negotiate agreements jointly. This study focuses on the growing subset of PTAs between pairs of countries that are highly unequal in their level of development and the size of their economies.

Figure 1.1 is a graph of the growth of these agreements over time. Until 1991, North–South PTAs were limited to a handful of agreements, mostly between the European Community and its close neighbors, such as the EC–Malta FTA of 1971. The turning point came in the early 1990s, when countries in Latin America and many former communist countries began to seek PTAs, and when the United States, the creator of the GATT regime and the biggest importer, turned to North–South agreements. By the mid-1990s, the trend was in full swing.

Notably, the number of North–North agreements has in fact decreased in recent years, as several central and east European countries have joined the EU (Pomfret 2007). North–South agreements as defined

---

[6] Whalley (2008) offers a thorough overview and warns against alarmist double-counting of PTAs.
[7] Iceland, Norway, Switzerland, and Liechtenstein.

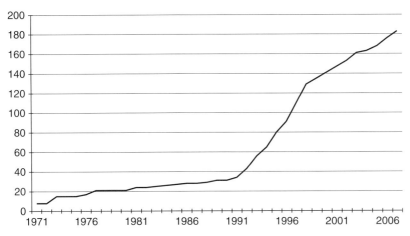

Figure 1.1 Growth of North–South PTAs, 1971–2007.
Source: WTO Secretariat; McGill Trade Agreements Database, http://ptas.
mcgill.ca.

here are experiencing the fastest growth of all PTAs.[8] Almost all are
classified as FTAs rather than as customs unions, the sole exception
being the 1996 EU–Turkey agreement.

Advanced developing countries such as Chile, Mexico, or Thailand
are preferred partners in today's agreements. Prior to liberalization in
the developing world, commercial interests from the North were limited
to resource extraction, "tariff-jumping" investment by multinational
firms, or, in the case of many "developmental states," closely circumscribed domains of export-oriented production. Liberalization creates
new opportunities and thus the incentives for interested parties in
industrialized countries to lobby for agreements to secure preferential
access.

In Latin America, unilateral liberalization represented the first step in
overcoming the legacy of import-substitution industrialization.[9] During
most of the 1950s–1980s, multinational firms produced outdated products, protected by high tariffs, for domestic sales in markets such as

---

[8] See also Fiorentino *et al.* (2006) for a slightly different classification that reaches a
similar conclusion.
[9] Imports were to be substituted by domestic production, protected by high tariffs
and quotas on imports. For a succinct description of these policies and their
unintended effects, see Krueger (1995a), esp. chapter 1.

Mexico, Brazil, and Argentina. Using various performance requirements, for example the sourcing of a percentage of inputs or mandatory
export of a share of the production, governments attempted to harness
the benefits of foreign capital (Caves 1996; Greenaway 1992). To
compensate multinational firms for high tariffs and host country
requirements, governments struck deals that sheltered investors from
competition and offered economic rents (Evans 1979). While the provision of services remained in the hands of governments, the high tariffs
and restrictions made exports and investment by smaller firms from
developed countries infeasible. FDI sought markets, but under the
specific conditions of the import-substitution policy of the host country.
As Latin American countries began to liberalize in the late 1980s and
early 1990s in search of foreign capital, they became attractive for a
different kind of investment integrated with world markets.

Despite important differences from Latin American countries, Asian
"developmental states" (Wade 1990) attracted similarly inward-oriented
FDI. Multinational firms, in this case mostly from Japan, enjoyed exclusive market share arrangements for their products. While export-oriented
investment caught the attention of many scholars, it was nearly always
limited to a few industries – mostly computer parts and consumer electronics manufacturing in east and southeast Asia, especially in Taiwan,
Singapore, and Malaysia. Following the 1997 Asian financial crisis,
liberalization has reached this region as well.

As other sources of capital such as bank loans have dried up, countries in both regions have been forced to compete for investment. In this
competition, governments see direct investment as preferable to volatile
portfolio capital flows. Table 1.1 shows the growth in total net FDI
inflows since 1987.[10] From a low base of less than 10 percent of global
FDI, developing countries received a growing share of capital flows
during the 1990s, with a peak of almost 36 percent in 1997. Although
China's share of FDI to developing countries alone made up a third on
average, other developing countries received massive inflows as well.
The growing share flowing to developing countries drew on a steadily
larger volume of global capital: measured in constant US dollars, foreign direct investment flows have grown more than sixfold since 1987.

---

[10] To facilitate comparison, all dollar figures throughout the book have been
   deflated to constant values using the US consumer price index with the year 2000
   as base.

Table 1.1. *Net global FDI inflows and country shares*

Year	Global FDI (US$ billion)	Country shares as a percentage		
		High-income countries	Developing world	Of which China
1987	178	90.3	8.1	1.8
1988	209	85.2	12.2	2.0
1989	248	86.6	11.9	1.7
1990	251	84.2	11.9	1.7
1991	186	73.7	22.1	2.8
1992	194	67.7	29.8	6.6
1993	249	66.4	30.3	12.5
1994	275	60.3	35.4	13.6
1995	357	64.5	31.7	10.9
1996	398	62.3	34.1	10.7
1997	491	59.6	35.9	9.4
1998	722	71.4	24.2	6.3
1999	1,119	79.5	16.2	3.5
2000	1,518	83.5	10.9	2.5
2001	779	72.5	21.7	5.5
2002	708	75.1	21.8	6.7
2003	608	69.7	25.0	7.3
2004	708	62.9	29.1	7.1
2005	929	66.4	27.5	7.5
2006	1160	65.8	27.2	5.8

Source: World Development Indicators Online 2008. All figures
deflated to constant US$2,000.

Moreover, the raw figures obscure qualitative differences. While high-income countries still receive close to two-thirds of total direct investment, much of this FDI consists of the acquisition of existing firms. A larger proportion of FDI to developing countries is made up of "greenfield investment" that leads to the construction of new production facilities. As is repeatedly stressed in UNCTAD reports (e.g. 2004a), FDI is by now the most important source of foreign capital for developing countries.

In various ways these investment flows are linked to international agreements. For developing countries, combined free trade and investment agreements offer an institutional package that locks in unilateral liberalization and provides guarantees for investors beyond WTO commitments (Fernández and Portes 1998). These benefits resemble those promised by the growing number of bilateral investment treaties (BITs), another product of the competition for foreign capital (Elkins *et al.* 2006). In addition to these advantages, trade agreements with an industrialized partner, even with only modest tariff reductions, give a developing country an edge over competitors with similar factor endowments (Ethier 1998a, 1998b, 2001). Both benefits explain why developing countries seek bilateral agreements with developed countries.

Less obvious is why these developed countries should take up the offer. Most developing countries are negligible export markets. In terms of national income, Mexico offered US firms barely 6 percent additional market size when NAFTA entered into force.[11] Foreign direct investment, however, creates powerful incentives for multinational firms to offer political support for PTAs beyond what the potential for conventional exports would lead us to expect.

Following the reintegration of many developing countries into the world economy, they attract manufacturing FDI to serve as export platforms to (mostly) developed-country markets. Sometimes, labor-intensive stages of production are moved to developing countries. At other times, multinational firms relocate the manufacturing of mass-market goods to low-cost countries, but keep the production of key components and high-end products at home. In addition, manufacturing FDI entails exports of machinery (capital goods) and inputs such as parts (intermediate goods) to the FDI host. One of the most important purposes of PTAs is to liberalize the trade in goods generated by FDI – much more so than the regulation of FDI in manufacturing itself or the reduction of tariffs on other exports.

Manufacturing FDI also creates a market for related services, for example insurance of exports or financing of direct investment. Moreover, since most developing countries have only recently begun to open their financial and telecommunications service markets, FDI in services represents a considerable share of the capital flows to emerging markets. Provisions for FDI in PTAs therefore apply in large measure to these flows.

---

[11] In concrete numbers, a GDP of merely US$466 billion compared with US GDP of US$7.7 trillion, adjusted for purchasing-power parity.

Perspectives on preferential trade agreements

Earlier theoretical traditions in International Relations explained PTAs as a symptom of hegemonic decline and the inability of the United States to keep the multilateral trade regime open and non-discriminatory. Neoliberalism conceived of trade agreements as one cooperation problem among many, arguing that greater numbers of states engaged in negotiations make it more difficult to come to an agreement. PTAs can therefore be seen as the inevitable by-product as many countries join the WTO, mounting transaction costs make negotiations more difficult, and governments look for alternative venues for trade liberalization.

These interpretations still have purchase today. Mansfield and Reinhardt (2003) show that the growth of WTO membership, the recurrent negotiation rounds, and, in particular, the participation in trade disputes motivate states to seek PTAs as an insurance policy: should WTO rounds fail or end up deadlocked, states secure export markets. Likewise, PTAs can serve as coalition-building strategy to increase bargaining power or to "obtain countervailing market access" (Mansfield and Reinhardt 2003: 830) for countries that lose in WTO disputes. Moreover, the growth in the sheer number of PTAs will lead states to pursue such deals, as institutional templates become available and competitors use them to secure outlets for their exports.

Yet although PTAs improve market access, the gains are often circumscribed. Usually, both parties reserve the right to use the WTO as an avenue for settling claims, even if the PTA contains elaborate dispute settlement mechanisms. PTAs with the United States in particular do not offer protection from US trade remedy laws. While a stalled multilateral negotiating round leads countries to a search for alternative venues for trade deals, it cannot be the only factor at work. The number of North–South PTAs exploded *after* the last WTO round, while earlier waves of PTAs reached their peak during GATT negotiations as countries sought to gain leverage, as Mansfield and Reinhardt show.

System-level explanations also offer only limited insight into the cross-regional variation in the spread of preferential trade agreements: PTAs have spread quickly in the Western hemisphere, but have only recently arrived in Asia (Ravenhill 2003), reigniting scholarly interest in turn (Aggarwal and Urata 2006; Dent 2006; Pempel 2006). The peculiar pattern of how PTAs have spread across the globe and the recent surge in North–South agreements invite a search for additional causal factors.

As Haggard (1997) has argued, the foremost reason for the impasse at the WTO table is the convergence or divergence of state interests, in particular over the seemingly intractable issue of agricultural liberalization. Katada *et al.* (in press) submit that major economic powers often prefer to deal bilaterally with a weaker partner because they can control the negotiating agenda to favor their internationally oriented businesses while protecting declining sectors. While this argument sheds light on some of the benefits of bilateral deals for developed countries, it cannot explain why states rarely chose this route until the early 1990s. Why do the interests of states converge on preferential rather than multilateral liberalization? Why has this convergence manifested itself so strongly in recent years?

Despite a multitude of studies, we have few answers to these questions. Economists have focused on the effects of PTAs on national and world aggregate welfare from a Pareto-optimality perspective. Most economists agree that multilateral liberalization is preferable to bilateral agreements. Just how preferable depends on the Pareto criterion: PTAs could still be desirable as long as they make some countries better and none worse off. The classic formulations by Viner (1950), Lipsey (1957), and Meade (1955) argued that PTAs can be welfare enhancing if more trade is created than diverted away from more efficient countries outside the arrangement. Kemp and Wan (1976) raised the prospect that PTAs can be constructed in a way that makes at least one member better off, but does not affect outsiders. Later contributions found that welfare effects tend to be ambiguous (Panagariya 1999, 2000).

With the second wave of regional trade agreements in the 1980s, the focus shifted from these "static" considerations to "dynamic issues": are PTAs "stumbling blocks" or "building blocks" (Bhagwati 1991) towards global free trade? Krishna (1998) argues that trade diversion reduces the incentives for parties to a bilateral agreement to reduce trade multilaterally. Levy (1997) even contends that bilateral PTAs can make multilateral liberalization politically unviable, while McLaren (2002) warns that PTAs can induce member countries to make relation-specific investments that inhibit future multilateral liberalization. Much of the criticism depends on how much trade is actually being created by PTAs, with recent studies suggesting a much stronger positive effect (Baier and Bergstrand 2007; Magee 2008). These benefits also help to explain the motivation for "natural" – that is, geographically close – partners to form PTAs. Yet it is doubtful how relevant these findings are for today's agreements between distant partners. The most prominent study of PTA formation motivated by welfare gains (Baier and Bergstrand 2004) relies on a dyadic dataset that ranges only until 1996, with almost 60 percent of the PTA formation outcomes driven by two political entities, the EU and EFTA.

To understand the motivation behind North–South PTAs, we need to focus on the two different forces that tend to influence the foreign economic policy of individual states: reactions to policies of other countries and to domestic political demands. Government policy often reflects the interests of strong and well-organized societal groups (Grossman and Helpman 1994), although mediated by the domestic institutions that offer or restrict access to governments (Mansfield and Busch 1995; Nelson 1988).

Since multinational firms are responsible for most international trade, their interests are an obvious starting point for the analysis. In Milner's framework, governments balance producer and consumer interests. Public officials therefore seek the support of industrial sectors, some of which will be in favor of liberalization. Firms support regional liberalization because it allows the mutual reduction of tariff barriers by "trading scale economies across industries" (Milner 1997: 91), in effect balancing costs and benefits between exporters in the two partner countries.

Along similar lines, Busch and Milner (1994: 270) put the growing importance of exports and intra-industry trade at the centre of their explanation of firm preferences. Producers that can achieve economies of scale in home markets are more competitive globally, leading them to demand regional trade agreements. This demand will be most pronounced when firms are competitive in terms of technology and management but lack the sizable home market to achieve the optimum efficiency. Milner cites the example of Canadian firms that supported NAFTA. Chase (2005) develops this approach further by showing that support for regional trade agreements since the end of World War I corresponded closely to the economies of scale that important industries achieved depending on their level of technology.[12]

---

[12] But see Thompson (1994), who argues that Canadian firms were particularly opposed to further liberalization. Since Canada and the United States had signed an FTA before NAFTA was proposed, Canada's initial interest in NAFTA was limited to the protection of the gains made in the CUSFTA (Cameron and Tomlin 2000: 63–64).

However, adding market size through North–South PTAs may not be the key to achieving economies of scale. Most developing country markets are too small to move firms down the cost curve towards greater efficiency. The drive to achieve greater economies of scale offers a convincing account of PTAs between developed countries or the political support for a large common market like that of the European Union, but without a commensurate explosion in returns to scale, it does not explain the exponential growth of North–South PTAs in recent years.

In a series of papers, Chase (2003, 2004) seeks to address this problem, arguing that multinational corporations lobby for regional agreements with developing countries because of the growth in offshore processing. Many of these firms, however, face a legacy of sunk investments originally made under protectionist host country policies. They therefore press for barriers to non-members to provide breathing room while they restructure.

Temporary relief is one aspect of non-tariff barriers, but not the most important. A growing literature demonstrates how rules of origin and other barriers have become a strategic policy instrument that firms try to manipulate to their advantage (Duttagupta and Panagariya 2003; Krishna 1998; Krishna and Krueger 1995; Suominen 2004). When a host country still retains high MFN tariffs – typical of many developing countries – rules of origin and tariffs interact to raise the costs for non-member firms. If member firms mainly source inputs from within the FTA, then ROOs are a costless device for insiders to extend protectionism to the host country and to gain the political support of intermediate goods producers. ROOs therefore either divert trade to producers in the PTA while inducing producers from non-members to relocate production into the PTA, or they create additional costs for outsiders.

The discriminatory aspect of PTAs, I argue, is one of the greatest attractions for multinational firms. The account in this book expands on political economy models that predict that preferential agreements are most likely to be formed when they divert trade, because the gains to exporters then outweigh the costs to import-competing industries (Grossman and Helpman 1995; Panagariya and Findlay 1996). The unintended consequence of such trade diversion is the reaction by other countries. Excluded parties can counter PTAs in two possible ways: they can either form PTAs among themselves, or they can attempt to join an existing agreement to prevent trade diversion. Baldwin (1996) calls this the "domino effect of regional trade agreements."

Although the domino theory appears to be an apt description of the progressive expansion of the EC/EU, it faces a fundamental challenge: only in the rarest of instances have PTAs been shown to divert trade, and even these findings are sensitive to econometric specifications (Magee 2008). Even NAFTA, with its unusually restrictive rules of origin, has not had measurable negative effects on trade with non-members (Aussilloux and Pajot 2002; Krueger 1999). In fact, when a developing country signs a PTA, in most cases its trade with members and non-members alike increases significantly. North–South PTAs often coincide with other economic reforms in developing countries and should in principle boost growth by attracting foreign investment. Moreover, "beachhead" FDI from outsiders in one country in order to serve the markets of the parties to the agreement will increase trade as its complement. As a result, many PTAs appear to have the counterintuitive effect of creating trade with the outside world. Neither the diversion of trade in finished goods based on comparative advantage, economies of scale, or stalled multilateral negotiations at the WTO seem to account fully for the recent explosion of North–South PTAs. Changing the focus to foreign direct investment explains this outcome.

Firms, states, and their investment in protection: an overview of the argument

North–South PTAs offer a variety of advantages to firms, depending on the sector in which investment takes place. In many service industries the first firm to enter a developing country market opened through a PTA enjoys advantages over later entrants. In manufacturing, PTAs allow firms to lower the cost of an internationally fragmented production while preventing competitors from non-member countries from obtaining the same benefits. These benefits are less evident at an aggregate economic level, but are clearly visible at the level of individual firms.[13]

In services, the structure of many markets confers important first-mover advantages. Many service industries are textbook examples of

---

[13] Since within PTAs FDI flows primarily from North to South, the following refers to the developed country as the "home" country, the developing economy as the "host."

oligopolies or natural monopolies, in which efficient production requires a dominant market share. First-movers with enough capital can buy up existing assets – such as telecommunications networks or branches in retail banking – and attain a commanding position. These firms will be able to offer their products at a lower cost than later entrants because with a larger market share first-movers produce on a greater, more efficient scale. Competitors would have to make significant investments before reaching profitability. Preferential liberalization therefore threatens to shut out competitors. Because the first-mover advantage is the result of market structures rather than the reduction of barriers, this applies even if host country laws on FDI are subsequently made non-discriminatory – that is, if liberalization is multilateralized later. In addition, first-mover firms may attempt to influence important regulations in a way that raises rivals' cost of market entry. As emerging market countries move towards the liberalization of services, the overhaul or, in some cases, initial creation of regulatory regimes becomes necessary, e.g. in the provision of financial services and the protection of investor and intellectual property rights. With the primary exporters of these services located in developed countries, this process creates an interest in influencing the regulation to adapt models used in the home country, thus lowering the barrier to entry for their providers and raising them for others (Wunsch-Vincent 2003).[14] In manufacturing, liberalization creates the opportunity to use the advantages of specific locations in the production of goods. Capital-intensive production takes place in developed countries that offer access to high technology and research and design facilities and personnel. Labor-intensive stages of production are outsourced to the developing world. This vertical fragmentation of production leads to an increase in intra-industry trade, or trade in the same industry in differentiated goods. Unlike intra-industry trade between developed countries, however, the traded goods are differentiated by "quality": developing countries are more likely to export low-cost goods, while developed countries export high-cost, high-quality goods. For example, while many car manufacturers produce their upscale vehicles in their home country, entry-level cars are produced in less developed countries. A typical case is the German car

---

[14] See also Mattli and Büthe (2003) for the importance of international standards and regulations in providing advantages to some firms over others.

manufacturing company Volkswagen that assembles most of its high-end models in Germany, but produces its entry-level Polo and Golf models in the Czech Republic and Brazil.

Moreover, such investment implies an enormous increase in trade in intermediate goods: parts production often takes place in specialized factories to achieve efficient production scales. The same parts are then shipped to different locations. Fragmented production thus creates a demand for tariff reduction in home and host countries. While transport costs are less and less important, not every country is equally attractive as a location of production. Proximity to developed country markets, as well as other factors such as available primary materials, turn access to these locations into competitive advantages.

The decisions firms make in a globalizing world explain their interest in the reduction of barriers to trade and investment in general, but not the popularity of preferential agreements. Unilateral or multilateral liberalization could lower tariff barriers between developed and developing countries, allowing trade and investment to produce efficiency gains without a multitude of different rules. Politics, however, opens the door to preferential treatment. While a North–South PTA allows firms to produce abroad where costs are lower, it also exposes the home market to foreign competition; nothing would prevent firms from third countries from investing in the developing partner country and using it as an export base. Firms and labor in the North will therefore try to minimize the threat of entry of competitors. When two countries with very different wage levels liberalize bilateral trade, firms and workers in manufacturing industries will often try to raise the barriers for outsiders.

In this situation, non-tariff barriers such as ROOs, an essential part of all preferential agreements, can be structured to increase the cost of production for firms from non-member countries. Despite earlier liberalization, developing country tariffs are still higher than the MFN tariffs of developed countries. Sufficiently strict rules of origin in an FTA interact with the remaining tariff to extend protection: firms from within the PTA can produce in the host country, and import intermediate goods from and reexport goods to the home market without costly tariffs. By contrast, firms from non-member countries can only import parts from home at a high price – if they exceed the rule of origin, they pay the initial tariff on the intermediate good, and often the MFN tariff on exports to the developed country as well. The barriers against outsiders created by a PTA therefore benefit both firms and workers in the partner countries.

Theoretically, firms would be induced to switch to suppliers from within the FTA, the classic case of trade diversion. However, firms often cannot easily change suppliers with whom they have long-standing relationships. Principal suppliers within the FTA may have close ties to the competition. Assuming that they do not choose to exit and surrender the FTA market to their competitors, how do non-member firms react?

Since they cannot influence the ROOs in the first PTA, non-member firms have to tackle the second part of the protectionist policy: the MFN tariff of the host country. Without tariffs, rules of origin lose much of their force. The obvious reaction is to lobby the host government to lower its duties. But unless negotiated within the framework of a PTA, the rules of the GATT prescribe that MFN tariffs can only be lowered for imports from *all* member countries. There is little that foreign firms can offer to motivate a developing country to do so since the political costs for the host country governments would normally be too high, unless they can convince their home governments to strike a deal with the host country. To retain their competitiveness, non-member firms therefore seek recourse with their home governments. The defensive reaction of these non-member firms is an unintended consequence of the first PTA – they likewise call for a PTA with the same developing country. Since intermediate and capital goods exporters in non-member countries are hurt by the same ROOs and tariffs, they become allies in this undertaking. Likewise, excluded service firms that witness preferential liberalization will try to level the playing field. Even though firms from non-member countries may not have been interested in a PTA with the host country originally, they will now come to support it to prevent exclusion from an important host of FDI. In response, their home governments also negotiate PTAs with the host country – the dominos fall, causing an endogenous proliferation of bilateral trade agreements driven by FDI in developing countries.

This account also helps to explain the variation in the spread of PTAs across the globe. Developing countries in the Americas were the first to liberalize their economies and to attract FDI in manufacturing and services. The important trade and investment links and the discriminatory measures of PTAs almost immediately triggered defensive PTAs. The cumulative effect of these agreements eventually reached more distant countries in Europe and Asia.[15] When the Asian financial crisis forced liberalization on several developing countries in the region, the endogenous dynamic came into full force again.

In sum, two factors emerge as the driving forces behind North–South PTAs: concentrated interests in FDI-exporting countries have a strong incentive to lobby for preferential agreements because they confer specific advantages over competitors. To be politically attractive, these agreements must have a discriminatory effect on trade and investment with non-members. This effect manifests itself mainly for firms from other countries that are disadvantaged in their ability to use developing countries as export platforms, or that are excluded from services markets. These firms push their home governments for defensive agreements[16] to remain competitive.

Methodology

If this study's central claim of an endogenous proliferation of PTAs holds, then its explanation presents a challenge for standard comparative methods. While comparative analysis has developed a nuanced set of approaches for different problems (George and Bennett 2005; King *et al.* 1994), it ultimately rests on two assumptions: that the cases are completely independent and, if several cases are affected by the same common external force, that this factor is truly exogenous. Usually the analyst pairs cases according some variation of Mill's (1843) "method of difference" to identify the variable(s) that are responsible for variation in outcomes while other factors are held constant, even if they are common influences such as having been part of the same colonial empire. Such research designs have demanding requirements for "unit homogeneity" (King *et al.* 1994: 91–94). More recent studies of the effects of globalization (e.g. Tiberghien 2007) have assumed that an external force affects all cases equally, so that domestic institutions and interests explain the

---

[15] See also Dent (2006: 49–50) for how Asian PTAs mimic extra-regional models. The effect is also partly captured in the empirical work of Mansfield and Reinhardt (2003): countries are more likely to sign PTAs with geographically proximate countries and important trade partners, especially when these countries are signing preferential agreements.

[16] Use of the terms "offensive" and "defensive" in relation to agreements seems to have been coined by officials at Japan's Ministry of the Economy, Trade, and Industry (METI).

variation in outcomes. The cases in this book, by contrast, are assumed to be interdependent. The model proposed is dynamic in the sense that the conclusion of one PTA will trigger several others. How can a model like this be tested without resorting to circular reasoning?

As argued by Büthe (2002: 485), modeling sequences of events offers a solution: Sequence "allows us to have causal feedback loops from the *explanandum* at one point in time to the explanatory variables at a *later* point in time only" (emphasis in original). Accordingly, I develop a model that predicts a sequence of decisions and feedback effects. Differences in the cases will therefore manifest in *variation over time* in the outcomes dependent on the strength of the causal factors.

To test this model I develop individual analytic narratives for each case study, emphasizing process-tracing (George and Bennett 2005: 211–81) to identify the constraints and variables that matter to the actors in their decision-making. In developing these accounts, the model provides the cast of actors, their interests and strategies (McKeown 1999). I begin by outlining two ideal types of North–South PTAs, an "offensive" type of agreement in which outsiders are discriminated against, and a "defensive" type that counters these effects. I then develop a model that establishes causal relations. My cases are dyads of countries with different factor endowments in which foreign direct investment flows predominantly in one direction. The independent variables are the political demands made by firms and other actors such as labor unions in the capital-exporting countries, while the actual institutional outcomes (trade and investment liberalization in preferential trade agreements) form the dependent variables. One of the most important sources of variation in outcomes is the strength of trade and investment links and resultant political demands within a particular dyad compared with other dyads involving the same host country. Consider the (not entirely) hypothetical example of South Africa as a host country for FDI. The strongest trade and investment links exist between the EU and South Africa, followed by the United States and Japan. The FTA between the EU and the South Africa affects more US firms than Japanese competitors, so that *ceteris paribus*, we are more likely to see a political reaction in US trade policy than in Japan.

The case studies are based on qualitative data collected through the analysis of interest group publications, documented lobbying activity such as congressional hearings, and over seventy interviews with decision-makers in government and the private sector. Given different political systems, such data cannot be truly "symmetric" (King *et al.* 1994: 48) in the sense that a uniform method of collecting information is used in all cases: lobbying in Japan leaves no visible paper trail, while evidence of comparable activities in the United States is often publicly available. These problems preclude a cross-sectional quantitative analysis of the effect of lobbying. Detailed process-tracing is the only feasible technique for testing hypotheses in this situation. To isolate the competition between major developed countries from those characterizing the bilateral relationship with the developing country, I focus on cases in which the trade policy of the latter remained constant.

The first case study focuses on NAFTA, the "original" and, in terms of trade and investment flows, still the most important North–South agreement. Since most of its clauses have been in effect for over a decade, it is possible to analyze outcomes among members as well as longer-term reactions among non-members to this offensive move. The North American deal also provided the institutional template for a variety of other agreements.

I then compare two defensive agreements: the EU–Mexico FTA as a response to NAFTA, and the Japan–Mexico FTA as countermove to both prior agreements. In particular the case of the EU–Mexico "Association Agreement" and the time lag to the conclusion of the Japan–Mexico "Economic Partnership Agreement" strengthen the argument: given the stronger investment interests, the EU moved faster to counter the effects of NAFTA. The European initiative in turn spurred Japan on to pursue its own FTA with Mexico. Mexico's policy remained consistent throughout the negotiations of all three agreements: it proposed each of them, but then negotiated defensively for all of them with the exception of specific agricultural exports.

In a third step I include cases in which the competitive dynamic is restricted to only one sector: services in the case of the FTAs of the United States and the European Union with Chile, and manufacturing in the cases of the Japanese FTAs with Thailand and Malaysia. The cases also changed the roles of key actors. In Chile, the United States and the European Union competed neck and neck after the United States' initial objective of Chile's accession to NAFTA had failed. Again, Chile's trade policy remained consistent in all the cases studied here: Chile sought FTAs with all major trade partners.

Finally, in the cases of the Japanese FTAs with Thailand and Malaysia, I focus on differences in the bilateral trade and investment relationship with the partner countries to bring the differing political coalitions into relief. Malaysia had fewer export interests regarding Japan compared with Thailand, leading to a quick conclusion of the negotiations with the former compared with the protracted bargaining with Thailand. These cases provide evidence that North–South agreements are unlikely to liberalize trade beyond the narrow interests of multinational firms with investment in the partner countries and their suppliers. It is noteworthy that the Japanese agreements with the ASEAN countries have likewise triggered defensive countermoves by the United States and the EU.

Caveats, limitations, and contributions

As with most political agreements, it is impossible to identify a single variable as decisive for the conclusion of an individual PTA. This applies to both the theoretical and the empirical dimensions of this study. In the case of NAFTA, concerns about the stability of the southern neighbor and the resulting flows of immigrants into the United States played a role in motivating the free trade agreement. The agreements with Chile also had an important function for the United States and the EU by setting high standards for the protection of intellectual property rights, reflecting the rule-making function of PTAs as described by Katada *et al.* (in press). Japan's trade agreements undoubtedly have a strategic diplomacy aspect, especially since China has started to negotiate trade agreements with important providers of natural resources and food products in southeast Asia and the Pacific.

On a theoretical level, the explanation put forth in this work does not endeavor to capture all the forces at work in the current proliferation of preferential trade agreements. PTAs can also be used to express political support when strategic interests are at stake, as in the case of the United States–Jordan FTA and the follow-up initiative to establish a regional free trade zone in the Middle East. Likewise, in cases of PTAs between countries of very similar levels of development, other considerations, such as achieving economies of scale, will be of central importance. As a final limitation, this study does not attempt to provide a generalized explanation of the policy choices of the developing country partner. A theoretical appraisal has been put forth by Shadlen (2005), while Cameron (1997), Grugel and Hout (1999), Pastor and Wise (1994) and Haggard (1995) offer individual country studies in Latin America and southeast Asia. My focuses is specifically on the convergence of interests between North and South that favors the narrow kind of liberalization evident in recent PTAs.

The book offers three specific contributions. First, it breaks new ground by explicitly theorizing and tracing the competitive dynamic between North–South PTAs. The argument helps to resolve two long-standing puzzles in international political economy by explaining the regional variation in preferential trade agreements and the sudden surge in their popularity since the mid-1990s.

Second, the study underscores the importance of the political interests in developed countries that emerge with foreign direct investment and vertical trade integration. It shows that multinational firms exercise a profound influence on the character of North–South trade agreements that often results in special interest politics running counter to the spirit of free trade. Prominent critics of preferential deals such as Jagdish Bhagwati and Anne Krueger (Bhagwati and Krueger 1995) have issued early warnings of such an outcome based on grounds of principle. This study shows that the convergence of interests between developed and developing countries on flows of foreign direct investment from North to South only exacerbates the issues these scholars have highlighted.

Finally, it presents evidence against the case that preferential trade agreements can provide support for multilateral liberalization at the level of the WTO: given the political temptation to create non-tariff barriers to make North–South agreements feasible, these deals will satisfy multinational firms, a key constituency that previously offered the necessary counterweight to protectionist forces in the WTO. But liberalization is likely going to be limited to the goods these firms want to trade. The onerous rules and regulations typical of North–South PTAs will prevent many smaller firms from developed economies and most exporters from developing countries from realizing the gains of liberalization.

In addition to the agreements analyzed here, the account can be applied to a growing number of cases. Because of the weight given to the interests of services firms, US PTAs with South and Central American countries are likely to disadvantage firms from the EU. European negotiating positions vis-à-vis the Andean Community and the four Central American countries have been accordingly influenced by considerations of equal access for FDI. This also holds for Canadian initiatives, often in the tailwind of US PTAs. Although these two countries' PTAs with Colombia have important security dimensions, they also affect the relative position of European firms. Japanese PTAs with southeast Asian countries, as well as the EU's Mediterranean agreements, have in turn stimulated various bilateral initiatives of the United States, including agreements with Morocco, South Africa, and the ASEAN countries. Moreover, with some qualifications the argument can be extended to cover initiatives between developing countries where foreign direct investment flows predominantly in one direction, such as South Korea–Mexico and South Korea–Chile. As more advanced developing country firms from Brazil, China, and India invest in other developing countries, these new FDI home countries will likewise be pulled into a global competition.

The organization of the book

The study is organized as follows. Chapter 2 establishes the theoretical argument for when and why preferential trade agreements between developed and developing countries become viable, and why they trigger a round of countermoves towards bilateral agreements. The explanation is developed based on a simplified model of two countries exporting FDI and one seeking to attract it, building on theories of vertical integration of production across country borders.

Chapter 3 focuses on NAFTA as the first case study. Under pressure from multinational manufacturing and service industries, the United States begins to target individual states for market opening, while promoting the same issues in the WTO from the mid-1980s on. Bilateral investment treaties and service negotiations form the templates that ultimately lead to the respective chapters in NAFTA, which in turn becomes the model for future FTAs. The chapter takes stock of the lobbying efforts of various industries before and during the negotiations, relating them to the selectively protectionist outcome and tracing to the demands of firms the emergence of NAFTA's strict rules of origin.

Chapter 4 shows that following the conclusion of NAFTA, European manufacturers and service providers began to lobby their governments to seek solutions against the discriminatory arrangement. Given the strong interest of European service providers, in particular the Spanish financial sector, the EU moved quickly to the conclusion of an intermediate "framework agreement," followed by a fully fledged FTA. Lobbying takes place around the Directorate General for Trade of the

European Commission and the Article 133 Committee (coordinating member states' interests and Community trade policy), in which Spanish interests clashed with protectionist forces from France. In the manufacturing sector, German automotive firms, in particular Volkswagen, emerged as key supporters of a bilateral agreement with Mexico.

Chapter 5 focuses on the Japanese reaction to NAFTA. Since investment by Japanese firms was concentrated in the manufacturing of electronics and automobiles, the discriminatory effect of NAFTA was limited to a smaller number of companies, many of them located in Mexican export processing zones (EPZs). Japanese electronics and automotive firms first unsuccessfully exhausted all possibilities of liberalization between Mexico and Japan. The eventual conclusion of the EU–Mexico agreement convinced policymakers in the trade and foreign affairs bureaucracy to move towards a policy of free trade agreements.

Chapter 6 traces the competitive dynamic between firms from the United States and the EU in the negotiations for a free trade agreement with Chile. Although investment in Chile is mostly limited to the service sector, the competitive dynamic was sufficient to motivate the United States and the EU to seek FTAs to secure equal access. Due to the lack of fast-track authority, the United States was unable to conclude an agreement with Chile before the EU. As a result of the EU move, intense lobbying in the United States drove the rapid conclusion of an agreement with evidently defensive aspects.

Chapter 7 focuses on two cases in which manufacturing industries dominated the negotiations. In the Japanese FTA negotiations with Thailand and Malaysia, the automobile industries and electronics industries played central roles, supported by a variety of intermediate goods producers. For the first time, Japanese firms are producing goods in southeast Asia not for exports to the US market, but for reimport to Japan. In both agreements, the vertical integration of trade strongly shapes the pattern of liberalization, leading to rapid tariff reductions on some goods and blanket exclusions for others, mostly "sensitive" agricultural products. Mirroring the agreements in Latin America, both the United States and the EU react by announcing negotiations with Malaysia and Thailand.

Chapter 8 summarizes and concludes that preferential trade agreements between North and South are first and foremost the product of the greater importance of foreign direct investment. The resulting pattern of liberalization that privileges the interests of multinational firms has implications for how PTAs will impact the multilateral trade regime. While the current proliferation of PTAs does not herald the reemergence of protectionist blocs, it threatens to undermine the support of important industries for multilateral negotiations, because their demands are met in bilateral and regional arrangements. At the same time it creates a patchwork of competing rules that mainly benefit the concentrated interests of a few multinational firms but offer less effective liberalization for smaller firms or those from developing countries.

2 | *Framework for analysis*

G OVERNMENTS liberalize international trade for a variety of economic reasons. Often, they respond to the demands of export-oriented industries (Milner 1988). At other times, they seek trade agreements because they hold causal beliefs that free trade increases the welfare of societies (Simmons and Elkins 2004). But these factors cannot explain why states would prefer preferential over multilateral or unilateral liberalization. Unilateral market-opening, although economically desirable, is rare. Without a foreign partner to offer reciprocal liberalization, governments frequently have difficulties in overcoming the resistance of domestic groups that would compete with imports.[1] Multilateral liberalization not only embodies the sovereign equality of nation-states and "diffuse reciprocity" (Ruggie 1993), but can also be shown to increase global welfare more than preferential trade agreements under a variety of conditions (Krishna 2005).[2] Yet the choice between different venues for liberalization is not well explored.

The general trend towards PTAs has no doubt been encouraged by the ever-longer multilateral negotiating rounds. With more than 150 members, the WTO is an unwieldy organization (Mansfield and Reinhardt 2003; McLaren 2002). Since most international commerce still takes place between the "Quad," consisting of Canada, the United States, the EU, and Japan, lately plus China, greater numbers do not automatically imply more trade. Faced with rising negotiating costs but diminishing returns to multilateral liberalization, countries may simply look for alternatives.

But a general propensity to sign more PTAs does not tell us much about the choice of partners. At times, the choice is primarily political,

---

[1] The seminal studies are Bailey *et al.* (1997) and Gilligan (1997a).

[2] Limao and Olarreaga (2006) empirically show that this effect is especially pronounced for small countries. Brown *et al.* (2006) find the same effect in a computable general equilibrium model of hub-and-spoke networks of PTAs.

for example if countries try to create "security externalities" of increased trade with an allied state (Gowa and Mansfield 1993) or to secure access to natural resources. The latter loomed large in NAFTA in the United States–Canada negotiations, while the Japan–Australia FTA may well have been driven by both goals. Most importantly, our explanations have only limited purchase when we look at the most recent wave of preferential trade agreements. During the last fifteen years the majority of new PTAs have been signed between countries with very different factor endowments, wage levels, and per capita incomes. Developed countries often team up with partners that offer only very small export markets. However, trade in finished goods is not in fact at the heart of these agreements.

One of the most important changes in the economic relations between developed and developing countries since the end of the Cold War has been the massive flow of foreign direct investment from North to South. Preferential trade agreements facilitate the flow of investment in several ways. In services, PTAs often liberalize FDI regimes, allowing firms from developed countries to invest in markets where it is necessary to supply a service. In manufacturing, they support firms in their efforts to move production into developing countries with lower wages.

The differences in factor endowments and the resulting capital flows, I argue, have consequences for the politics of North–South PTAs. Specifically, I make three claims about how trade and investment liberalization is shaped by governments and firms.

North–South PTAs require discriminatory barriers. Manufacturing firms from the developed country that invest in the developing country will try to create trade barriers that raise costs for competitors from non-member countries.

The trade generated by foreign direct investment rather than exports of finished goods assumes central place in North–South bilateral trade agreements. Many developing countries have become "export platforms," places to invest not because they are markets in their own right, but because they can be used by multinational firms to produce goods for exports to the home country. In principle, multilateral liberalization allows this as well. But since the non-discriminatory reduction of trade barriers enables competitors from other countries to benefit, it exposes the home market to competition. In the absence of discriminatory rules, the developing country could become the back door to the developed country market. Since entry into mature manufacturing industries is relatively easy – often a precondition for production in a developing country – firms will try to use explicit policies to raise the costs for competitors. Often, the political price of North–South liberalization is discrimination against non-members. A related dynamic is at work in service industries.

Service market structures form entry barriers. Service firms that invest in the developing country will support North–South PTAs because they create first-mover advantages.

In many services industries, trade barriers and market structures create conditions in which the first firms to enter a market enjoy advantages over latecomers. At times, these advantages consist of regulatory barriers that directly limit market shares or the number of participants. Technical and legal standards may be easier to comply with for multinational firms from a jurisdiction with similar rules. More subtly, the characteristics of service industries may create first-mover advantages even in the absence of regulatory barriers. The structure of markets characterized by economies of scale gives an advantage to firms that are the first to buy up existing assets. Here as well, firms will be concerned about the entry of competitors, although they may not deliberately try to raise barriers against outsiders. But the end result will still be a strongly preferential liberalization.

The key to the argument I make in this book is that the discrimination embedded in these offensive North–South PTAs tends to engender a reaction. The immediate effect will often be a diversion of investment into the developing country. Some firms may choose to "jump" over the new barriers and avoid discrimination by investing within the PTA zone rather than exporting their necessary parts and components into it. Some may choose the developing country over alternative locations because of the preferential access to a major market. Others may now be deterred from investing because discriminatory barriers created by the PTA are too high. In all these instances, firms from non-member countries will be forced to make decisions based on criteria unrelated to economic efficiency or corporate strategy. Policies that impose costs on competitors from non-member countries will create an incentive to lobby for defensive agreements that restore access.

Discriminatory North–South PTAs trigger defensive agreements. Firms from non-member countries with substantial FDI in the developing country will likewise call for a PTA.

The most vocal non-member firms will be those that have already "sunk" investments into the host country and now see their profits eroded. But newcomers that plan to invest will likely support such a PTA as well. The threshold at which firms from non-member countries become active will be lower if the barriers created by the PTA are particularly costly, and a presence in the host country is important to preserve commercial opportunities. But once the endogenous, competitive trend of bilateral PTAs comes into motion, it is hard to stop – as competitors level the playing field by getting their own bilateral deals, it becomes more costly to stay on the sidelines. Consequently, at later stages, even much weaker investments and trade interests will suffice to trigger a reaction. Countries can no longer afford to rely on the multilateral system alone.

In other words, once the first PTAs with important host countries have been signed, the competitive dynamic between countries becomes the driving force of bilateral deals. Although the discriminatory clauses of PTAs are trade barriers, not investment rules, they affect the trade stemming from foreign direct investment. FDI and the resulting trade in intermediate goods create a particular coalition of producers, and FDI and intermediate goods trade are especially susceptible to the discriminatory effects of bilateral trade agreements.

Importantly, the interests of developed and developing countries converge on such discriminatory measures. Many developing countries seek PTAs with developed economies in order to attract FDI (Ethier 1998a, 1998b, 2001; Grugel and Hout 1999; Oman 1994). If FDI is being diverted to them instead of their competitors, they benefit as well. Developing country governments sometimes also hope to increase their exports of goods in which they have a comparative advantage, such as agriculture. But if anything, preferential trade agreements are even less likely than the WTO to offer such market access. This chapter presents a framework for the analysis of these factors.

Interest groups and trade policy

My approach follows Frieden's (1991: 15) definition of "modern political economy." Political economy in this sense assumes rational, goal-oriented, and utility-driven actors, who attempt to influence government policies that affect the return they achieve on their assets. This does not imply that their actions are collectively rational – in fact, much of the following analysis is concerned with actions that may be individually rational, but lead to collectively suboptimal outcomes.

Actors operating in markets where policies directly influence the return on assets, for example by raising the barriers to entry of competitors, will be prepared to make efforts at lobbying if the expected increase in return on their assets exceeds the cost of lobbying. Assets also influence how economic actors organize themselves vis-à-vis the government. For example, firms with comparable assets will have similar preferences over policy, even though they may be direct competitors in the marketplace. If actors choose to lobby to influence a government policy, the similarity in preferences may motivate them to form a coalition if their common interest overrides the competitive element of the marketplace.[3]

Based on these assumptions, I analyze the role of interest groups, in particular firms, in demanding changes in government policies. The pursuit of these preferences takes place in the context of political institutions that shape how decisions over foreign economic policy are made. Institutional differences could therefore lead to variation in policy outcomes across cases. Institutions matter in the political process by affecting the way in which coalitions are formed and what "access points" interest groups have for their lobbying. In principle, they could have a strong effect on the specific character of liberalization achieved in a PTA. However, my focus is on policy convergence – the rapid increase in PTAs – rather than variation, the domain of institutional analysis. If we observe convergence on a policy choice such as North–South PTAs despite institutional differences in the participating countries, then actor preferences are the only remaining possible cause. Accordingly, I mainly consider the institutional background in my case studies in order to be able to trace the lobbying process. In some instances, institutions delayed the conclusion of PTAs without affecting the ultimate outcome, while in others they had limited influence on the degree of liberalization, but they do not explain the popularity of North–South PTAs.

How do government decision-makers formulate trade policy, given domestic actors with defined preferences? I follow classic public choice works in assuming that politicians, just like other actors, are

---

[3] Although rarely acknowledged by political economists today, this assumption was first made by Marx: the relation to the means of production determines the political interests.

utility-maximizers whose goal is reelection. When using trade policy to increase their election chances, they have three options (Grossman and Helpman 1994): they can increase consumer welfare (which would imply lower prices), raise firm profits, or improve the fiscal position of the state through greater tariff revenues. The latter plays a marginal role for all but the lowest-income countries. Benefits in consumer welfare are likely to be small and highly dispersed. Under this assumption, and holding political institutions constant for the moment,[4] politicians are susceptible to political pressure from concentrated groups. Consequently, politicians will prefer trade policies that raise firm profits, provided they do not negatively affect consumer welfare to the point where the decisions of voters change. Individual leaders may matter in particular instances, but given the number of North–South PTAs, they are not likely to be a systematic factor. For example, the close ties of the US administration of George Bush Sr. to Texan business and banking, in turn with interests in Mexico, may have been a positive factor for the NAFTA initiative, or at a minimum will have heightened the awareness of certain aspects of the deal.

Like politicians, bureaucrats enter the picture primarily by responding to the demands of interest groups. A broad literature has addressed the role of bureaucrats in formulating economic policy, in particular in the context of the "developmental state" (Aoki *et al.* 1996; Wade 1990; Weiss 2000; Woo-Cumings 1999). Since in many countries bureaucrats are sheltered from direct political pressures, they are seen as an independent political force. Yet a long tradition of public choice theory argues that bureaucrats are just like other rational actors, albeit with longer time horizons and different rewards (Downs 1967). Moreover, even within the developmental state tradition, some authors acknowledge that firms can counteract bureaucratic initiatives because of asymmetries of information (Okimoto 1989). Bureaucrats can expect little reward for policies that maximize national welfare but are unresponsive to, or even costly for, organized domestic interest groups. If, on the other hand, officials pursue policies that benefit firms, they can gain rewards, often in the form of lucrative positions after leaving office. Washington is notorious for its former officials-turned-lobbyists, but

---

[4] Alt and Gilligan (1994) provide a useful discussion of how ideal-typical collective action problems, producer interests, and political institutions interact to shape trade policy outcomes.

other capitals, in particular Brussels, also have their share of "consultants" recruited from among retired officials (Hayes 1993). In Japan, bureaucrats often move into important positions in private companies they previously regulated, following a brief period of retirement (Curtis 1999: 233–34). Finally, even trade officials with the best intentions are constrained in how much time they can spend studying the potential effects of their policies, if these could in fact be reliably predicted. In consequence, they often have to resort to specific input from industry in trade negotiations. This study therefore assumes that bureaucrats primarily act on behalf of their constituents.

This does not require that the concrete initiative for a PTA comes from the private sector. Government bureaucrats may put forward the negotiation of trade agreements because a new set of responsibilities allows for career advancement and justifies an increase in resources. Yet for whatever reasons a PTA is proposed, any agreement of economic relevance will have distributive effects. Accordingly, even if governments decide to pursue a PTA for non-economic reasons, such as strengthening ties with an ally, if the PTA affects trade and investment they usually need the support of important social groups. Governments will therefore be receptive to the economic interests of these groups, among the most important of which are firms.

Assumptions about firms

Firms engage in the political process on the basis of their preferences, which in turn can be derived from their characteristic assets and their position in the market and vis-à-vis political institutions. My assumptions about firms build on work by Milner (1997) and Chase (2005) on the role of economies of scale. Technological change over the last eighty years has increased the "minimum efficient scales" of production, requiring larger markets. Accordingly, firms have supported regional integration in the form of preferential trade agreements to different degrees, depending on their technology and the resulting economies of scale. Moreover, as Gilligan (1997a) shows, with imperfectly competitive markets trade liberalization can lead to intense lobbying by firms. If firms become increasingly productive with longer production runs, then changing the variety of the good produced is often costly. If a few firms with increasing returns to scale have previously divided up a market by differentiating their products, the entry of new producers with "close" varieties forces them to adjust and to differentiate their products again. Because of the high fixed cost production, such adjustment will be costly and lead to vehement lobbying against foreign entry.

These frameworks provide elegant accounts of the tendency to form ever-larger markets. In particular until the mid-1990s, many observers expected world trade to fracture into a three-bloc world, with attendant reductions in global welfare compared with a multilateral regime (Krugman 1993). Yet while PTAs have proliferated rapidly in recent years, we cannot argue that there has been a similarly explosive growth in scale economies. Moreover, the frameworks do not explain well why east Asian countries that did not pursue regional trade agreements in the past are now doing so, or why preferential trade agreements are not really regional, but rather form a "lattice" (Dent 2006) or a "noodle bowl." My model synthesizes these approaches with recent work on vertical integration to account for the network-like structure of PTAs.

Often firms compete with other interest groups over access to political decision-makers. To increase their political influence, firms can form horizontal coalitions with other firms in the same industry, or organize vertically along "rent chains." Rent chains are composed of those who earn rents because of their interaction with a firm, for example suppliers and employees (Baron 1995). The existence of vertical rent chains will tend to reduce collective action problems and thereby encourage firm lobbying. Such chains are most likely to be formed when firms are engaged in oligopolistic competition – that is, when their strategic behavior can influence their profits. Baron (1999: 29–31) cites the example of the lobbying around the corporate average fuel economy bill (CAFE) in the United States. Since strict CAFE standards would hurt US manufacturers producing big and inefficient vehicles, automotive firms not only lobbied individually but also mustered the support of suppliers, dealers, and even some consumers organized in the National Cattlemen's Association – a powerful vertical coalition. Rent chains will be particularly important for the lobbying activity of firms when the economic interests in a trade agreement cannot be divided clearly along sectoral or industry lines.

In this study I derive the goals that firms pursue from their links with foreign direct investment in emerging markets. These links depend on the motivations for FDI. Why would multinational firms invest in emerging markets rather than export from their home countries? According to the "eclectic theory" of the multinational enterprise

(Dunning 2002), firms invest overseas because of ownership, location, and internalization advantages. Different combinations of these advantages attract different types of FDI. The following refers to "home country" as the developed country in which the multinational firm is based, and "host country" as the developing country in which the firm invests.

Resource-based international production seeks the ownership of specific resources that are generally bound to a certain location. Examples are extractive industries such as mining and petroleum, whose possible locations are primarily determined by geological rather than political or economic factors. Since trade in resources is rarely subject to import tariffs, these industries are only occasionally the focus of trade-policy-related lobbying.[5] By contrast, *import-substituting* FDI reflects the location advantage of access to protected markets. Particularly from the 1950s to the 1980s, developing country policies sought the substitution of imports with domestic products (Krueger 1995a: 1–14), erecting high tariff and non-tariff barriers to protect infant industries. Multinational firms responded with "tariff-jumping investment" to serve protected markets (Evans 1979). While many developing countries still show the vestiges of import-substitution industrialization, most opened their manufacturing and service markets to foreign investment in the 1980s and 1990s.

In some of these sectors and industries, FDI is a precondition for market access. In services in particular, a commercial presence ("mode 4" in the GATS)[6] is necessary for business activities that require proximity to customers. Once countries open their service markets for the first time, they attract *market-seeking* FDI of this kind, as witnessed by flows of direct investment to emerging market countries in the last two decades. Finally, multinational firms undertake *efficiency-seeking* FDI (also referred to as vertical investment) to specialize their manufacturing activities according to the benefits of the location – in emerging market countries primarily low labor costs. To internalize this benefit, a division of labor across borders but within the multinational firm or with its

---

[5] They are, however, often the target of "resource nationalism" when the price of commodities rises to historical highs. History repeats itself more than thirty years after Vernon (1977) published his seminal *Storm over the Multinationals*.

[6] The General Agreement on Trade in Services (GATS) divides the supply of services into mode 1 – cross-border trade, mode 2 – consumption abroad, mode 3 – commercial presence, and mode 4 – movement of natural persons.

suppliers becomes a second important driving force of FDI in emerging markets. My framework focuses on the last two kinds of foreign investment.

Emerging markets and the economics of vertical integration

Recent FDI in emerging markets has two main objectives: benefiting from different factor endowments and opening new markets. In the manufacturing sector multinational firms often invest because of the former. Since labor is relatively abundant in developing countries and capital relatively scarce, it is more efficient to produce labor-intensive goods in developing countries, all else being equal. As a result, developed countries export physical- and human-capital intensive "high quality" goods, while developing economies produce "low quality" exports with greater labor input (Falvey 1981). The result is trade within industries, but in vertically differentiated goods, or vertical intra-industry trade (Greenaway *et al.* 1994). The products do not have to be truly "high-tech": for instance, Italy exports expensive fabrics and suits to Turkey, but imports cotton t-shirts and socks. Vertical trade contrasts with horizontal intra-industry trade in similar goods, as in the bilateral sales of mid-sized vehicles between Japan and Germany, and commercial exchange based on comparative advantage.[7]

Firms engage in vertically integrated FDI when there is a gap in factor prices between host and home economy (usually in that labor is cheaper in developing countries), when the market of the host economy is relatively small, and when transport costs between home and host are low (Carr *et al.* 2001; Markusen 1995; Markusen *et al.* 1996).[8] Markets for high-quality and luxury goods in the developing country will be much smaller than for basic goods, so high-quality finished goods are likely going to be exported from the developed country in small quantities. Accordingly, the developing country serves mainly as an export platform to developed country markets (Ekholm *et al.* 2003). This also explains why conventional exporters of finished goods are less

---

[7] Fontagné *et al.* (2006) develop a measure of vertical intra-industry trade based on a minimum difference in unit prices. The data requirements, however, are relatively demanding, so that the calculation is only possible for very recent periods for countries that report complete trade data.

[8] Implicitly, these authors also make a political assumption: Factor prices are not equalized because labor migration to the developed country is restricted.

interested in reciprocal trade liberalization with small, developing countries than with major developed markets, and why they have less to gain than firms engaged in overseas production.

Production of both high- and low-quality goods in different locations, however, requires the shipping of goods across borders. Capital goods such as production machinery are mainly supplied from developed countries and have to be exported to the developing country. Intermediate goods such as parts, components, and other inputs have an additional characteristic: their efficient production often requires achieving minimum economies of scale at the plant level. Automotive engine plants, for example, achieve efficiency at an annual production of at least 250,000, while the production of parts sometimes requires figures of several million per year (Husan 1997; McAlinden 1997). Enjoying the benefits of different production sites while achieving economies of scale implies a specialization of plants and an increase in trade of intermediate goods, much of it intra-firm or with close suppliers (Feenstra and Hanson 1996; Head and Ries 2001; Head *et al.* 2004; Slaughter 2000).

Accordingly, to make vertical FDI viable, three other conditions have to be fulfilled: the benefits of location should not be outweighed by the cost of transportation, the fixed cost of FDI, or the transaction cost of moving goods and capital across borders. Transaction costs are greatly increased by tariff and non-tariff barriers, making them potential aims for lobbying. Firms will try to reduce tariff and non-tariff barriers on intermediate, capital, and finished goods as much as possible. This applies both to the multinational firm that produces the final good as well as to its suppliers of intermediate and capital goods, henceforth referred to as upstream producers.

When creating a framework suitable for vertical manufacturing FDI, developing countries face a legacy of protectionist policies. While developed country MFN tariffs on manufactured goods are generally below 10 percent, most developing countries still charge higher import taxes. Moreover, average tariffs often hide tariff peaks in certain commodity classes, some of which may be of particular interest to foreign firms.

Besides erecting high tariff barriers, developing countries pursue policies to harness foreign investment to stimulate the development of local industry. Local content requirements promote a domestic base of supply industry, employment requirements create jobs, and technology transfer requirements and domestic equity participation quotas foster domestic human capital (UNCTAD 2001: 3). However, the measures impose costs on investors by forcing them to allocate their resources differently than they would in the absence of any measure. These costs are shifted to the home country or other markets (Caves 1996; Greenaway 1992: 146–47). Multinational firms therefore make considerable efforts to lobby both home and host governments to reduce these trade barriers.

A preference for free trade, however, does not predict a choice as to how to achieve liberalization. Firms could also lobby home and host countries to reduce tariffs unilaterally on only the goods of their interest. Alternatively, offshore processing programs allow such tariff reductions without true liberalization on an MFN basis and provide many of the benefits of vertically integrated production across borders. Under these programs, firms ship intermediate goods to EPZs in developing countries, where labor-intensive stages of the production process take place. Subsequently, goods are reexported to the home or other countries. Often, more capital-intensive stages of production take place in the home country, leading to back-and-forth trade of the same good in different tariff categories. Home countries often only tax the value added abroad. Furthermore, host countries frequently offer incentives and MFN tariff rebates. EPZs are therefore often referred to as in-bond factories because no import tariffs are paid in them. Offshore assembly programs are used by the United States and the EU (Feenstra *et al.* 2000). Numerous developing countries offer EPZs to attract manufacturing FDI (McIntyre *et al.* 1996; Warr 1989, 1990), the most well-known example being Mexico's program for maquiladoras – in-bond factories along the US–Mexican border. However, in recent years EPZs have become less common as manufacturing industries have seen a wholesale shift to developing countries. More and more, vertical intra-industry trade appears to supplant production-sharing arrangements in which developing countries are mere processing locations (Fontagné *et al.* 2006). As a result, host economies are providing not just cheap labor, but also basic parts and components.[9]

Preferential trade agreements facilitate North–South integration, but they are not just liberalizing policy measures. Rather, they promise specific benefits to their supporters that multilateral liberalization cannot supply. The next section addresses this issue.

---

[9] It is noteworthy that much of the supply industry on which multinational firms draw stems from earlier periods of import-substitution industrialization.

Preferential agreements as exclusive clubs

Unlike multilateral negotiations in the WTO, preferential trade agreements can be shaped to favor multinational firms from the capital-exporting partner. Trade and investment liberalization helps firms in lowering the cost of multinational production, particularly if a developing country functions as an export platform to the host market. Yet if liberalization took place multilaterally or unilaterally, nothing would prevent firms from third countries from enjoying the same benefits. European firms could invest in Mexico and export to the United States. Japanese firms could build factories in eastern Europe to serve EU markets. PTAs, by contrast, offer the benefits of liberalization, but can raise the barriers for these outsiders and protect the home market.

Since a growing share of trade between developed and developing countries is vertical intra-industry in nature, discriminatory policies tend to focus on these goods. In preferential trade agreements, two tools serve this end: the prohibition of tariff rebates and the negotiation of tight rules of origin.

Closing the back door: rules of origin

In both customs unions and PTAs, rules of origin define whether a good qualifies for tariff-free shipping across borders among the member countries. They are necessary because goods within a PTA are often either produced with input of parts imported from non-members or produced abroad with parts originating in the PTA and then reimported. In customs unions, the rules can in principle be kept simple. Often they stipulate that a percentage of parts has to originate in the PTA. For example, if a good is produced in the EU, but less than 50 percent of the parts originate there, the common MFN tariff is applied when the good is shipped to another EU member country. However, even such simple rules can strongly discriminate against certain kinds of trade. For example, until recently the EU rule of origin system did not allow "cumulation," or the adding-up of component shares between different EU partner countries. For example, an apparel manufacturer based in Morocco could not use Turkish textiles and expect to count them towards fulfilling the origin requirement, even though both countries have preferential trade agreements with the EU.

Rules of origin in FTAs are more complex. Since in an FTA each member country applies its own external tariff, rules are necessary to prevent transshipping. In the absence of such rules, goods would enter via the member country with the lowest external tariff. For example, trucks from the EU or Japan would be imported into Canada with a 6.1 percent tariff (presumably at a port close to the United States to keep transport costs low) and transshipped to the United States tariff free, rather than the exporter paying the 25 percent tariff imposed by the United States. Without rules of origin, FTAs would be very liberalizing, because they would exert pressure to lower tariffs to the lowest level applied by any member. Weak rules of origin would thus clearly further the goal of "open regionalism," or regional agreements that boost multilateral liberalization. In practice, this is rarely the case.

Although many rules of origin are highly technical, they can be grouped into three categories according to the test of origin they apply (Falvey and Reed 2000: 1):

value added test – rules that require that the last production stage taking place within the PTA adds a minimum value, or that a minimum value of local content is used;

change in tariff heading test – rules that confer origin status if the final product is classified under a different tariff heading than its intermediate goods input;

technical tests – rules setting out that certain production activities or specific parts confer origin status.

Within these broad categories ROOs can be highly specific. Often they are negotiated at up to a ten-digit level of tariff disaggregation. At other times they exclude inputs completely from non-member countries. Consider the rule of origin for dairy products in NAFTA contained in Chapter 4 of the Annex to the main text: a change in tariff heading to 04.01 to 04.10 (dairy products including cheese) confers NAFTA origin, unless the change is from a specified list of tariff items of the member states. This seems innocuous unless the reader knows that the latter items include any dairy product consisting of more than 10 percent milk solids. Translated into plain language, if a cheese producer wanted to make cheese in Maine to sell it in Quebec, she could use any non-NAFTA input to do so – except for milk.

Due to their ostensibly technical nature, rules of origin have only recently attracted the attention of political economists (Hirsch 2002;

Jensen-Moran 1996; Krueger 1993). Empirical tests of their effects are even more sparse, since measurement of the restrictiveness of ROO regimes across agreements are plagued by difficulties caused by the highly specific character of the regimes. Comparisons are often restricted to industries within a particular agreement.[10]

This relative dearth of research contrasts with the political importance of ROOs for firms, suggested by the intense lobbying around the design of these rules. For example, during the NAFTA negotiations, ROOs were among the last items on which negotiators reached agreement (Cameron and Tomlin 2000: 168–75). More than a fifth of the final text is taken up by rules of origin. Consequently, ROOs need to be seen as an independent policy instrument that attracts the lobbying efforts of firms and labor; given different external tariffs, tight rules of origin can be used to export protection within a preferential trade agreement (Chase 2008; Falvey and Reed 2000). Perhaps the most direct evidence of this is that even customs unions such as Mercosur impose complex ROOs even though with a common external tariff they cannot be explained by the need to prevent transshipment (Cadot *et al.* 2006: 13).

If ROOs stipulate a minimum local content, then they distort the use of inputs towards intermediate goods producers located in the FTA. If the cost of importing an intermediate good from a more efficient producer located outside the FTA is normally lower, then sufficiently strict ROOs and remaining MFN tariffs can combine to make it more expensive than sourcing from a less efficient producer in the FTA. Due to their distorting effect, rules of origin can initially make FTAs politically viable, as shown formally by Duttagupta and Panagariya (2003). ROOs, seen as a policy affecting the return on assets of firms, are crucial in mustering the political support necessary for the conclusion of PTAs, by creating vertical rent chains that sometimes extend into both negotiating countries. Based on their discriminatory effect, we can deduce the preferences regarding rules of origin that firms will have.

Multinational manufacturing firms differ in their preferences over rules of origin depending on their supply networks. Primarily, the

---

[10] See Chase (2008) for a study of the political economy determinants of ROO restrictiveness in NAFTA, and Estevadeordal and Suominen (2004) and Garay and Cornejo (2001) for examples of measures of ROO regimes and their difficulties.

share of regional content that a firm uses determines the desirability of ROOs.

Hypothesis 1a. *The more a firm sources regionally rather than globally, the higher the rules of origin it demands.*

High regional content characterizes incumbent firms with existing supplier linkages rather than newcomers (Graham 1994: 116). Often, firms maintain high levels of imports from their home country and other important production sites. But this may not always be the case: if the suppliers are outside the partner country, firms will attempt to resist the negotiation of strict rules of origin (Chase 2008). By contrast, intermediate goods producers in the FTA have a strong incentive to lobby for strict ROOs, because it creates an artificial barrier for suppliers from outside the FTA.

Hypothesis 1b. *The more intermediate goods producers compete with extra-regional producers, the higher the rule of origin they demand.*

It follows that intermediate goods producers and multinational firms may or may not lobby for the same rules, depending on their relationship to regional production. Suppose that a multinational firm sources *only* from within the proposed PTA and that all its suppliers are located in the two member countries. Then we would observe the extreme case of a coherent vertical coalition of the end-user firm and its suppliers that would lobby for a rule of origin of 100 percent. By contrast, if a multinational firm prefers to source from outside the proposed PTA but there are potential, more expensive, intermediate goods suppliers in the PTA, then the latter would demand higher rules of origin thresholds than their customers – possibly preventing the emergence of a coherent vertical coalition. This might be the case if the developing country has developed a domestic industrial base of suppliers.

Host countries will usually collaborate in negotiating rules of origin to some extent, if these rules favor domestic producers of intermediate goods. At the same time, as outlined below, strict rules of origin will also act as a deterrent to outsiders. Host country governments will therefore have to balance competing aims. On the one hand, they want to attract FDI from more than one developed country, which weighs against strict rules of origin. On the other hand, domestic intermediate goods producers will call for tighter rules that would extend protection to them. Since rules of origin interact with other host country barriers to trade, the same logic applies to tariff liberalization.

Labor's preferences over rules of origin are straightforward: the higher the threshold imposed by the rule of origin in a PTA, the greater the protective effect. A 100 percent requirement still allows for some shifting of production within a PTA according to different wage levels, but effectively bars any intermediate goods imports from non-member countries. Labor organizations in developed and developing countries will therefore demand the strictest rule of origin possible.

How will industries differ in the restrictiveness of the ROOs demanded because of other characteristics of the production process? Based on an analysis of NAFTA lobbying, Chase (2008) argues that greater economies of scale induce firms to demand higher rules of origin thresholds, because the entry of competitors will push firms into less efficient scales of production. However, the NAFTA case does not allow us to differentiate clearly between the effect of FDI and increasing returns to scale (IRS). The industries for which Mexico (and to a lesser extent Canada) attracted FDI from non-NAFTA countries (autos and consumer electronics) and that made up the lion's share of manufacturing exports from Mexico to the United States also happen to be characterized by IRS. But do scale economies by themselves trigger the demand for a high threshold in the rules of origin?

If this were true, then we would observe a strong relationship between restrictions on FDI (or entry of foreign competitors) and the restrictiveness of ROOs. Consider the US auto industry. US MFN tariffs on cars (but not trucks) have historically been low. Even episodes of "negotiated protectionism" (Aggarwal *et al.* 1987) have only temporarily resulted in import restrictions, soon to be circumvented by Japanese manufacturers by investing in the United States instead. If US automakers were concerned about losing market share because this directly pushes them up their cost curve, they would have had as much incentive to lobby for restrictions on FDI as for reductions in imports. But this has never occurred (Crystal 1998). Only when FTAs created the risk of production in low-wage countries (Mexico and, at the time with a weaker currency, Canada) did US firms push for barriers in the form of rules of origin. This indicates that FDI by outsiders *in the low-wage partner* triggers demands for ROOs, rather than scale economies by themselves. Similar effects are at work in export processing zones.

Closing the back door: export processing zones

Following the same principle, firms will want to ensure that rules of origin are applied to goods produced in export processing zones. In a

PTA, export processing zones are redundant for member country firms, since goods cross borders tariff-free. Just like PTAs in the absence of rules of origin, export processing zones are a potential back door for non-member firms. As an incentive for foreign investors, many developing countries (and some developed countries such as Canada) offer rebates on MFN tariffs for the import of capital and intermediate goods that cannot be sourced in the host country. Although common practice in EPZs, tariff rebates present a threat to the developed country partner, because non-member firms could invest in the export processing zone and export to the home market. Consequently, home country firms will need to close this entry point by lobbying against tariff rebates and for an application of MFN tariffs and rules of origin.

Hypothesis 1c. *The more competitors import parts from outside the host country, the more likely home country manufacturing firms will try to ban exemptions from the MFN tariff for imported parts.*

Manufacturing firms' preferences depend primarily on their link to foreign direct investment. This also applies to the service sector, although the competitive advantages conferred by PTAs result from market structures as much as from rules and regulations.

Getting a head start: foreign oligopolists in services

Service firms occupy a middle ground between investors in manufacturing and exporters. Often, service negotiators raise the same demands in bilateral and multilateral negotiations. However, once preferential service liberalization occurs in a PTA, the market and regulatory structure of the service sector tend to raise barriers to outsiders.

In principle, services liberalization could be pursued unilaterally, preferentially, or multilaterally. In fact, most services markets are opened by the host country governments themselves. By contrast, developing country commitments in the GATS are limited (Sauvé 1995), leaving an increasingly important role to preferential agreements to liberalize remaining sectors and lock in existing commitments (Stephenson 2000; Stephenson and Nikomborirak 2002).

Service providers that supply host country markets across borders ("mode 1" in the GATS) rarely have strong preferences for bilateral over multilateral liberalization. They seek investment liberalization because it is a precondition for market access, for example if a PTA offers the chance for liberalization under GATS Article V (free trade area in services). Alternatively, if multilateral negotiations are more difficult because of the large number of players involved, bilateral negotiations could be easier. Practitioners argue, however, that the main difficulty in services liberalization lies in the domestic work of adapting laws, regulations, decrees, and procedures, making multilateral and bilateral liberalization equally hard to achieve (Stephenson 2002). This suggests that if PTAs are more successful in services liberalization, the reasons lie in the specific trade-offs of the deal.

Services PTAs offer particular benefits for firms that need to establish a commercial presence by investing in the host country, especially in industries characterized by economies of scale. In this situation, "sunk" investments, or capital that needs to be committed in order to contest a market, but that is not recoverable, often call for considerable sales to be profitable. The bigger the initial investment, the greater the economies of scale. Examples of this kind of industries are banking and most other financial services, power generation and distribution, and telecommunications.

In financial services, dominant firms often enjoy market power that allows them to price competitors out of the market (Berger *et al.* 2004). In industries that require investments in distribution such as energy and telecommunications, firms can acquire existing networks and control access by competitors entering the market later. In retail markets with many branches, first entrants can achieve economies of scale in marketing and back office operations (Williams 2003). If previously protected banking markets in developing countries are opened for the first time, more efficient foreign firms rapidly establish footholds (Claessens *et al.* 2001).

As shown by the Stackelberg-Spence-Dixit model (Tirole 1988: 309–11), these market structures can be used by first-movers to deter later entry by competitors. The effectiveness of such barriers depends on the relationship between economies of scale, sunk investments, and prices. If later entrants are efficient enough to compete with incumbents by offering lower prices, they can draw customers to them and can overcome these challenges. However, when the incumbent is a foreign multinational competing with other foreign firms, it is unlikely that firms differ much in their productivity. Consequently, the dominant firm may be tempted to set prices low enough to deter entry.

Although many agreements merely lock in existing unilateral commitments, some PTAs open up opportunities for investment in service

markets for the first time. In this situation, the question of economies of
scale and entry deterrence can assume particular prominence. From a
purely legal perspective, such liberalization is rarely preferential. For
example, the United States pushed for the liberalization of many
Mexican service industries in the NAFTA negotiations, but the legal
implementation in Mexican law took place on a non-discriminatory
basis. Yet in many situations, the demands for liberalization will come
from service firms that have already invested and who are constrained
by limits on ownership imposed by the host country. For example, a
bank might have the maximum legal market share allowed by a host
country prior to liberalization. If this limit is abolished, the rule in itself
may be non-discriminatory. But this does not automatically translate
into equal access. A dominant bank might try to rapidly expand its
market share until it is able to deter entry. The relationship between
economies of scale and first-mover advantages is expressed in hypothesis 2a.

Hypothesis 2a. *The greater the economies of scale in a service industry
in relation to a host country market, the greater the first-mover advantage created by preferential liberalization, and the more services firms
with FDI in the partner country will support it.*

More rarely, liberalization measures are also legally sequenced. In
these situations, sequential liberalization from preferential to multilateral could allow firms to capture markets and prevent competitors from
entering later (Fink and Mattoo 2002; Harms *et al.* 2003). At other
times, the regulatory structure directly determines whether a PTA will
exclude outsiders. Often, a country will open its service markets bilaterally first, but then adapt its domestic laws and regulations to allow
market entry on a most-favored-nation basis. However, in industries
such as telecommunications, regulators often limit the number of
licenses granted to operators. In this situation, late entry is not pena-
lized, but completely blocked until the next licenses are offered.[11] Even
though service firms may not be the first to push for preferential liberalization, they cannot afford to let the opportunity pass.

Finally, the politics of standard-setting influence the negotiation of
North–South PTAs. International product standards, or technical specifications of the design and characteristics of manufactured goods, can
act as a trade barrier and are, unsurprisingly, the object of lobbying

---

[11] I am indebted to Pascal Kerneis for clarification of this point.

activities. However, while standard-setting negotiations between the United States and the EU are embedded in domestic institutional frameworks that often go back to the nineteenth century, as Mattli and Büthe (2003) show, North–South agreements leave much more room for multinational firms to advance their particular interests. Many developing countries have yet to prescribe standards for manufacturing and services industries, but do not have domestic interests that favor one over the other. Often, standards are minimally different with negligible consequences for trade and investment (for example, Mexico uses letter-size rather than A4 paper), at other times they involve decisions over multi-million dollar investments, such as whether to use the European GSM standard for mobile telecommunication or the CDMA standard common in the United States and Japan.

Services industries are a hotly contested field for standard-setting, since virtually all activities from accounting to energy generation require compliance with government-set regulations. By pressing a developing country to adopt a particular standard, developed countries can create first-mover advantages for their service providers. Other countries may try to establish open standards or "technology neutrality." The United States specifically includes standard-setting in the trade agenda (Wunsch-Vincent 2003). Moreover, major services firms in telecommunications may have a rent chain of manufacturers that produce equipment that complies with a certain standard and who have a vested interest in its promotion over competing rules. The next hypothesis sums up these predictions.

Hypothesis 2b. *The more important standards are for a particular industry and the more specific these standards, the greater the first-mover advantages in a PTA.*

If these propositions hold, they describe a key constituency for the liberalization of trade and investment between developed and developing countries. If a PTA creates first-mover advantages, firms seeking investment opportunities in services will throw their weight behind a preferential deal.

The discussion so far shows that various firms have specific interests in preferential trade agreements. The following section argues that host countries are likely to collude with these interests, making preferential agreements easier to achieve. By contrast, firms and economic groups that will resist liberalization efforts have no such allies. Although they are protectionist, they do not mount a principled opposition to preferential agreements. Rather, import-competing industries oppose liberalization in general.

Import-competing sectors and protectionism in North–South PTAs

Success or failure of firm lobbying depends on relative political influence compared to protectionist forces. As in all trade negotiations, protectionists are found at home and in the partner country. In this sense, PTA negotiations do not differ from other deals across domestic and international levels, the subject of the seminal contributions by Evans *et al.* (1993) and Moravcsik (1993, 1997, 1998). According to the logic of two-level games, governments negotiate at two tables: one for the deal with their counterparts, the other for ratification by domestic constituents in the respective institutions. The preferences and relative strength of domestic coalitions thus determine the leeway international negotiators have for an agreement.

The governments of developing countries often set out to negotiate PTAs with developed countries with the specific aim to attract foreign direct investment. The principal goal is not to achieve better access to the developed country market in a PTA relative to what could be obtained in the WTO. Rather, the developing country government merely needs to obtain slightly better access than competing countries with similar factor endowments – although "exchanging development for market access" (Shadlen 2005: 750) often entails making asymmetrical commitments that constrain developing country policies beyond WTO rules. The political coalitions in support of North–South PTAs are unlikely to result in much market opening in other fields in which developing countries are competitive, such as agricultural exports. Rather, these agreements tend to be driven by a narrow set of interest groups.

Multinational firms are likely to succeed in pressing their points in preferential North–South agreements. Not only are they often important employers offering higher-paid jobs than domestic firms, but also buyers of intermediate goods produced in the host country. In negotiations over tariffs and rules of origin, their views will therefore be represented at both sides of the table.[12] Consequently, they will be

---

[12] Putnam (1988: 459) briefly considers the effect of such transnational linkages on negotiations.

more successful in their lobbying than conventional exporters, who are less likely to have allies in the partner country.

Contrary to intuition and frequent press reports, conventional exporters of finished goods are often the least interested in bilateral North–South deals. Their return on assets is less likely to be favorably affected by preferential liberalization. Since differences in factor prices also imply differences in per capita income and purchasing power, exporters of expensive, developed country products stand to gain less by supporting a PTA with a developing country than multinational firms. Occasionally, a firm may be highly dependent on one particular market to sell its products.[13] Yet given the limited purchasing power of developing countries, they will rarely be such crucial markets. We can expect exporters to make less effort than firms that undertake FDI in the partner country. Unsurprisingly, if a potential PTA partner is a sizable market, the prospect motivates more lobbying by finished goods exporters and market service providers than access to a small country.

Note that the dominance of multinational firm interests also implies that intermediate goods producers from the home country will lobby strongly, but will be less successful than investors if they have import-competing counterparts in the host country. The familiar contest between export-oriented and import-competing firms plays out in the negotiation of preferential deals just like in multilateral rounds. Resistance to negotiating a PTA will therefore come from the usual suspects: import-competing firms and industries. For them, a preferential agreement is yet another threat to the protected home market. Moreover, since bilateral negotiations make it much easier to assess the concrete danger of cheaper imports, protectionists may actually have an informational advantage compared to multinational bargains, and may face fewer counterbalancing forces interested in exports (Gilligan 1997b). However, two factors may allow PTAs to be negotiated faster than multilateral agreements. First, not every partner country exports goods that compete with domestic producers. In this situation, negotiators have more freedom to strike a deal. Second, although the institutional context in the form of GATT Article XXIV limits the scope of exclusions, governments can still carve out a few sectors. Preferential trade agreements are supposed to cover substantially all trade, but given the right configuration of

---

[13] I thank Stephan Haggard for making this point.

domestic coalitions, excluding a few sectors may suffice to reach agreement.

Hypothesis 3. *The more an import-competing firm will be exposed to trade with a particular PTA partner, the more it will oppose the agreement.*

Although the contest between import-competing producers, buyers of imports, and export-oriented industries plays out in a preferential setting as in the multilateral arena, North–South negotiations will inevitably be characterized by stark asymmetries. In the words of Cameron and Tomlin (2000: 15) on NAFTA, "This meant that a US negotiator could say to his Mexican and Canadian counterpart, 'You want access to our $7 trillion market, and you offer in exchange access to your $250 and $500 billion markets? You are going to have to pay for that access, and here is what it is going to cost you …'."

These asymmetries imply that North–South PTAs will rarely offer substantial market access gains for those exports in which developing countries have a comparative advantage – often agricultural products. The "push" of firms that invest and the "pull" of developing country governments that want to attract FDI often suffice to bring about preferential trade agreements. As the case studies in this book show, North–South PTAs, indeed, offer little liberalization of "sensitive" goods such as agriculture.

Will organized labor oppose North–South PTAs? Moving manufacturing into developing countries is likely to make some jobs redundant. On the other hand, it also increases demand for high-end products. Moreover, labor opposition to PTAs may be hampered by organizational characteristics. Firm-based labor unions, for example, will have difficulties mounting a strong opposition because their economic interests in a PTA depend largely on the products they make. For some products, sales might increase because of a PTA; for others they might decline. Broader industry-based unions face the challenge that PTAs are in the interests of some members but not of others. Overall, unions may not be able to overcome the informational difficulties in coming to a coherent position.

But, perhaps more importantly, FDI flows from North to South tend to precede PTA negotiations by years, a point taken up in chapter 2 in the analysis of NAFTA. This turns labor opposition to North–South PTAs into a rearguard defense, although it may be enough to extract concessions and side-payments. Yet it is striking that, during dozens of

PTA negotiations, labor organizations, with the partial exception of US unions, have either remained passive or were so powerless when they chose to mount resistance that they could be ignored by governments.

Alternatives to PTAs

A reciprocal preferential trade agreement is only one among several international institutional choices for regulating policies for trade and investment. The principal alternatives are bilateral investment treaties (BITs) and greater efforts at trade and investment liberalization in the multilateral sphere. The former do not offer the same benefits with regard to trade and exclusivity, while the latter are much more demanding in terms of the political coalition required to support them.

In legal terms, BITs are international agreements that guarantee the property rights of foreign investors when they commit capital to a particular host country. Recent research supports the claim that developing countries compete for FDI by means of BITs (Elkins *et al.* 2006), although the evidence of their effectiveness remains mixed (Büthe and Milner 2004; Egger and Merlo 2007; Neumayer and Spess 2005; Rose-Ackerman and Tobin 2005; Walter 2002). While a growing number of North–South PTAs incorporate BIT-like clauses or chapters, their functions only partially overlap. Most recent North–South PTAs include clauses that broadly liberalize the investment environment of the developing country, among them a general right of establishment for foreign investors from the other members of the agreement. By contrast, the majority of BITs do not infringe the rights of states to screen and potentially exclude investments if this is done in a transparent fashion and according to a due process of law (UNCTAD 2007). A notable exception are BITs negotiated by the United States after the introduction of the 1987 treaty template that generally include preestablishment rights (Vandevelde 1993), although some developing countries (including China) have not concluded BITs with the United States for precisely this reason.

BITs appear to be an effective means of protecting investors from expropriation, but they are less important for multinational firms in manufacturing than for investors in natural resources. Since multinational manufacturing firms provide employment and, if they export, generate foreign exchange revenue, they create their own political constituency that offers considerable protection, so that expropriation has historically been of much less concern in this sector (Kobrin 1987). Manufacturing firms are therefore less likely specifically to demand BITs.

Still, many host countries have historically applied a variety of "host country operational measures" or trade-related investment measures (TRIMS), such as requirements to employ local personnel or to use a minimum share of local inputs with the goal of nurturing a domestic supply industry (UNCTAD 2001). These policies are of greater concern to multinational manufacturing firms than the risk of expropriation, but they tend to affect those multinational firms that are also concerned about trade barriers. Since these firms' interests are better served by a PTA than a BIT, the elimination of TRIMS becomes part of the goal pursued in North–South trade agreements.

The remaining investment-related risk for multinational firms is the temptation of host governments to raise tariffs on goods that they need to import for their production. Solving this hold-up problem calls for tariff reductions followed by guarantees against sudden reimposition. However, locking in low tariffs appears secondary to their reduction. Again, multinational manufacturing firms enjoy the same leverage based on the employment they provide, and most countries do not completely relinquish the right to reimpose tariffs at least temporarily, but create an apparatus to maintain the flexibility to levy anti-dumping duties if they have recently signed PTAs (Kucik and Reinhardt 2008). North–South PTAs will offer only limited guarantees against host country tariff impositions if the partner countries' interests diverge too widely.

By contrast, services firms are much more sensitive to the risk of expropriation than manufacturing companies. The profitability of services FDI in industries such as telecommunications and infrastructure often depends on long-term contracts. It is unsurprising, then, that infrastructure firms have resorted to arbitration clauses in BITs in instances of contract violations. For example, more than a dozen prominent arbitration cases at the International Centre for Settlement of Investment Disputes (ICSID) were brought against Argentina in the aftermath of the 2001 financial crisis and the end it put to 1-to-1 convertibility of the Argentine peso to the dollar. Most of these cases revolved around infrastructure user fees that are now paid in pesos, effectively reducing their value to a fifth of what investors expected at the time the contracts were signed.

Yet again, PTAs offer advantages that BITs cannot provide. Most importantly, WTO members can draw on an institutional template in

GATS Article V that permits preferential trade agreements in services. The GATS explicitly recognizes FDI, referred to as "commercial presence," as a mode of provision for services. In addition, many of the guarantees provided by BITs, such as non-discrimination and transparency, are commitments all GATS signatories have made on a multilateral basis. Most developing countries, however, have refrained from liberalizing services trade and investment in the WTO negotiations (Sauvé 2000). The actual opening of investment regimes in services industries takes place either unilaterally or on a preferential basis (Hoekman and Sauvé 1994; Stephenson 2000).

The second alternative to North–South PTAs would be comprehensive tariff reduction and services liberalization on a multilateral basis. PTAs might simply be a second-best alternative because multilateral negotiations at the WTO are stalled. Without any doubt, negotiations among more than 150 states are bound to be lengthy, especially as the WTO's remit is expanded into more and more issue areas. However, interpreting PTAs as the result of a better multilateral alternative leads to different theoretical predictions for lobbying coalitions and the design of preferential agreements.

If PTAs merely substituted liberalization efforts at the WTO, we would observe very similar lobbying coalitions in favor of tariff reductions. Export-oriented sectors would support liberalization, while import-competing sectors could be expected to resist it in line with the established results of endogenous tariff theory (Barton *et al.* 2006: 15; Magee *et al.* 1989; Milner 1988, 1999). Issue-linkage might occur, in which the most competitive sectors in each country gain access to the other partner's market in exchange for overcoming domestic resistance (Davis 2004). As a result, tariff liberalization should broadly follow patterns of comparative advantage, although asymmetries between developed and developing countries will circumscribe liberalization by the North. Moreover, in the design of the PTA, we would expect a different emphasis in the lobbying aims. A firm from the North that primarily targets the market of a developing country would focus on bilateral tariff reductions, and possibly press for bans on MFN tariff reductions (duty-drawbacks) for third parties if these pose a competition in the developing country market. However, if the developing country imposes higher tariffs, these firms would have no incentive to demand particularly strict rules of origin.

In services, the dividing line is less clear, since the benefits of preferential over multilateral liberalization are often highly specific to

Table 2.1. *Predictions based on different motivations for North–South PTAs*

	PTAs have specific benefits	PTAs as substitute for WTO
Coalitions for and against	Individual firms with FDI in host country; rent chains specific to partner country; import-competing sectors oppose	Sectoral coalitions, export-oriented vs. import-competing; coalitions form along industry lines
Trade-offs	Narrow liberalization that exempts inefficient sectors	Broad market opening based on comparative advantage
Design	High non-tariff barriers against third parties, ROOs	By definition no strict ROOs

individual firms and dependent on the mode of provision of services – if FDI or "commercial presence" is required, they tend to be more pronounced than in the case of cross-border trade. Both services and manufacturing are more likely to show lobbying along broad industry lines in multilateral negotiations, while preferential liberalization is often driven by organized political demands of individual firms that take the lead in a rent chain, but whose interests may differ from similar firms that have no investment in the host country. These rent chains reinforce the "private goods" character of many North–South PTAs and favor narrow liberalization outcomes and high barriers against outsiders. Table 2.1 contrasts the coalitions, liberalization outcomes, and design features that we would expect to see, depending on whether PTAs have intrinsic benefits because they are discriminatory or merely substitute for stalled WTO negotiations.

If the arguments put forth so far hold, they help to explain why preferential liberalization has become desirable for many firms. Foreign direct investment from developed to developing countries has expanded rapidly in the last two decades, stimulating increasing flows of vertical intra-industry trade. But the accelerating proliferation of these agreements outpaces the growth of FDI and trade by far. As I argue in the next section, the discriminatory aspects of PTAs that make them politically attractive have unintended consequences: they motivate excluded parties to seek their own bilateral agreements with FDI host countries. Although even PTAs concluded as alternatives to the WTO because of the slow progress of liberalization may cause reactions from other countries, this outcome is made more likely by the narrow liberalization and high barriers against outsiders in North–South PTAs.

The endogenous dynamic of PTAs

If firms are successful in pursuing their preferences in PTA negotiations, then they gain an advantage over competitors from other countries. Strict rules of origin, the abolishment of MFN rebates for producers in EPZs, and the structural features of service markets either impose costs on incumbents from non-member countries or raise the barriers for new entrants. Firms from non-member countries face an unpleasant choice: they can either forsake the host country as a market and location for investment and absorb the cost increase to stay in the market, or they can try to level the playing field to remain competitive.

Non-member firms' reactions to exclusion

Once the PTA is in place, how does the situation present itself to firms from non-member countries? Take the following stylized situation of three countries: two developed home countries A_1 and A_2, and D, a developing host country. To simplify, country D imposes a uniform MFN tariff of 15 percent; countries A_1 and A_2 levy a 5 percent uniform tariff. Under the assumptions outlined above, D attracts FDI in manufacturing and services from A_1 and A_2 because of the differing factor endowments. In the absence of a PTA, all intermediate and capital goods from A_1 or A_2 are taxed at the same MFN rate. Host country D can rebate the MFN tariff on these goods for *all* foreign firms if they manufacture for export, and all firms pay the same 5 percent MFN tariff when they export finished goods to either A_1 or A_2. Figure 2.1 presents this situation.

Firms from either A would prefer tariff reduction by D. Lowering the barriers to trade reduces the cost of vertically integrated production and makes FDI in D more profitable. Often, a host country will attract more FDI from one developed country than from the other, due either to geographic proximity, lower barriers because of similar language and legal institutions, or differences in firm strategy. Geographically close countries have been labeled "natural" partners (Frankel *et al.* 1995) because of low transport costs. For these idiosyncratic factors, one

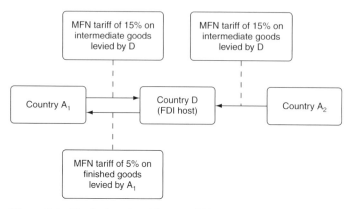

Figure 2.1. Vertical trade without a PTA

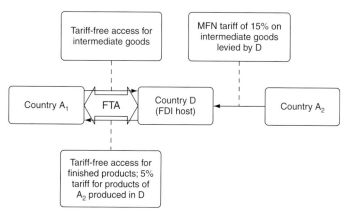

Figure 2.2. Vertical trade with a PTA and rules of origin

country pair will negotiate a first PTA. Now assume that the first, offensive PTA is in place, with strict rules of origin and a ban on the rebate of MFN tariffs, as depicted in figure 2.2.

In this scenario, the excluded firms face different costs in a vertically integrated production across borders. Intermediate and capital goods pay the MFN tariff of the host country, which is now prevented from offering rebates. Moreover, firms from A_2 may even have to fulfill the rule of origin requirement to avoid paying a second tariff, the MFN tariff upon export to A_1! For A_2's service firms, the first-mover advantages created by the PTA between A_1 and D penalize them when they seek to enter the market. Upstream producers from A_2 will be the worst affected, since multinational firms from A_2 are forced to switch to regional suppliers from within the PTA.

What are the options for firms from A_2? As so often in political economy, the choice is between voice and exit in Hirschman's (1970) classic formulation. The simplest choice would be to de-invest. Firms could forgo the opportunity of using country D as an export platform to supply A_1's market, relocate production to a country with similar endowments, and export from there while paying MFN tariffs. But if the benefits of production in D – proximity to the market of A_2 combined with low wages – still outweigh the increased cost, non-member firms are likely to invest more rather than less. Since such a location of production creates a competitive advantage, non-member firms will try to maintain this access.

If firms from A_2 indeed choose to preserve or raise current levels of FDI, then they have a strong incentive to try and convince the host government of country D to lower its most-favored-nation tariffs. This is the likeliest and least costly response, but one that will rarely suffice. Firms from A_2 can offer little in return for such a host country concession other than the promise of staying in the host country. But the most-favored-nation principle implies that any liberalization outside a PTA has to be extended to all GATT members. If unilateral liberalization was not previously feasible for D, then the first PTA will not change this situation. The next-best response to the PTA between A_1 and D is to counter with an agreement between A_2 and D. Eliminating the tariff between A_2 and D takes away the force of the rules of origin: goods produced in D with parts and components that are imported tariff-free at worst face the MFN tariff when exported to country A_1 – recall that this tariff is likely to be very low.

Hypothesis 4. *The more important country D as an investment location for firms from A_2 and the higher the barriers created by the offensive PTA, the more likely that the firms will lobby for a defensive PTA.*

The importance of country D as an investment location in terms of FDI interacts with the trade barriers created by the first PTA. Firms will base their decision on the trade-off between the cost of lobbying home and host government and the potential losses incurred by the first, offensive PTA. If they consider the location and sunk investments as crucial for their profitability, they will likely press for a defensive PTA. To this end, firms need not demand further liberalization from the host country than what was conceded in the first PTA between A_1 and D – achieving the same reduction of barriers to trade and investment suffices. Ideally, a defensive PTA will incorporate a "ratchet clause" that ensures matching commitments if host country D accelerates its liberalization with A_1.

Given the functional similarity of domestic regulations for services to tariffs for manufacturing industries, a defensive PTA is most effective at leveling the playing field when the barriers created (or preferentially removed) by the first PTA are regulatory in nature. The subsequently negotiated PTA will then focus on technical issues such as standards or "technology neutrality." If, on the other hand, the offensive agreement has created significant first-mover advantages, they may sometimes outweigh the benefits of a later PTA. Firms from A_2 might choose to exit by selling their assets, or forgo the chance of later entry. A more subtle effect might be a shift in emphasis of the lobbying targets. For example, if a particular service can be supplied through FDI as well as cross-border, but the route to a commercial presence is difficult because of large economies of scale, then firms from A_2 may choose to press for improved market access through the alternative mode of supply.

The propositions outlined above regarding the preferences of firms can be directly extended to the defensive agreement. Barriers for non-members target immediate competitors, so that the coalitions of firms lobbying for counter-agreements are often very similar. The lobbying efforts by firms in A_2 parallel the initial efforts made in A_1 – with one key difference: higher barriers for non-members imply a lower threshold at which firms become active, because the potential losses provide stronger incentives to lobby. Because of this effect, the unintended – and, as I argue, most undesirable – consequence of bilateral deals between developed and developing countries is that they engender their own proliferation.

As in the case of offensive PTA initiatives, opponents to defensive PTAs in general are firms in import-competing sectors, typically comprising agriculture in developed countries, capital in developing countries that might be exposed to competition from entering multinational corporations (MNCs), and less efficient producers. These need not always be present in all cases. For example, if the United States or the EU negotiates a PTA with a developing country, agricultural producers in the South might suddenly be import-competing because of the subsidies offered in the North.

Whether workers join a coalition against a defensive PTA depends largely on their sector and even their wages, since highly skilled workers

Table 2.2. *Predicted lobbying coalitions in offensive and defensive PTAs*

	Offensive PTA		Defensive PTA	
	North (home)	South (host)	(North) home	(South) host
For	MNCs in manufacturing and services		MNCs in manufacturing and services	
	Suppliers	Suppliers	Suppliers	
		Labor	Labor	Labor
		Agriculture		Agriculture
Against	Import-competing firms	Import-competing firms	Import-competing firms	Import-competing firms
		Domestic capital		Domestic capital
	Labor			Suppliers
	Agriculture		Agriculture	

may not be as fearful that their jobs are being displaced. Especially in firms producing intermediate goods, labor can sometimes gain from restoring a level playing field. Note also that suppliers in the developing host country are more likely to resist a defensive PTA if it robs them of the benefits of investment diversion into the host country – unless the effect of the offensive PTA is so strong that outsiders leave the host country. In practice, labor may again face an informational challenge and fail to differentiate between offensive and defensive PTAs, or may not voice any opposition at all.

Table 2.2 sums up the predicted coalitions that will emerge when an ideal-type of a North–South PTA is negotiated. The principal difference is that suppliers in the host country have very little to gain from a defensive PTA since they would lose the cost advantage created by ROOs. Labor's position is more likely to be in opposition to an offensive agreement, but in favor of a defensive PTA, subject to the qualifications laid out above.

Clearly, if a defensive PTA undermines much of the protectionism built into the offensively negotiated agreement, the first developed country (A_1 in the stylized facts above) has an incentive to try to prevent agreements that level the playing field. No existing agreement, however, contains clauses that directly constrain the sovereignty of a country and its freedom to sign subsequent PTAs. Yet more subtle interference may be common. For example, the same multinational firms from A_1 that pressed for discriminatory clauses may also lobby the developing country government to prevent a defensive PTA that erodes their protective barriers. Even if they fail to stall completely negotiations of a defensive agreement, they may slow down the tariff reductions.

At other times, firms from A_1 may anticipate that their advantages will be only temporary, but still be of use. Some firms may support a PTA because it provides "breathing room" for firms to complete the restructuring of their operations to export (Chase 2004). Services firms may only be interested in the first-mover advantages created by a PTA because they already have enough of a foothold in the host country to expand quickly. Yet even if the gains are only temporary, the time horizon of many firms (or rather, their management) may be short enough to warrant considerable lobbying efforts. For example, it took almost a decade for the first defensive PTA to materialize in reaction to NAFTA – longer than most chief executives are in office.

Conversely, firms from A_2 may lobby D's government to avoid being excluded by an offensive PTA. Again, if they cannot prevent such an agreement, they may try to slow down the preferential liberalization or weaken its non-tariff barriers such as its rules of origin. Whether they succeed will depend on their political influence with the host government, usually as a function of the employment they provide, their importance as buyers of products of the local supply industry, and the foreign exchange they generate. For example, a firm from A_2 that focuses on the domestic market might have less influence than a firm from A_1 that promises exports back to the home market.

Intensifying the competition

While political support for the first PTA stemmed from FDI flows to the emerging market, based on strategic decisions by firms about desirable production locations, the countermovement can result from much weaker trade and investment linkages. The initial PTA offers the prospect of lower costs for production fragmented across borders and improves on the status quo. The decision to support a PTA therefore involves an element of uncertainty, because firms do not know ex ante whether their lobbying efforts will really pay off.

For firms from non-member countries, however, the case is clear: if strict rules of origin are established and MFN rebates for non-members are proscribed, they are worse off than before. These firms will immediately feel the effect of import taxes and administrative costs of compliance with rules of origin. Since the initial PTA *raises* the barriers, firms have greater incentives to seek a reduction in these impediments to trade and investment. Similarly, services firms are able to observe directly the acquisitions made by first-movers, the regulatory barriers to FDI, and soon even the revenue stream of their competitors if they are public companies.

Once a number of bilateral agreements have been signed, it becomes more costly for governments to stay on the sidelines. While firms at first might accept discrimination in a few markets, the cumulative effect of a growing number of PTAs may spur them on to lobby for defensive moves. Given these circumstances, government decision-makers will have an incentive to anticipate and preempt the initiatives by other countries by actively seeking PTAs. But this effect motivates even more countries, despite weak trade and investment linkages, to opt for bilateral deals. Once countries have gone down the road of PTAs, the proliferation of bilateral trade agreements becomes endogenous.

Systemic implications

What implications for multilateral trade liberalization can be derived from the framework presented here? Although this study does not address the welfare effects of PTAs, its findings suggest that the current proliferation of bilateral agreements may be less liberalizing than its proponents argue. The unfolding competitive dynamic produces a network of PTAs – the "spaghetti bowl" effect (Bhagwati and Panagariya 1996) – each with different rules that reflect the preferences of firms. PTAs therefore create an enormous burden for firms as they seek to comply with documentation and tracing of origin rules.

In particular, firms from developing countries and small and medium-sized enterprises face capacity problems in fulfilling these requirements. Anson *et al.* (2005) estimate that up to 47 percent of Mexico's preferential access gains to the US market in 2000 were absorbed by administrative costs related to NAFTA tracing rules. Depken and Ford (1999) show that NAFTA documentation requirements are strongly biased against smaller firms to the point where they may further industrial concentration within sectors and depress trade between the United States and Mexico. Kunimoto and Sawchuk (2004) report that small Canadian exporters often prefer to pay the US MFN tariff than deal with NAFTA's complex ROOs. But such complex non-tariff barriers to trade are by no means limited to NAFTA: Brenton (2003) argues that the European Union's "everything but arms" initiative in offering least-developed countries better access to its markets is much less effective than had been assumed, mainly because of complex ROOs that limit the ability of developing countries to use tariff preferences. In another study Brenton and Ikezuki (2006) estimate that the cost of compliance is the equivalent of an *ad valorem* tariff of 6.7 percent for access to the United States, 8.5 percent for exports to the EU, and 5.6 percent for shipments to Japan. Given these considerations, the liberalizing effect of bilateral agreements may primarily help multinational firms that can afford to do the paperwork. Yet if these firms actually benefit from ROOs, as is argued in this study, then each PTA will create a group of supporters with a vested interest in their continuation.

But do PTAs at least create a pro-free trade constituency? Again, much depends on the investment undertaken by firms. Take a situation in which two countries with similar factor endowments conclude a PTA. These types of country tend to trade in similar goods that are differentiated to suit different consumer tastes. Intra-industry trade will be horizontal rather than vertical in nature. In the standard example, Japan and the EU trade high-quality automobiles with each other. Production of these goods requires economies of scale to be competitive. As Milner (1997: 81) argues, "firms would rather export from existing plants to attain optimal scale than invest abroad." But since firms also become more competitive within the PTA, they will want to export more to non-members. This requires reciprocal tariff concessions. These predictions closely conform to the bargaining observed between countries of similar levels of development, such as Canada and the United States. Moreover, these countries in practice tend to have low MFN tariffs. PTAs of this type could be stepping-stones to global free trade.

By contrast, as McLaren (2002) has argued, PTAs may be "insidious" because producers may make specialized investments in anticipation of preferential agreements. In this sense trade partners are unnatural, because their specialization towards each other is a product of a PTA. Moreover, in North–South agreements, multinational firms are undertaking much of the export-oriented investment. Vertical intra-industry trade within a region creates incentives to extend protection rather than to truly liberalize. If, at the same time, PTAs exclude uncompetitive sectors, then they are unlikely to bolster global free trade.

The simplest countermeasure, at least in principle, is multilateral tariff reduction. With lower MFN tariffs charged by the host countries of FDI, rules of origin lose their potential to divert trade. But if the propositions put forth here hold, then the host country should have little incentive unilaterally to reduce its tariffs, but would rather hold on to its preference margin to attract FDI. At the same time, preferential liberalization with the most important host countries of FDI will take away support for multilateral efforts by fulfilling key demands of multinational firms. Moreover, if states carve out protected sectors such as agriculture, then the multilateral trade institutions will be left with the most intractable problems of protectionism. The case studies in the next chapters evaluate existing agreements in the light of these concerns.

3 | NAFTA – *the original sin?*

I T is difficult to overstate the importance of the North American Free Trade Agreement for the evolution of the global trade regime. NAFTA marked the first preferential trade agreement across the North–South divide negotiated under Article XXIV of the GATT. It also signified a major diversion off the course of multilateralism by the United States, the co-founder and often the most important promoter of the international institutions that "embedded" liberalism (Ruggie 1982) in the post-World War II era. The United States had negotiated only two free trade agreements previously – the United States–Israel FTA, signed in 1985 to extend strategic support to Israel (Destler 1986: 26), and the 1987 Canada–United States FTA (CUSFTA), the result of a turnaround in Canadian policy after almost a century of resisting US advances. Neither agreement, however, had much potential to affect outsiders. Israel's regional political isolation left it entirely dependent on European and US trade in any case. Canada lowered its MFN tariffs below US levels in the Uruguay Round and participated actively in the GATS, thereby limiting the discrimination against outsiders.

Mexico's desire to sign a trade agreement with the United States surprised even the most prominent experts and inspired a considerable body of research (Bulmer-Thomas *et al.* 1994; Cameron 1997; Grinspun and Cameron 1993; Pastor and Wise 1994). Perhaps most importantly, NAFTA became the template for a multitude of North–South agreements across the globe. The agreement triggered reactions by the EU and Japan, as well as Mexico's neighbors in the region, and kicked off the avalanche of North–South PTAs.

Why would NAFTA, arguably an agreement between three already very integrated economies, have any impact on the global trade regime beyond its region? To answer this question in the following chapters we need to take a closer look at the specific form of the trade and investment liberalization and rules of origin in NAFTA, and the interests that shaped this outcome.

Contrary to the rhetoric of free trade, preferential trade agreements became attractive to key industries when many US manufacturing firms were on the defensive, while liberalization in the more competitive service sector made little progress in multilateral negotiations. For US multinational firms, NAFTA offered an opportunity to seize the benefits of the liberalization undertaken by Mexico, an important host country for FDI from the United States. NAFTA did not, however, trigger the flows of FDI to Mexico, although together with the depreciation of the peso after the 1994 financial crisis it probably gave it an additional boost. As the chapter shows, Mexican liberalization had proceeded far enough to attract considerable investment from the United States. Key manufacturing industries began restructuring their operations towards export-oriented production well before NAFTA was on the agenda.

Once under way, the NAFTA negotiations were decisively influenced by the preferences of US firms towards a selectively protectionist outcome in precisely those industries where outsiders could use Mexico as an export platform to the home market. Under increasing competitive pressure, US firms tried to secure the locational benefits of FDI in Mexico for themselves. In conjunction with Mexico's remaining barriers to imports and investment from the rest of the world, NAFTA therefore held the potential to discriminate strongly against outsiders, triggering the defensive reactions by the EU and Japan.

NAFTA was obviously more than a purely economic agreement. As a case study, it is overdetermined. The agreement was also meant to further Mexican development to help stem an influx of undocumented immigrants into the United States – a hope that, seen from more than a decade later, was not fulfilled. Already during his 1980 presidential campaign, Ronald Reagan spoke of a vision of free market access across all of North America. NAFTA also locked in economic reforms, gave a strong impetus to Mexico's democratization (Cameron and Wise 2004), and encouraged massive US support for Mexico during the 1994 financial crisis (Cameron and Aggarwal 1996). For both the United States and Mexico the agreement was at least as much the fulfillment of a political vision as a trade-focused bargain. Many US manufacturing industry associations lobbied for a particular design of the agreement rather than free trade per se.

But NAFTA is also close to the ideal type of North–South PTA. Mexico's liberalization efforts attracted considerable inflows of foreign direct investment, leading to a vertical integration of production with the United States. Free trade between the two partners facilitated the mutual specialization, but it also threatened to open the back door to the US market. Implementing NAFTA therefore carried the political price of strict rules of origin – rules that in turn would generate an unanticipated response by triggering defensive agreements. The agreement therefore presents clear evidence of how the micro-level decisions made at the behest of individual industries and even firms have repercussions at the systemic level of international economic relations.

Bilateralism in US trade policy

US trade policy preferences began to move away from unconditional support for multilateralism with shifts in comparative advantage, in particular the rise in the United States of service industries and the concurrent decline in manufacturing. Starting in the late 1970s, services were pushed on to the negotiating agenda by US business groups (Freeman 1998: 184). In 1984, Congress, stirred on by the 1981–82 recession and the uncompetitive exchange rate of the first Reagan administration that – at least as alleged by US firms – battered the industrial heartland of the United States, passed a new Trade and Tariff Act. The 1984 Act expressed the congressional reaction to growing concern among import-competing industries, a shrinking and specialized constituency for free trade (Richardson 1991), and limited success in pushing the services and investment agenda at the 1982 GATT Ministerial Meeting in Geneva (Destler 1986: 226; Frankel 1997: 5; Krueger 1995b: 87; Schott 1983: 4–45, 1989: 4). In May 1985 the Advisory Committee for Trade Negotiations, an important body in which business interests are transmitted to the US administration, issued a report on a potential future GATT round. While groups advocating the new issues of services, intellectual property, and investment strongly supported a new multilateral round, most manufacturing industries appeared reluctant, and instead called for an aggressive trade policy in defense of US import-competing industries (Ostry 1990: 27–28). The shift to a preferential trade policy took place in the context of declining competitiveness in the manufacturing sector.

Following the mandate of the 1984 Act, the USTR developed a series of bilateral instruments for trade and investment liberalization. One element was a program of bilateral investment treaties. European countries, trying to provide their investors with a minimum of legal guarantees against expropriation by developing countries, had been active in signing BITs for over twenty years. BITs usually follow a common template, or model BIT. The US approach differed from European policy in that the 1987 and 1991 US model BITs also liberalized investment: they prohibited the use of performance requirements and scheduled previously closed sectors of the host country for opening to foreign investment (Vandevelde 1993).

The new BIT was first implemented in the 1991 United States–Argentina treaty, which became the template for investment chapters in future free trade agreements. Neither the United States–Israel FTA nor the CUSFTA, however, contained clauses equivalent to the US model BIT. NAFTA broke new ground in creating a legal framework that closely reflected new economic realities: investment and trade are linked in the economic integration with emerging markets, as Mexico's liberalization and the resulting changes in the character of FDI show. Yet, as argued in the previous chapter, if the host country maintains high barriers to the outside world, preferential trade liberalization discriminates strongly against firms from third countries. Mexico took major unilateral steps to liberalization during the 1980s; important tariff and non-tariff barriers, however, remained.

Mexico's unilateral liberalization

Like many developing countries, Mexico followed an economic policy of import substitution until the mid-1980s. Foreign direct investment was restricted and burdened by performance requirements such as domestic content quota and export-balancing requirements. Importers required licenses and paid high tariffs. The 1973 Ley para Promover la Inversión Mexicana y Regular la Inversión Extranjera reserved key sectors of the economy, in particular resource extraction and public utilities, for the state or exclusive Mexican ownership. All other activities had a 49 percent ceiling on foreign participation, subject to approval by the National Foreign Investment Commission. The guiding principles were the protection of Mexican-owned companies, an increase in local employment, the use of local inputs, and the transfer of technology (UNCTC 1992: 13).

Central to the Mexican development policy was the promotion of a domestic automotive industry. With this goal in mind, the government issued several decrees to guide foreign investment. Between 1962 and 1983, four auto decrees mandated a 60 percent local content quota to stimulate the development of the local auto parts industry, while banning imports of assembled cars. Given the rapid growth of Mexico's economy, which averaged 6 percent per year until 1982, the US "Big Three" automakers, along with Nissan and Volkswagen as well as (briefly) Renault, invested in Mexico despite these policies (Peres Nuñez 1990: 18). However, the protected market structure led to "low production runs, high prices and poor quality" (Calderón *et al.* 1995: 22). Transplant factories and especially parts manufacturers worked below efficient scales of production compared with plants in the developed world. Restrictions on FDI, especially in the supply industry, prevented multinational firms from achieving economies of scale (Peres Nuñez 1990: 22). Still, the sector generated jobs, many in the Mexican-owned parts industry, and began to export successfully, especially when the 1977 decree allowed 20 percent of the automakers' production to be shifted to the maquiladoras (Robert 2000: 183–84). While automotive parts production was not as efficient as in the developed world, the import-substitution policies nurtured what later became the basis for the rapid restructuring of Mexico's auto industry by fostering the necessary human capital for the export boom of the second half of the 1980s.

In contrast to the import-substitution industries, the maquiladora sector was open to 100 percent foreign ownership, provided that 80 percent of the production was exported. Under the former US tariff classifications 806 and 807, products could be exported to Mexico, processed, and reimported into the United States. Duty was only levied on the value added abroad. In addition, in a duty-drawback scheme, the Mexican government rebated the import tariff on intermediate goods (parts and other supplies) from third countries, again provided that the final product was exported. Effectively, foreign investors that wanted to use Mexico as an export platform to the US market did not pay any import duty. The maquiladoras attracted considerable investment from US firms, but also from Japanese and European multinationals. These firms used their US subsidiaries to qualify for the US export processing tariffs, but often imported capital and intermediate goods from outside North America using the duty-drawback scheme.[1]

---

[1] In addition, several other foreign automotive companies assembled complete knock down kits (CKDs), essentially finished cars that had been taken apart again to be shipped to Mexico, in very small production runs during the 1960s, until later decrees restricted such activities. See Bennett and Sharpe (1985: 52–53).

Besides textiles, much of this investment was concentrated in auto parts and electronics manufacturing (Calderón *et al.* 1995: 23). Most prominent among these was the production of color television sets, accounting for 4 million units in 1989. Combining sets and exports of subassembly parts, 65 percent of color televisions sold in the United States in the same year were either wholly or partially produced in Mexico's maquiladoras (Koido 1991: 23).

Unlike manufacturing, the service sector was completely closed to foreign investment. State-owned companies provided key services such as telecommunications. No foreign investment was permitted in financial services with the exception of Citibank, the only foreign bank allowed to operate since 1929. State-owned development banks such as Nacional Financiera provided long-term lending for firms, while most other investment was based on the retained earnings of firms. The Mexican central bank mandated the holding of government bonds and set interest-rate ceilings. In 1974, the government sought a consolidation into a universal banking system along German lines (Welch and Gruben 1993: 1–3). Finally, in the crisis year of 1982, President José López Portillo nationalized all Mexican banks and merged them into several larger institutions to stem the flight of capital (Ramírez 1989: 91). In that year, despite several decades of rapid growth, Mexico plunged into a severe crisis, brought about by the collapse of the oil price and the resulting difficulties in servicing its spiraling foreign debt. By 1983 the Mexican government saw itself forced to open the foreign investment regime to attract capital from abroad. Facing severe balance-of-payments problems, the administration of Miguel de la Madrid (1982–88) agreed to an austerity program designed by the International Monetary Fund (IMF). Central elements were the opening of the economy to foreign competition with the aim of joining the GATT, culminating in Mexico's formal admission on July 25, 1986, a promotion of non-petroleum exports through the expansion of maquiladoras, the liberalization of the FDI regime, and the privatization of public companies (Ramírez 1989: 99–100).

Over the course of the decade, Mexico embarked on a rapid and sweeping liberalization effort. In accordance with the 1983 National Development Plan, the National Foreign Investment Commission issued new guidelines indicating that most sectors no longer required authorization for joint ventures with less than 49 percent foreign participation. Beginning in 1985, many projects with up to 100 percent foreign capital were approved (Ramírez 1989: 106). The May 1989

Table 3.1. *Liberalization of the Mexican import regime, 1985–90*

	1985	1986	1987	1988	1989	1990
Coverage of import licenses[i]	92.2	46.9	35.8	23.2	22.1	19.9
Coverage of reference prices[ii]	18.7	19.6	13.4	0	0	0
Maximum tariff	100.0	45.0	40.0	20.0	20.0	20.0
Production-weighted average tariff	23.5	24.0	22.7	11.0	12.6	12.5

[i] Share of total imports.
[ii] Percentage share of tradable output.
Source: USITC (1990).

decree on "Regulations of the Law to Promote Mexican Investment and Regulate Foreign Investment" changed the application of the 1973 law by allowing 100 percent ownership in 73 of the 74 economic categories defined in the statute. Mexico's applied average MFN tariff was lowered to a fifth of prior rates, or 9.8 percent on a trade-weighted basis (Lustig 1998: 129–33) and 12.5 percent on a production-weighted basis, as table 3.1 shows. From a highly protectionist trade regime, Mexico quickly moved to open its economy.

Through a sweeping reduction in tariffs, Mexico had already unilaterally taken important steps to attract manufacturing FDI before NAFTA was negotiated. Although import-substitution industrialization failed, forcing on Mexico an opening to the outside world, it created the industrial basis for the subsequent reorientation towards exports. Geographical proximity to the United States and a pool of low-cost labor made Mexico attractive for manufacturing FDI that produced for the US home market.

The service sector remained closed to foreign participation until much later. Mexican banks remained in state hands until 1991, although the de la Madrid administration divested the non-bank assets of the nationalized banks. Finally, the government reprivatized the banks and returned to the universal banking system with the Financial Groups Law of 1990 (Gruben *et al.* 1993). Foreign direct investment therefore primarily flowed into manufacturing.

The Mexican export platform: FDI as restructuring agent

As multinational firms reacted to Mexico's liberalization efforts, the country began to attract considerable inflows of FDI into its manufacturing sector. Unlike earlier periods, though, this FDI sought efficiency rather than market access. Mexico offered the central locational advantage of a pool of low-cost labor close to the US home market. Liberalization coincided with a change in the strategies of multinational firms, especially from the United States, that sought to use developing countries as export platforms. The strategic shift, however, took place before a trade deal between the United States and Mexico was a realistic option. The turning point for the flows of US FDI into Mexico, in both quantitative and qualitative terms, came several years before NAFTA. Since this integration was in full swing before NAFTA, the arguments of US firms in favor of strict rules of origin stand out as obvious protectionism. US manufacturers enjoyed de facto free trade with Mexico even without a trade agreement, thanks to the EPZs created by the maquiladora program, but only NAFTA offered the chance to raise the cost for Japanese and European competitors.

US FDI in Mexico before NAFTA

US FDI in Mexico picked up in the late 1980s, with considerable flows into automobile production, rubber products (for car tires and gaskets), and electronics. These flows of FDI needed very little encouragement in the form of international agreements. In a 1989 survey by the Organisation for Economic Co-operation and Development (OECD) of US CEOs, most respondents perceived Mexico's opening as driven by underlying structural forces rather than domestic politics, forces that precluded a rolling back of liberalization in any case (Peres Nuñez 1990: 53). A second indication of the turning point for US FDI in Mexico is found in the trend in total FDI stock over time. Figure 3.1 shows changes in the stock of US FDI in Mexico between 1966 and 2006 as published by the Bureau of Economic Analysis (BEA). We can estimate the point(s) in time at which the trend turned by fitting a piecewise linear relationship and estimating which assumed "break" minimizes the squared deviations from the actual data by conducting a series of F-tests.[2] The time point with the biggest F-test value is indicated in the graph by a vertical line.

---

[2] See the chapter appendix for details of the estimation and also Graham and Wada (2000) for a similar analysis with older data.

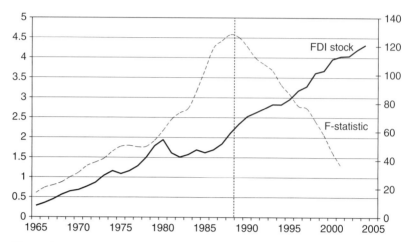

Figure 3.1. US FDI stock in Mexico in US$, logarithmic scale (left axis), F-statistic of test for structural break (right axis)

A linear relationship with a cusp at 1989 fits the data better than any other breakpoint, suggesting that the change in the trend in 1989 was more important than any other trend change before or after. This does not imply that NAFTA had no effect at all on foreign direct investment flows – it gave the FDI flows a further boost, as described in the chapter appendix – but its function as a commitment device appears less important for the decisions of US firms to invest than the policies implemented earlier. Before 1989 the FDI stock grew at an approximate rate of 3.2 percent per year, whereas after that year the growth rate approximates 6.2 percent. Assuming that most projects take about two to three years of planning, it appears that unilateral liberalization, not the at the time unforeseeable free trade agreement, caused a more important shift in the FDI trend. Changes in the character of FDI, analyzed in the next section, corresponded to the quantitative trend change.

Retooling Mexican factories for export

As inflows into Mexico picked up, US FDI also underwent important qualitative changes. In the late 1980s, four factors coincided in Mexico: trade liberalization, an energy cost 50 percent lower than that paid by foreign investors in southeast and east Asia in 1987, very low labor costs following the depreciation of the peso in the wake of the debt

Table 3.2. *Exports by US firms based in Mexico, 1983–99, US$ million*

	Total sales	Total exports to the US	Percentage intra-firm	Percentage of total sales	Total exports to other countries	Percentage of total sales
1983	11,491	1,645	89.0	14.3	393	3.4
1984	14,298	2,271	94.4	15.9	685	4.8
1985	15,832	2,856	95.1	18.0	671	4.2
1986	12,815	3,207	95.9	25.0	764	6.0
1987	14,351	4,223	97.0	29.4	850	5.9
1988	17,946	4,917	97.5	27.4	790	4.4
1989	20,143	5,349	98.5	26.6	1,081	5.4
1990	22,924	6,015	98.4	26.2	953	4.2
1991	28,662	7,421	97.4	25.9	755	2.6
1992	34,334	8,489	98.5	24.7	873	2.5
1993	36,558	9,676	97.8	26.5	1,130	3.1
1994	43,748	12,426	95.4	28.4	1,333	3.0
1995	39,255	14,470	95.4	36.9	1,774	4.5
1996	49,540	19,887	94.5	40.1	3,411	6.9
1997	57,995	21,460	96.0	37.0	4,766	8.2
1998	67,947	22,232	94.3	32.7	5,161	7.6
1999	84,891	22,667	91.4	26.7	7,207	8.5

Source: Bureau of Economic Analysis, author's calculations.

crisis, and slumping domestic demand (Peres Nuñez 1990: 64). US manufacturing firms therefore sought to restructure existing plants for production for export. A crucial element of this strategy was the specialization of existing plants to achieve greater economies of scale (Calderón *et al.* 1995: 16). Given the changing circumstances in the host country, the new investment was different in character from earlier, market-seeking and tariff-jumping FDI.

The extent to which US firms used Mexico as an export platform is striking. Figures from the Bureau of Economic Analysis in table 3.2 show that between 1983 and 1999 the share of total sales that was exported to the United States grew from 14.3 to 26.7 percent, with a peak of 40 percent in 1996, when the effects of the Mexican currency crisis depressed domestic demand. Virtually all of these exports were intra-firm trade or trade between close affiliates. Notably, the share

Table 3.3. *Sales by US firms back to the United States, by industry*

	Sales		Industry shares		
	Value, US$ million	Percentage intra-firm	Machinery	Transportation equipment	Electric equipment and electronics
1985	2,720	95.1	*d*	74.9	*d*
1986	3,076	95.9	1.7	76.2	17.0
1987	4,029	97.0	2.1	*d*	13.3
1988	4,559	97.5	3.5	73.7	15.6
1989	5,043	98.5	6.6	61.9	19.3
1990	5,692	98.4	5.5	*d*	*d*
1991	7,009	97.4	4.3	70.1	17.3
1992	8,096	98.5	3.8	*d*	*d*
1993	9,029	97.8	3.1	*d*	22.6
1994	11,060	95.4	4.7	*d*	18.7
1995	12,144	95.4	*d*	*d*	*d*
1996	13,182	94.5	4.6	65.7	18.6
1997	20,784	96.0	14.0	62.7	11.2
1998	21,608	94.3	*d*	61.7	9.6
1999	22,054	91.4	4.8	*d*	18.3

d Data suppressed by the BEA to protect the identity of respondents.
Source: Bureau of Economic Analysis, author's calculations.

of intra-firm trade did not change much between 1983 and 1999, suggesting that NAFTA played only a minor role in stimulating a greater integration of US firms' operations.

The following discussion of the manufacturing sector focuses primarily on the automotive and electronics industries, since between 1985 and 1998, these two industries taken together accounted for between 71 and 93 percent of exports by US affiliates back to the home market, as shown in table 3.3.

Exports of automobiles and auto parts made up a third of all Mexican exports to the United States, and 14 percent of imports. This development resulted from the combination of Mexico's liberalization, the change in US firms' strategies, and the locational benefits of production in Mexico. The next section takes up these issues in greater detail.

Export orientation in the automotive industry

While manufacturing in the electronics and electrical equipment industry mostly took place in maquiladoras, the automotive sector was divided into parts producers in maquiladoras, assembly plants, and a domestic Mexican supply industry. Because of its central role in the Mexican manufacturing sector and the importance of the industry in providing jobs, achieving greater efficiency in the automotive industry was vital to overcome the economic crisis. At the same time, given the dominance of foreign multinational firms that preferred to import parts or even finished vehicles from abroad, the Mexican government tried to promote the industry's export orientation. The 1983 auto decree required automakers to reduce the number of models per factory line and firm. Additional lines were only allowed if they were "self-sufficient" in generating foreign exchange – that is, did not contribute to balance-of-payments problems and more than 50 percent of production were exported (UNCTC 1992: 10). The 1989 auto decree reduced the local content requirement from 60 to 36 percent for assemblers and 30 percent for parts producers. However, the auto parts industry retained enough political influence to prevent a thorough liberalization and retained a ceiling of 40 percent for foreign ownership.

Under the more liberal host country policies, the production of cars in Mexico became rapidly more competitive. Technology consultants Booz, Allen, and Hamilton estimated in a late 1980s study that car manufacturing in Mexico would be fairly competitive with around 50 percent foreign components; production with 70 percent would be highly competitive globally (cited in Peres Nuñez 1990: 121). The currency depreciation made Mexican wages highly attractive just when productivity and quality of workmanship began to reach international standards (Womack 1991: 43, 52–54). The US Big Three manufacturers seized the opportunity to implement strategies to produce entry-level, small cars in Mexico, hoping to defend their market share at home from competition by Japanese automakers (Calderón *et al.* 1995: 24).

Starting in 1986, General Motors transferred virtually all of its production of wire harnesses and upholstery, and a considerable share of subassembly work to maquiladora factories. By 1990 the process was largely completed, with GM having thirty maquiladora plants in operation (Womack 1991: 39). Ford expanded its stamping and assembling facilities as well as its production capacity for engines in Chihuahua.

The production of the compact car model Fiesta was completely relocated from Germany and South Korea to Mexico. Two new models began rolling off the lines in Cuautitlán. Chrysler began producing the Neon and smaller Dodge models in Toluca and transferred the production of light trucks to Saltillo (Moreno Brid 1996: 27). By contrast, the two other foreign car manufacturers, Volkswagen and Nissan, did not yet change their strategies proactively (Peres Nuñez 1990: 119). VW only exported engines as a defensive move because of the 1983 auto decree requirements, and even briefly entered the business of exporting honey to meet its foreign exchange balancing requirements (Maxfield and Shapiro 1998: 89). Nissan did shift to overseas sales, but concentrated its efforts on other Central and South American markets (UNCTC 1992: 63).

The different responses to the changed circumstances were reflected in the export figures in the following years. The automobile industry became Mexico's most successful exporter of manufactured goods. As shown in table 3.4, in 1987 more than 60 percent of the production of Chrysler and Ford in Mexico was exported, with between 91 and 100 percent of these exports going to the US market. By 1992, automotive exports represented 16 percent of all Mexican exports to OECD countries, most of which went to the United States. The Mexican operations of the US Big Three occupied ranks 6, 7, and 12 respectively of all exporting enterprises from Latin America in 1993 (Calderón *et al.*

Table 3.4. *Exports of vehicles by company, 1987*

Firms	Total vehicle exports (units)	Export share of production	Main export market	Share of main export market in exports
Chrysler	62,811	61.1	USA	91
Ford	51,773	60.4	USA	99
GM	32,272	44.1	USA	100
Nissan	16,107	18.7	Central America	73
Volkswagen	85	0.1	–	–
Others	25	0.1	–	–
Total	163,073	–	–	–

– Missing data.
Source: Peres Nuñez (1990: 119), author's calculations.

Table 3.5. *Passenger car sales by principal export market, percentage shares*

	1978–82	1983–87	1988–1992
Mexican market	49.7	31.4	12.3
Dual market	46.8	46.8	53.3
Export market	0.4	21.8	34.4

Source: Moreno Brid (1994).

1995: 21). For US automotive firms, Mexico was the primary export platform for entry-level vehicles for the home market.

Moreover, the US Big Three specialized their plants in Mexico towards the production of a few models that could be sold in developed country markets. Outdated models for the Mexican market only were phased out, while models for sale in the United States were also introduced in Mexico. Between 1978 and 1992, US manufacturers' production almost doubled, from 296,000 to 577,000 units, suggesting that they were reaching economies of scale through longer production runs. Table 3.5 breaks these figures into their component shares.

In the automobile industry, US firms changed to a vertically integrated strategy during the 1980s. Entry-level models would be produced in Mexico, while the small demand for high-end vehicles could be satisfied through exports from the United States. The low transport costs between Mexico and the home market attracted considerable stocks of vertically integrated FDI. Much of this took place in the maquiladora sector, especially in the production of intermediate goods.

Growth in the maquiladora sector

Concurrently with the rapid growth in the automotive sector, the export-processing zones known as maquiladoras expanded rapidly. Employment increased tenfold between 1980 and 2000, with about 65 percent of the capital of automotive parts maquiladoras coming from the United States (Carillo 2000: 59). The considerable growth potential of the maquiladora sector ensured that the duty-drawback schemes would be linked to the question of rules of origin in the NAFTA negotiations. Most maquiladoras used very few Mexican inputs; in a comprehensive study of maquiladoras in northern and central Mexico,

Wilson (1992: 101–19) finds that factories in the electronics and auto parts industries sourced virtually all materials from outside Mexico, usually the United States. Surprisingly, maquiladoras owned by non-US firms and factories in low-technology industries such as footwear, apparel, glass, and toys sourced the most domestically, although they could have benefited from duty-drawbacks.

The example of the auto industry is reflected elsewhere. Research into corporate strategies has shown that in the electronics and household appliances industries, the integration of Mexico into a North American production network had already picked up speed in the late 1980s. The primary aims were to increase the volume of Mexican operations to achieve economies of scale, and to integrate Mexican operations into the US network to gain efficiency in research and development and marketing (Blank and Haar 1998: 34).

In the NAFTA negotiations, the firms' strategies described so far translated into often highly specific demands regarding the nature of the liberalization. US firms lobbied negotiators to ensure that the free trade agreement gave them preferential access to Mexico for trade and investment.

The NAFTA negotiations: a preference for protectionism

In February 1990, President Carlos Salinas de Gortari of Mexico launched his initiative for a trade agreement with the United States. The government, led by a few, mostly Harvard-trained, economists like Jaime Serra Puche at the Economics Secretariat SECOFI (Secretaría de Comercio y Fomento Industrial), Pedro Aspe at the Finance Ministry, and Salinas himself, saw a free trade agreement as a chance to attract more foreign capital from the United States to stimulate development by sending a signal that Mexico would not fall back into its old protectionist ways. More importantly, the agreement would lock future governments into a liberal economic policy – a measure primarily aimed at the domestic opposition – force Mexico's less efficient sectors into a process of rapid economic adjustment, and ultimately lead to greater macroeconomic stability (Pastor and Wise 1994: 484).

Key firms in the US service industry were mainly interested in market access, since Mexico's outdated infrastructure in telecommunications and its underprovision with services in general offered enormous potential. For US manufacturing industries, the advantages of an FTA were less clear. While Mexico still imposed some performance measures (in particular the export requirements of the 1989 auto decree), these were apparently not much of a deterrent for foreign investment that had sought out the Mexican production location. If firms were concerned about US tariffs (since Mexico rebated its own tariff under the maquiladora system), it would have been easier to lobby the US government to reduce the tariffs unilaterally on the goods these firms wanted to import. Such efforts have traditionally been common in US trade policy, accounting for a rather open trade policy and forming a counterweight to protectionist interests (Destler *et al.* 1987: 43–56). Reducing MFN tariffs on particular items, however, had the disadvantage that non-US manufacturers could follow the example set by the US Big Three and use Mexico as an export base to enter the US home market. By contrast, NAFTA offered a means to raise the barriers to investing in Mexico for non-NAFTA firms. If free trade with Mexico was to be negotiated, then it had to be flanked by measures to protect the US home market.

Industry support for NAFTA in the United States came from a relatively narrow set of sectors. As Chase (2003) shows, firms from sectors characterized by economies of scale and those with regionally integrated production in Mexico and Canada were the most supportive of the deal. Import-competing sectors and labor opposed NAFTA just like any other liberalization measure. The demands for strict rules of origin, by contrast, depended primarily on whether firms sourced inputs from non-NAFTA countries, and on the threat of foreign firms using Mexico as a back door to the United States. Strict ROOs were negotiated in a variety of industries, from textiles to dairy and automobiles, and combined with Mexico's remaining barriers to the rest of the world to provide the preferential margin to secure the Mexican investment location.

Negotiating rules of origin

Considering the importance of the share of automobiles and automotive parts in the exports of US firms from Mexico to the home market, it is unsurprising that the industry was one of the most vocal during the NAFTA negotiations. The related tariffs and rules of origin became one of the most contentious aspects of the talks. US negotiators were mainly concerned with protecting the Big Three and their auto parts suppliers from potential European and particularly Japanese competition

(Cameron and Tomlin 2000: 91–92; Carlsen and McCarthy 1991). The respective demands of different firms directly reflected their stake in the negotiations, based on their relation to the Mexican and, to a lesser extent, Canadian market and production location.

As predicted, the more production was regionally concentrated in North America, the higher the rule of origin that a firm sought (Chase 2008). Ford and Chrysler demanded a rule of origin of 70 percent, since they exported most of their Mexican production but sourced parts virtually exclusively from within North America. By contrast, General Motors preferred a 60 percent threshold because of its joint venture with Suzuki in Canada, which used Japanese parts (Eden and Molot 1992: 15; Molot 1993: 9). Intermediate goods producers demanded an even stricter ROO. Parts producers asked for a constraining rule of origin of 75 percent, or at a minimum a rule that guaranteed that the "powertrain" (engine and transmission) would be wholly produced from North American parts (Robert 2000: 196). Since the US firms sourced very little from outside North America (the biggest parts producers, Delphi and Magna, were located in Michigan and Ontario), the auto industry formed a vertical rent chain that pushed for discriminatory measures.

Testifying before the House Subcommittee on Trade in September 1992, Christopher M. Bates of the Motor & Equipment Manufacturers Association stated that "since the outset, we have pushed for a NAFTA agreement structured to ... prevent Mexico or Canada from serving as an export platform to the United States for vehicles and components assembled using high concentrations of non-North American content" (US Congress 1992: 297). In a 1991 proposal, the Big Three called for the NAFTA rules of origin to

EXPAND employment and increase the international competitiveness of the North American automotive industry.

ASSURE that the benefits of the full NAFTA only accrue to companies that have made meaningful manufacturing and research and development commitments in North America. There should be no opportunity to inflate content levels or manipulate compliance through accounting, cost allocation, or pricing practices. (Chrysler Corporation, cited in Robert 2000: 196)

The rule of origin question became closely tied up with a demand by the Big Three to differentiate in the phasing-out of tariff and non-tariff barriers between incumbent firms and newcomers. Similar to the rules of origin, the aim was to slow down the entry of new firms that could invest in Mexico. Firms were to be divided into a tier I of incumbents (Chrysler, Ford, GM, Volkswagen, and Nissan) and a tier II of new-comers.[3] Specifically, the Big Three lobbied US negotiators to press for a differential phase-out of the Mexican automotive decrees (Cameron and Tomlin 2000, 92): "US negotiators must ensure that the evolving competitive environment under a NAFTA does not disadvantage the position of existing investors in Mexico relative to those who may wish to enter" (Chrysler Corporation, cited in Robert 2000: 196). Mexico's remaining non-tariff barriers were to be phased out over a fifteen-year transition period, with a more rapid elimination for incumbent firms. US negotiators also pushed for an elimination of the trade-balancing requirement in the 1989 auto decree, whereby a firm producing in Mexico would have to export 2.5 times the value of its imports (Robert 2000: 192). Finally, the United States sought the complete elimination of the auto decrees with respect to parts suppliers.

These demands presented a problem for Mexican and Canadian negotiators. Although the Big Three had important manufacturing plants in Ontario, Toyota and Honda also produced cars there with significant shares of imported parts. Mexican negotiators were under pressure from the domestic parts industry, which sought the imposition of a higher threshold by the rule of origin as well, but knew well that a prohibitively high threshold would deter investment by non-NAFTA firms and therefore run counter to a key policy objective. In the end, the Mexican government retained the auto decree to protect its parts man-ufacturers, but pushed together with the Canadians for a lower thresh-old (Cameron and Tomlin 2000: 91–92). The ROO for automobiles would prove too restrictive for European and Japanese firms, but during the negotiations few anticipated that the deal would have repercussions beyond NAFTA.[4] Labor (the United Auto Workers, UAW) demanded an even stricter rule of origin of 80 percent. However, since the UAW would likely be opposed to the final agreement regardless of the rule of

---

[3] *Inside US Trade*, September 23, 1991; Motor and Equipment Manufacturers Association (1991).

[4] Cameron and Tomlin (2000) state that the positions of Nissan and Volkswagen shifted during the negotiations, leading Mexico to accept higher thresholds imposed by the rules of origin than originally demanded. I have not been able to corroborate this claim in my interviews with representatives of these firms (Tokyo, February 2003, and Brussels, June 2004).

origin, negotiators chose to ignore labor and focused only on the necessary trade-offs between the requests of firms (from inside and outside NAFTA) and parts producers (Mayer 1998: 121).

Textiles, one of the most notoriously protectionist industries, became the other contentious issue in the rules of origin negotiations. That the United States had any textile industry left at all was itself the result of tariffs and quotas under the Multi-Fiber Arrangement.[5] Just as in the auto industry, the textile rule of origin was the product of lobbying by a vertical rent chain. US textile and apparel manufacturers either directly owned or had very close contractual relationships with yarn and fabric producers. Mexico, on the other hand, had developed a substantial apparel industry in the maquiladoras that sourced yarn and fabric from non-NAFTA countries. US textile manufacturers demanded the equivalent of a 100 percent rule of origin, or "yarn forward," meaning that every piece of clothing would have to be made of North American yarns and fabrics. Mexico originally called for a lower threshold of "fabric forward," but also wanted to eliminate the quotas that restricted its exports – quantitative restrictions for access to the US market that were lower than those of many Asian countries. Near the end of the negotiations, Mexico accepted this deal. It was less problematic for Mexico to collude with the United States on this protectionist measure than in the auto industry, since in the textile sector the producers were Mexican-owned, while the suppliers were based in the United States, resulting in a vertical rent chain in line with hypotheses 1a and 1b. If no non-NAFTA firms could be deterred, it mattered less for Mexican producers where the materials they used came from. In Destler's (2006: 182) assessment, the restrictive rule for textiles was crucial in swinging the votes of the representatives from North Carolina, one of the traditional textile-producing states, from a 2–9 against fast-track in 1991 to an 8–4 in favor of the ratification of NAFTA in 1993.

The comparison between Canada (here essentially acting like a developing country) and Mexico is instructive, in that it underlines the effect of international sourcing on the attitude towards ROOs. Canadian negotiators, under pressure from a small, but politically well-connected firm based in Quebec, the home province of the prime minister, Brian

---

[5] For the seminal work on the origins of the regime that only ceased to operate in 2006, see Aggarwal (1985).

Mulroney, tried their best to resist a strict rule. The firm (Peerless Clothing) bought wool fabrics outside North America at a discount that irked US suppliers, and had managed to carve out a niche in the US market. However, the Canadian negotiators ultimately had to give in and agreed to freeze wool exports at 1992 levels as long as Canada retained its quotas (Cameron and Tomlin 2000: 137, 159).

Banning MFN rebates for non-NAFTA firms

For the rules of origin to work as effective protectionist devices, Mexico would also have to be barred from rebating its MFN tariff for non-NAFTA investors. Duty-drawback schemes of this type were an essential part of the Canada–United States auto pact that was maintained under the CUSFTA, as well as of Mexico's maquiladora scheme. The US negotiation objective was to abolish the maquiladora benefits as quickly as possible, while the Mexican side wanted to retain them as long as possible as an incentive for FDI from non-NAFTA countries. US firms had long criticized the fact that Japanese investors in the maquiladoras, although nominally based in the United States, imported most of their parts from Japan rather than sourcing them from the US or Mexican suppliers (Székely 1991: 20). Mexican negotiators reported that, just like in the automotive sector, US industries feared that outsiders would use Mexico as an export platform to enter the US market by using their US subsidiaries to process goods in Mexico (Silverstein 1992: 4). In particular the iron and steel industries, providers of the principal input for the parts used by US auto production in Mexico, "spearheaded … a steady call … for the prohibition of duty-drawback programs as part of NAFTA" (Maxfield and Shapiro 1998: 87). US firms had to close any back doors in the form of MFN rebates in order to harness the host country MFN tariff as a measure to protect its foreign operations.

Rapid liberalization in services

In the service sector, US negotiators pressed for market access at the behest of US firms organized in the Coalition of Service Industries (CSI).[6] Particularly strong demands came from banks with a regional

[6] *Business Mexico*, special edition, "Foreign investment in NAFTA: A US perspective," 2 (1) (1992), 25.

base in the southern US states as well as major credit card companies, which lobbied through the American Bankers Association, the Bankers Association for Trade and Finance, and the Texas Bankers Association.[7] Major banks like Citibank lobbied the negotiators directly and through the Senate Finance Committee.[8] From the perspective of these firms, the Mexican retail banking market was "underbanked," with only 21 million of the 48 million Mexicans aged eighteen and over having a bank account in 1994 (USITC 1990: 2–21).

Despite strong Mexican opposition, US negotiators regarded financial services as an essential component of NAFTA without which the deal would fail (Cameron and Tomlin 2000: 83). Mexico's banks had only recently been reprivatized in 1991 and were generally considered to be undercapitalized and uncompetitive, allowing US banks to enter the market with a clear advantage (Chant 1993). US and Canadian financial firms would be uniquely well positioned to offer financial services for foreign investors setting up shop in Mexico and to offer import–export financing. By serving customers all across the continent, financial services providers could therefore achieve economies of scale with regard to back office operations and marketing (Borrego 1991). Even in the case of remaining restrictions to cross-border trade in services, US firms expected to enter the Mexican market through takeovers of established Mexican banks (Russell 1992).

Central to market access was attaining national treatment for investment in services. Unlike the manufacturing sector, however, the US financial services industry did not specifically prefer a bilateral solution to a sectoral deal or multilateral negotiations. In this sense, NAFTA only represented a chance to achieve objectives that US firms also lobbied for in multilateral negotiations.

Similar objectives drove negotiations over telecommunications liberalization. Mexico's infrastructure was outdated, leading analysts to expect strong demand for an upgrading and the prospect of future investment (Frischkorn 1993). Market access consideration therefore guided lobbying efforts of US firms (USITC 1990: 2–9), although much of it was looking to the development of future technologies, since the Mexican state telecommunications company TELMEX had already been privatized in 1990. Directly linked to telecommunications was

---

[7] *United States Banker*, June 1992; *Wall Street Journal*, February 12, 1992.
[8] *Inside US Trade*, February 8, 1991.

the issue of government procurement, which would offer enormous opportunities for the provision of services to the industries that remained in the hands of the Mexican government (Cameron and Tomlin 2000: 93; Messmer 1992).

Investment liberalization in non-service sectors was closely tied to the question of guarantees for investors.[9] While the negotiations faced considerable difficulties over the language of Chapter 11 on investment in terms of its expropriation and compensation clauses (Cameron and Tomlin 2000: 112), the more important issue in terms of NAFTA's preferential liberalization was the question of national treatment. Initially, the non-finance US business community was unclear whether it sought unconditional MFN treatment by US investors in Mexico, or whether preferential liberalization of sectors was more desirable. Unlike the automotive industry with its differential liberalization targets, US negotiators pressed for a schedule for the immediate liberalization of sectors that were previously closed to FDI.[10]

Buying off labor-friendly politicians

In contrast to other North–South agreements, NAFTA stirred up considerable resistance from organized labor. The AFL-CIO (American Federation of Labor and Congress of Industrial Organizations) opposed outright the granting of fast-track authority, the mandate for the president to negotiate a trade agreement that would only be subject to a simple up-or-down vote in Congress.

Since trade agreements change tariffs and thus affect revenue, the US constitution grants Congress the right to pass the laws implementing an agreement. Given this division of powers, countries negotiating with the United States cannot be sure that an agreement will be binding unless Congress ties its own hands and agrees beforehand either to accept or reject what the president has negotiated. Since 1934 Congress has ceded this power almost without interruption, modifying the Trade Act in 1962, 1979, and 1988 to take into account the negotiation of non-tariff barriers in the Kennedy and Tokyo rounds. This fast-track procedure restricts the role of Congress – specifically of the House Ways and

---

[9] *Business Mexico*, special edition, "Foreign investment in NAFTA: A US perspective," 2 (1) (1992), 24.
[10] *Ibid.*, 24.

Means and Senate Finance Committees – to a simple up-or-down vote during a limited time frame. In the case of NAFTA, Congress extended fast-track in May 1991 by rejecting resolutions of disapproval. At this point, obtaining fast-track was unproblematic for the administration, since not only the agreement with Mexico but also the broadly supported multilateral negotiations depended on the president's authority to negotiate. In addition, potential Democratic opposition to NAFTA was split because senators from the southwest supported an agreement that would increase trade with Mexico, while politicians from rust-belt states opposed it (Cameron and Tomlin 2000: 72–76).

Labor's fundamental opposition to the agreement meant that union views were rarely considered during the negotiation of the agreement (Mayer 1998: 72–75). Only when ratification was in doubt, after George Bush Sr. had lost the presidential election to Bill Clinton, did labor gain enough influence to extract a concession in the form of the side agreement on labor. The agreement created a (largely toothless) trilateral commission to watch over the implementation of national standards that offered enough to secure the votes of Democrats with close ties to unions, especially the House of Representatives majority leader Richard Gephardt. Further concessions to labor were prevented by strong lobbying by business organizations, and by the risk of losing the support of Republican members of Congress, which was crucial for the ratification of NAFTA (Mayer 1998: 177–204).

The institutional setting of US trade policymaking, in which Congress plays a role in providing negotiating mandates and ratifying agreements, differs from most other countries, where governments can rely on near-automatic ratification of international agreements as long as they have a parliamentary majority. When members of Congress with close ties to labor, or more precisely, with import-competing industries in their districts, are in a position to block trade agreements, it is unsurprising that they do so. But even the NAFTA case shows that in North–South PTAs, the assent of labor is rarely necessary to create a coalition in favor of the agreement.

Preferential aspects of NAFTA and multilateral commitments

How much potential for trade and investment diversion was built into NAFTA? As the above discussion has shown, US manufacturing firms were intent on maintaining exclusivity. In the automotive sector, the final outcome in the negotiations was a 62.5 percent rule, a compromise between the US team and the Mexican and Canadian negotiators, who had sought a lower level. In addition to the restrictive rules, the US Big Three attained the requested two-tiered phase-out period of the remaining Mexican host country measures – faster for incumbents than for new entrants. Firms that had existing operations in Mexico (the Big Three, Volkswagen, and Nissan) were allowed to produce vehicles with a lower domestic content than new operations by competitors (Robert 2000: 161, 94).[11] Specifically, incumbents did not have to satisfy the 36 percent local (Mexican) content quota required under the 1989 auto decree as long as they fulfilled NAFTA's rule of origin, but could use the 1992 model year's content quota (Eden and Molot 1993). These factors jointly worked to the disadvantage of new entrants.

However, the automotive firms with the greatest unrealized economies of scale were Nissan and Volkswagen. Meeting the demands of the US Big Three and their suppliers in the NAFTA negotiations implied that the agreement would discriminate not only against newcomers, but also against incumbents that imported parts and capital goods from outside the NAFTA area, unless Mexico could be motivated to lower its remaining tariff and non-tariff barriers.

NAFTA also included the phasing out of the maquiladora benefits. The intended side effect was raising the costs for non-NAFTA producers. NAFTA granted a temporary extension of duty-drawback programs, but limited this to the lower of the two MFN tariffs.[12] Since the US tariff averages less than 4 percent, the higher Mexican tariff effectively raised the cost of importing intermediate goods by 10–15 percent. As of January 2001, the duty-drawback offered by Mexico has been completely eliminated and the MFN tariff is levied by the United States on goods that do not meet NAFTA's rule of origin requirements (Maxfield and Shapiro 1998: 88). In 1994, maquiladoras could only sell up to the equivalent of 5 percent of their exports into the domestic market. The ceiling was raised gradually by 5 percent per year, allowing US manufacturers increasingly to use maquiladoras as suppliers for assembly in Mexico (Robert 2000: 163). US manufacturers could therefore benefit from access to a world-class supply industry in Mexico.

The potentially negative effect of rules of origin on outsiders was by no means unexpected. In a 1991 report to Congress, the United States

---

[11] See also *Inside US Trade*, September 23, 1991.   [12] NAFTA, Art. 303(2).

International Trade Commission (USITC) clearly cited the implications for foreign producers based in Mexico, especially automotive and electronics firms, as well as their concerns about the possible discriminatory effect of an FTA. The same report noted that because of the small size of the Mexican market, the trade-creating effect of an FTA would be concentrated in intermediate goods serving US investment in Mexico (USITC 1991a: 4-19–4-26). A second USITC report pointed out that the investment liberalization clauses of NAFTA[13] enabled US automakers to wholly own parts suppliers in Mexico, which should further increase their competitiveness vis-à-vis firms from third countries (USITC 1991b: 4–7).

In contrast to regionally integrated industries, US industries that preferred to source globally opposed tight rules of origin. Most prominently, the computer industry procured most inputs from Asia and thus preferred free trade to regional integration (Wonnacott 1993: 14). IBM specifically opposed the inclusion of hard disks as a requirement for computers to qualify as North American (Cameron and Tomlin 2000: 90), since most hard disks were manufactured in Singapore. However, it did not resist the requirement that cathode-ray tubes for monitors be produced in North America – Japanese firms assembled monitors in Mexico with imported cathode-ray tubes (Johnson 1993: 12). The outcome was selectively protectionist, requiring high North American content for some products, but not for others. The USITC states, "although the rules of origin are complex, they reportedly reflect the needs and desires of the domestic [US] industry" (USITC 1993: 5-2, n. 5).

In the services sector the potential for investment diversion appeared as an unintended consequence of the preferential liberalization. In the financial services industry NAFTA guarantees national treatment for financial intermediaries, allowing US and Canadian banks to establish subsidiaries in Mexico. Mexico reserved the right to approve on a case-by-case basis the ownership of Mexican banks or securities firms by US and Canadian commercial or industrial corporations in accordance with its 1993 law on foreign investment. NAFTA also guarantees the right to purchase financial services in another NAFTA country.[14]

---

[13] NAFTA, Annex I, Reservations for Existing Measures and Liberalization Commitments, Schedule of Mexico, I-M-32.

[14] Except for Canadians, who remain "protected" from access to cheaper financial services.

Market access was originally limited to some extent by a cap on the share of the Mexican banking system that may be owned by US and Canadian banks. When NAFTA entered into force, the aggregate capital of US and Canadian banks operating in Mexico was limited to 8 percent of the capital of the Mexican banking system as a whole. The limit was scheduled to increase gradually until reaching 15 percent in 1999 and to be completely abolished on January 1, 2000, although Mexico reserved the right to restrict increases beyond 25 percent until 2006, when all restrictions were to be eliminated. Caps on the capital share of individual banks were allowed until 2000, with some limitations on acquisitions. Despite these remaining limitations, US banks did not hesitate to enter the market on a grand scale, from retail banking offered by Bank of Boston, Bank One, and Citibank to specialized financial services for certain industries provided by Chemical Bank and Nationsbank (Ioannou 1994).

Some of these caps fell in the wake of the 1994 peso crisis, as the Mexican government decided to open the sector to attract more FDI. In February 1995 the schedule for opening the financial services sector was accelerated to allow full takeovers of Mexican banks. However, even here a cap remained, since each takeover would only be allowed if the assets represented less than 6 percent of the entire financial system (Santín Quiroz 2001: 221). The preferential liberalization under NAFTA contrasts with Mexico's multilateral opening. As shown in table 3.6, Mexico's GATS commitments only allowed a 40 percent foreign equity participation in commercial banks, and restricted individual holdings to 20 percent. Until 1998, when the Mexican government lifted all limits on foreign bank holdings, NAFTA investors retained a considerable preferential margin.

In tourism as well as a range of professional services, NAFTA allows 100 percent foreign ownership compared with 49 percent under Mexico's law. Investment in services and exports from the United States to Mexico nearly doubled by 1999 according to BEA figures. In particular, financial services investment made up an increasingly large share of total FDI, as shown in table 3.7. Manufacturing investment had continued unabated since the late 1980s, as shown earlier, with the exception of a brief period following the 1994 Mexican currency crisis.

In the manufacturing sector, the interaction of high thresholds imposed by the rules of origin with Mexico's tariff rates implied highly discriminatory trade barriers by OECD country standards. Mexico's

Table 3.6. *Comparison of Mexico's NAFTA and GATS commitments*

	GATS	NAFTA
Commercial banks, deposits and lending	FDI up to 40%	Aggregate FDI up to 30% of capital in three largest banks after 1995
	Limit on individual holdings 20% Effective control must be by Mexicans	No limits after 2000
	Mode 1 – unbound	Cross-border purchases of financial services in Mexican pesos not allowed
Securities firms	FDI up to 40%	Aggregate FDI up to 30% of capital in Mexican securities firms
	Limit on individual holdings 20% Effective control must be by Mexicans	No limits after 2000

Source: Stephenson (2002: 200).

tariff rates under the WTO are usually bound at 50 percent. With the failure of the millennium round of the WTO, no further multilateral liberalization occurred after NAFTA and the Uruguay Round. Instead, Mexico even raised some MFN tariffs to higher levels, as shown in table 3.8 below.

Several MFN tariff lines were raised during the 1994–95 financial crisis to protect less efficient sectors such as textiles and footwear, and to bolster government revenue. Others, in particular tariffs on electronics and components, were a response to competition from producers based in China and sought to shelter production in Mexico. As a result, the margin between preferential and non-discriminatory duties widened considerably, reaching among the highest differences in the western hemisphere (Zlabudovsky and Gómez Lora 2007: 94–95). This compares with a phasing-out of tariffs in NAFTA during the same period.

Table 3.7. *US FDI in services in Mexico, US$ million, and industry shares*

	Services exports[i]	FDI in financial services	Share in total FDI stock	FDI in other services	Share in total FDI stock
1986	2,670.9	350.9	4.9	903.9	12.7
1987	2,154.5	423.5	5.7	847.0	11.4
1988	1,614.4	158.5	1.9	1,113.7	13.4
1989	2,274.8	d		1,014.6	9.6
1990	2,933.0	758.7	6.0	1,032.0	8.2
1991	3,550.3	793.4	5.4	1,263.6	8.5
1992	3,882.6	920.3	5.8	1,406.5	8.8
1993	4,235.1	2,382.9	13.8	1,276.3	7.4
1994	4,958.0	2,485.1	13.2	1,851.3	9.8
1995	4,852.0	2,604.6	14.2	1,641.6	9.0
1996	4,932.2	3,254.1	15.8	1,550.3	7.5
1997	5,520.2	4,583.2	18.2	1,579.4	6.3
1998	5,729.1	5,656.6	20.5	1,776.7	6.4
1999	6,240.0	5,883.4	15.5	3,105.2	8.2
2000	6,346.0	6,154.0	15.6	3,146.0	8.0
2001	6,828.2	d		2,994.2	5.8
2002	6,745.6	20,526.6	38.0	3,055.1	5.7

[i] Services exports from the United States to Mexico.
[d] Data suppressed by the BEA to protect confidentiality of firms.

Table 3.8. *Average MFN tariff applied by Mexico*

	1994	1995	1996	1997	1998	1999
Capital goods	11.7	11.7	11.5	11.4	11.4	14.5
Parts and components	11.4	11.8	11.3	11.2	11.2	13.9
Consumer goods	17.2	24.8	25.0	24.9	24.5	29.3
Unweighted average	12.4	13.7	13.3	13.3	13.2	16.1

Source: Presidencia de la República de México, *Informe del Gobierno*, Annex (September 1999), author's calculations.

By 1999 Mexico had eliminated tariffs on 65 percent of goods originating in the United States or Canada. The phase-out has been completed in 2009, making over 95 percent of Mexican imports from the NAFTA countries tariff-free.

Alternative accounts: the benign view of NAFTA

Did the US Big Three primarily lobby for NAFTA because it would allow them to fully integrate their production in North America? The export figures for US car manufacturers and the increase in investment prior to NAFTA suggest otherwise. If the Mexican host country measures had been really that onerous, it is unlikely that US firms would have increased their investment at all. The early turn of the trend towards more FDI in Mexico indicates that US firms may have found the tariff reduction in NAFTA beneficial, but did not see it as a precondition for production in Mexico. Moreover, although the volume of reexports of US firms to the home market kept growing, the composition of these exports did not change much following the conclusion of the agreement. It seems more likely that US manufacturers chose to refer to their onerous legacy of investment in Mexico because it did not appear blatantly protectionist. Conveniently, the same rules would apply to Japanese factories in Canada. Here US manufacturers sought to avoid a repetition of intrusions like Honda's production of Civic models in Ontario that sold well in the US market.[15]

Did NAFTA offer protection against the loss of the main export market? For the United States the Mexican market is simply too small for this argument to be credible. Yet for Mexico achieving a significant concession from the United States was never a realistic proposition. If securing market access had indeed been Mexico's main objective, NAFTA was a mixed bag. Just like the CUSFTA, the agreement preserves the application of US domestic laws on anti-dumping and countervailing duties. Following the CUSFTA precedent, NAFTA created the institution of binational panels to settle disputes over the propriety of the application of domestic trade remedy laws. But Mexico did not even have such laws in place at the time of negotiation, and thus had to commit to an overhaul of its domestic legislation, although it did press for changes in US trade laws during the negotiations (Cameron and Tomlin 2000: 47–49). Given the importance of US FDI as source of Mexican exports, it is unlikely that secure market access for conventional exports was high on Mexico's list of priorities.

---

[15] In 1991, US Customs had ruled that Honda Civics assembled in Ontario between January 1989 and March 1990 did not fulfill the origin requirement of the CUSFTA, set at 50 percent. *New York Times*, June 17, 1991.

By contrast, the political rationale for NAFTA is hard to dispute with hindsight. As described by Pastor and Wise (1994), greater macroeconomic stability ranked high among the objectives of Salinas' proposal for an FTA with the United States. The test of NAFTA's effectiveness came all too quickly, in the 1995 "Tequila Crisis." The crisis was triggered by a sudden loss of confidence by foreign investors in the ability of Mexico to finance its current-account deficit with foreign capital inflows. Devaluation, however, seemed too costly, as the government had begun to rely more and more on dollar-denominated bonds or "Tesobonos" for its international borrowing, after institutional investors refused to buy peso-denominated instruments. A depreciated peso would have made it much more costly to repay the dollar-denominated debt. When the government was finally forced to devalue the peso, international financial markets meted out swift punishment: Mexico's economy contracted 6.9 percent within a year, inflation spiked at 52 percent, and real average incomes shrank by 12 percent. Yet NAFTA fulfilled its strategic function by giving the United States a considerable stake in Mexico's economic well-being. Within weeks, the US Treasury had put together a $20 billion rescue package and leaned on unenthusiastic European countries to contribute another $10 billion (Cameron and Aggarwal 1996). Although the Mexican crisis did not represent a systemic threat to global banking, the comprehensive package stood in marked contrast to the limited financial support disbursed in the 1982 debt crisis, or later instances of Latin American countries running into financial trouble.[16] Cameron and Aggarwal (1996: 979) conclude that "The reason [for the generosity of the bailout] lies in the crucial importance of Mexico to the USA in the context of NAFTA, and the extent to which US business interests were affected by the devaluation." NAFTA not only committed Mexico to a liberal economic policy, but also gave the United States a considerable stake in the success of this choice.

Conclusion: raising the barriers to market entry

This chapter has argued that US manufacturing firms with export-oriented FDI in Mexico showed a strong preference for protectionism

---

[16] Katada (2001) offers an insightful comparison of the differing responses of industrial countries.

in the disguise of an FTA. Mexico's reintegration into the world economy and the subsequent negotiation of NAFTA offered US firms broad opportunities to create an export platform. US manufacturing firms benefited from an educated labor force with low wages in close proximity to the home market. As the case study shows, the restructuring of US direct investment in Mexico towards exports was well under way before NAFTA was a serious policy option, suggesting that it would have continued even without a formal free trade agreement.

The negotiation of NAFTA, however, offered US industries the chance to lobby for rules of origin that raised the costs considerably for outsiders when they invested in Mexico to serve the US market. In particular the Big Three auto manufacturers and their rent chain of parts producers sought the strictest rules of origin. This reflected their strategic position vis-à-vis competitors: once Mexico became feasible as an export platform for the production of automobiles, it would likely attract export-oriented investment from European and Japanese firms. Rules of origin would impose higher costs on these firms if they chose to start up production in Mexico. But despite the differential phase-out clauses of the Mexican host country requirements for incumbents and newcomers, non-NAFTA incumbents such as Nissan and Volkswagen would be hurt as well. Should they choose to export to the US market, strict rules of origin would induce them to buy from NAFTA suppliers. Through concerted lobbying efforts, US firms were able to achieve many of these goals in the actual negotiations.

The case also shows that in markets with high tariff and non-tariff barriers, or markets in which investment is a requirement for access, the investment and services provisions of a free trade agreement can be discriminatory. The preferential liberalization of the Mexican banking market offered significant first-mover advantages. It is unlikely that either lobbyists or negotiators in the United States anticipated that within a few years of the free trade agreement entering into force, the EU and Japan would seek both relief for their multinational firms active in Mexico and market access comparable with NAFTA. Unless Mexico could be motivated to reduce its tariff applied to the intermediate and capital goods imports of these investors, they would be at a severe competitive disadvantage vis-à-vis US and Canadian firms. The next two chapters consider the reactions to NAFTA.

Appendix: Estimating trend changes

In order to estimate breakpoints in the trend in US FDI stock in Mexico, 1966–2006, we can fit a piecewise linear function with one or more breakpoints following Andrews (1993) and Hansen (1992). A change in trend can be inferred if the function with cusp at t_1 fits *ln y(t)* = *rt+A*, where *y(t)* is the stock of US FDI in Mexico in year *t*, $1966 \leq t \leq 2006$, and *r* and *A* are constants, better than any other linear or piecewise linear function. We take the dependent variable in logarithmic form to be able to estimate an approximation of percentage changes. For every potential change point between 1966 and 2006, we fit an ordinary least squares (OLS) model that estimates $2\,k$ parameters for all the observations before and after the potential change point, and compute the error sum of squares (ESS). We then fit another OLS model for all observations with a restricted sum of squares (RSS) with *k* parameters. With *n* as the number of observations and *k* as the number of parameters, the formula is:

$$F = \frac{RSS - ESS}{ESS/(n - 2k)}$$

A Chow test has a value of 126.482 with a p-value of 2.2×10^{-16} at the year 1989. These tests are implemented in the package *strucchange* for the statistical programming language *R* (Zeileis *et al.* 2002). The number of breakpoints is ultimately an arbitrary choice, since a piecewise linear function with the number of breaks equal to the time points will always fit the data perfectly. Increasing the number of breaks gradually, however, reveals that they tend to coincide with major events: for five breakpoints, the model suggests the years 1972, 1978, 1989, 1994, and 2000. The first two fall into Mexico's oil boom period, while the latter two are the dates of NAFTA's entry into force and of the rise in US interest rates that caused the dot-com bubble to burst. This also suggests that NAFTA had an effect on FDI decisions, but that it was less important than the unilateral opening.

4 | *Iberian ties: the EU–Mexico free trade agreement*

W HEN President Salinas traveled to Europe in late January 1990 to advertise Mexico as an attractive investment location, he returned disheartened. European corporate and political leaders, mesmerized by the economic potential of central and eastern Europe emerging from communist rule, showed little interest in Latin America (Cameron and Tomlin 2000: 1–2). Yet in 1999 the EU concluded its first inter-regional FTA with Mexico. Three years later, EU Trade Commissioner Pascal Lamy (2002) referred to Mexico as a beautiful bride between two lovers, whom the EU "would like to tempt ... back closer to the centre of the bed, and invite ... not to sleep right on one edge of the mattress!"

What had made Mexico so attractive? The country had just emerged from a severe financial crisis that cast doubt on its growth potential over the next years. In European capitals, most government attention was focused on future EU enlargement. Many observers expected the negotiation of the Free Trade Area of the Americas, spanning from the Arctic to Tierra del Fuego, rather than a comprehensive trade and investment deal between Mexico and the then fifteen EU member states.

NAFTA's entry into force, however, fundamentally changed the parameters for foreign direct investment in Mexico. The rapid depreciation of the Mexican peso depressed domestic demand and reduced imports, but made Mexico more attractive as an export platform. Yet to the detriment of outsiders NAFTA ensured that only US and Canadian firms could fully benefit from these developments. By exerting pressure to switch from overseas suppliers to producers based in Mexico, NAFTA's rules of origin raised the cost of production for European and Japanese firms.

A weakened financial sector, in which the government lifted ceilings on foreign participation, offered the chance to enter a new market. The preferential access to the Mexican service market offered by NAFTA put European service providers at a disadvantage. The North American accord threatened long-term exclusion from the market, should US and Canadian firms manage to snap up the most attractive firms in the Mexican banking sector.

Mexico's multilateral trade policy did not help. The Mexican government first retained, and later even increased, the margin between NAFTA and most-favored-nation duties by lifting the applied rate to the bound rate, the maximum legally possible under the GATT. Within a few years, European exporters lost market share. Between 1990 and 1994, EU exports to Mexico grew by 64 percent, but then began to level off. During the first three years after NAFTA's entry into force, the EU's share in Mexican imports fell from 17.4 percent to 9 percent. Although initially mainly caused by the peso crisis, many European firms perceived the loss of sales in Mexico as the direct result of the competitive disadvantages created by NAFTA. While exports to Mexico made up only a small share of European trade, they originated primarily in two countries, Spain and Germany, the latter making up over half of EU–Mexico commerce. In 1995, Spanish exports to Mexico shrank by nearly 70 percent. The European firms affected by NAFTA were therefore geographically highly concentrated.

At the same time, FDI from the EU began to rise rapidly. As shown in table 4.1, European direct investment in Mexico more than tripled in the first five years after NAFTA's entry into force. In relative terms, however, the importance of the United States and the EU did not change. Although sectoral data on FDI stocks from the EU are not available, it is likely that most of the FDI from Germany was manufacturing-related, while most of the investment from Spain took place in the services sector, as discussed in this chapter. The increase in FDI without concurrent increases in trade suggests that European firms reacted to NAFTA by establishing or enlarging beachheads for production within the free trade zone that aimed at the US and Canadian markets rather than the reduced Mexican demand. In doing so, European firms incurred a higher cost than their competitors from within NAFTA: intermediate and capital goods from the EU faced a tariff 10–20 percent higher than those from the United States and Canada.

European investment in Mexico

Prior to Mexico's economic liberalization, most European firms that invested in Mexico focused on sales to the domestic market. While US

Table 4.1. *Stock of FDI in Mexico by source, and percentage share*

Year	Stocks US$ million				Percentage share	
	EU[i]	Germany	Spain	Total[ii]	US	EU
1990	6,382	1,914	348	26,625	45.99	23.97
1991	7,934	1,939	467	35,530	40.60	22.33
1992	8,810	2,000	1,323	40,649	38.48	21.67
1993	7,910	1,811	1,312	45,601	37.49	17.35
1994	6,684	1,527	832	36,841	51.11	18.14
1995	8,125	1,993	1,774	44,609	41.02	18.21
1996	8,669	1,663	1,667	50,085	41.25	17.31
1997	10,828	2,127	1,139	58,902	43.09	18.38
1998	18,661	4,115	1,761	67,440	41.91	27.67
1999	21,763	4,368	2,497	81,335	47.59	26.76
2000	26,849	4,073	5,132	97,170	40.50	27.63
2001	24,815	4,451	9,265	138,807	37.43	17.88
2002	25,218	4,443	12,692	156,391	35.25	16.13
2003	31,564	4,246	13,958	165,951	32.47	19.02
2004	45,942	4,407	22,953	181,554	33.64	25.30
2005	50,141	4,927	23,181	193,457	34.58	25.92
2006	48,159	4,675	22,550	205,570	35.85	23.43

[i] Includes Sweden, Finland, and Austria in all figures.
[ii] Total FDI stock from all countries.
Source: OECD, Eurostat.

manufacturing firms used tariff rebates and in-bond maquiladora man-ufacturing programs to produce for the home market, European pro-ducers aligned their corporate strategies with the requirements that Mexico's import-substitution policy imposed on foreign investors. The single most important European company in terms of jobs and total capital invested in Mexico was Volkswagen, directly employing over 16,000 workers. In the early 1990s, production by German com-panies represented close to 4 percent of Mexico's GDP. Of this figure, Volkswagen and its suppliers accounted for more than half, before considering parts manufacturers under Mexican ownership that pri-marily sold to the German car company.

In contrast to the US Big Three, Volkswagen's manufacturing and supply base was concentrated in Mexico's central region. Volkswagen began production in Mexico in 1964, when it established a manufacturing plant in Puebla, 90 km east of Mexico City. Between 1980 and 1991 Volkswagen dominated the domestic passenger car market with an average share of 30 percent (Asociación Mexicana de la Industria Automotriz 1993). In response to the 1977 auto decree, it built an engine plant and aluminum foundry and concentrated production on a single model (the Beetle, commonly known as *vocho*). Because of its strong links to Mexican parts manufacturers and the reliance on simpler, outdated technology for everything except engines, it achieved a higher domestic content than the US manufacturers.

In 1981, Volkswagen began exporting engines to Germany, starting with about 15,000 units and reaching a peak of 340,000 in 1990. However, the company exported much smaller numbers of finished vehicles, mostly to other Latin American countries, since stricter emissions standards imposed in the early 1980s ruled out sales of the old VW Beetle and Van to the United States. For reasons of cost and recurrent quality problems that threatened to undermine the VW brand value in the United States,[1] Volkswagen decided to close its plant in Westmoreland County, Pennsylvania, in 1988, leaving the Puebla factory as its only production site in North America. Volkswagen complied with the Mexican auto decrees through the export of engines.

The high quality of the engines produced in Mexico for the European market convinced Volkswagen's management that the production site could be used to supply the US and Canadian market, a decision further facilitated by the steady decline of the Mexican peso vis-à-vis the US dollar.[2] In 1991, Volkswagen invested US$1 billion in the Puebla plant, focusing on the production of Golf and Jetta models for the US and Canadian markets.

The major decisions on restructuring the Mexican operations coincided with the NAFTA negotiations. Following the 1994 Mexican peso crisis that depressed domestic demand, exports from Mexico became all the more imperative, including exports of Jetta models back to Germany. The company found itself in a quandary: continuing the production of the Beetle, a model based on 1930s technology, would become much less profitable if US competitors could offer more modern alternatives and if even Japanese vehicles produced in Canada and the

[1] Interview with Volkswagen manager, Brussels, June 2004.
[2] Telephone interview with Volkswagen manager, April 2004.

United States were eventually to be on sale in Mexico. NAFTA implied that the Big Three's Mexican production would not only be exported to the US market as under the auto decrees, but also sold in Mexico itself. The only option besides exiting the market was to overhaul the Puebla factory and to produce cars with long production runs, models that could be sold in all the NAFTA member countries and Europe, a market big enough to achieve efficient scales of production.

NAFTA's rules of origin posed a challenge to this strategy. While North American companies had access to their supplier networks to fulfill the regional content quota, Volkswagen did not. In 1992, Volkswagen acquired half of its inputs from Germany, 40 percent from Mexico and 10 percent from the United States. However, this percentage differed considerably from model to model. Whereas the old Beetle was 80 percent Mexican, the third-generation Golf/Jetta was to be assembled from up to 90 percent imported parts. Compliance with the rule of origin required an enormous strengthening of the local supply industry in terms of technology, quality, and efficiency. Volkswagen estimated that it would take ten years to develop adequate supplier networks. At the same time, neither Volkswagen nor its European suppliers could invest in Mexico's parts industry without restrictions, since Mexico still maintained the 49 percent ownership ceiling for non-NAFTA firms. Volkswagen therefore faced the competition from the US Big Three with a burdensome inheritance of the pre-liberalization era, and with a potentially much higher cost of restructuring, unless a significant share of components could be imported from Europe.

Because of the high volume of engine exports to Europe, Volkswagen also benefited from its participation in the Programa de Importación Temporal para Producir Artículos de Exportación (PITEX), whereby it could obtain full rebates of the value added tax on imported parts, provided the final product was exported. Like the maquiladora benefits, PITEX would not be applicable to exports to other NAFTA countries after 2001.

In 1996, on the occasion of the production mark of 22 million VW Beetles, the company announced its decision to produce the New Beetle, a model specifically aimed at the US market, and a further US$500 million in investments in its Puebla plant. Volkswagen's commitment to the use of Mexico as an export platform turned it into the most vocal supporter of an EU–Mexico FTA. Horst Palemberg, the German ambassador to Mexico, noted the possibility of such an agreement during an October 1996 interview with the Spanish magazine *Expansión*, but called the likelihood of such an initiative "still very remote."

Two other German automotive firms also considered the Mexican market. BMW entered the market by setting up a small assembly facility in Mexico in Toluca in 1994, but aimed at an annual output of only 10,000 vehicles[3] (BMW de Colombia 2004), exclusively for the domestic market. Mercedes-Benz set up a manufacturing plant for large trucks in the northern city of Santiago, but did not produce passenger cars in Mexico (Moreno Brid 1996: 26 n. 17). Since its truck manufacturing capacity in North America resulted from the purchase of the US company Freightliner, Mercedes-Benz imported very few components from outside North America, and thus did not face difficulties in complying with NAFTA's rules of origin.

The second principal force for an FTA was the financial services sector. With the prospect of a growing Mexican market, European firms began to eye expansion into Latin America. Although Mexico had secured broad exclusions for its banking system in the original NAFTA deal, the government decided to lift these restrictions to facilitate a rapid recapitalization in the aftermath of the peso crisis. Yet even after the relaxation of these rules, foreign ownership in the major retail banks Bancomer, Banamex, and Serfín was limited to 30 percent. No single foreign bank was allowed to gain control over more than 25 percent of the Mexican banking system. Moreover, European financial service companies faced additional costs because they had to use their US or Canadian subsidiaries to enter the Mexican market. Accordingly, the German insurer Allianz bought Aseguradora Cuauhtémoc in 1996 via its New York subsidiary. Dresdner Bank Ottawa acted as legal parent of Dresdner Bank México.[4] Of the seventeen applications for brokerage licenses submitted to the Mexican Ministry of Finance under the new NAFTA rules in 1994, seven were from subsidiaries of European companies. Four of thirteen applications for licenses for the insurance business were sent by European banks.[5] This strategy was hampered by the restrictions that both countries imposed on investment

---

[3] Asociación Mexicana de la Industria Automotriz, "Ubicación de las Empresas: Estado de México," 2004, available at www.amia.com.mx/ubicacion.html.
[4] *Expansión*, October 1, 1996.   [5] AFX News, August 19, 1994.

in financial services: the United States did not allow interstate banking, while Canada did not permit any foreign control over domestic retail banks.

Spanish banks made major investments in Mexico after the initial steps of liberalization undertaken by the Mexican government. Following a process of concentration via mergers and acquisitions in the Spanish domestic market, Banco Bilbao Vizcaya (BBV), Argentaria, Banco Santander, and Banco Central Hispano (BCH) emerged as major players. Further mergers in 1999 resulted in the current groupings Banco Bilbao Vizcaya Argentaria (BBVA) and Banco Santander Central Hispano (BSCH), the two major banks representing the main Spanish investors in the Mexican financial sector.

Using their competitive advantage arising from familiar legal and cultural backgrounds (Toral 2005), these banks invested heavily in Mexico, where together they held 33 percent of the total capital of all foreign banks. In 1996, BBV took over the Mexican bank Probursa, making it the fifth-biggest retail bank in the country, and bought a 30 percent share of the administration of the pension fund Profutura (Banco Bilbao Vizcaya 1998).

Santander had already entered the market in 1996, buying a 75 percent stake in Banco Mexico, the fourth-biggest retail bank,[6] and a 71 percent stake in Banco Santander Mexicano, in addition to administering the second-biggest and twelfth-biggest pension funds in the country, Afore Santander Mexico and Afore Génesis respectively (Calderón and Casilda 1999: 20–30).

Like their US counterparts active in the region, these banks' interests in regional trade agreements and service sector liberalization have to be seen in a broader context. BBVA and BSCH hold shares in the Spanish telecommunications firm Telefónica, a major investor in both Mexico and Chile, as well as in other Spanish utilities and energy companies such as Repsol that have focused on Latin American markets (Calderón and Casilda 1999: 22). Moreover, they also provide financing for foreign direct investment by European companies in the region. BBVA and BSCH are the only banks in the global market that hold greater investments in Latin America than in their home country (Calderón and Casilda 1999: 38), and together had investments of about US$100 billion in 1999, or about 93 percent of all investment by the Spanish

---

[6] *El País* (Madrid), October 24, 1996.

financial sector in the region (Rozas Balbontín 2001: 28). By 2002, BBVA had 22 percent of its assets in Mexico and made 18 percent of its profits there, while BSCH had 31 percent of its assets in Latin America, generating 67 percent of its profits (Barth *et al.* 2005). However, as long as Mexico restricted foreign ownership, these banks were at a perceptible disadvantage compared with their NAFTA-based competitors.

For all these primarily European firms, the external commercial policy of the European Union offered a potential recourse to secure their competitive position. Spain's representatives in the European institutions became key supporters of a services deal with Mexico. While some of the most active lobbying efforts took place before the actual negotiations, the Spanish members of the Committee of Permanent Representatives of the EU (COREPER) continued to press for a deal that included services even after Mexico lifted most restrictions in late 1998. US banks had gained a head start in investment in Mexico that could allow them to dominate retail banking, especially since Mexican migrants to the United States could be targeted as customers for remittance services. If future Mexican governments decided to restrict the market shares of individual banks, European financial services firms were the most likely to lose out. The complex institutional structure of the EU required industry representatives to voice their interests to both European Commission and member state representatives.

The institutional background: trade policy in the European Union

As European firms faced problems of declining competitiveness, they turned towards the EU institutions responsible for conducting the common trade policy of the Communities.[7] The institutional setting primarily determined the pattern of lobbying and the access points for private-sector interest, but it also had a direct effect on the outcome: since the European Commission did not have a mandate to negotiate a comprehensive investment chapter along the lines of NAFTA Chapter 11, the final text of the EU–Mexico FTA referred only to the

---

[7] Since the common external commercial policy stems from the Treaty of Rome, the correct legal term refers to the European Communities (EC). For simplicity, the following only refers to the European Union (EU).

bilateral investment treaties that several member states had signed with Mexico. Several of these agreements were negotiated immediately prior to the start of the FTA talks, including the 1997 Mexico–Germany BIT, flanking the trade negotiations with investment protection clauses.

These limitations on the negotiating competence of the European Commission reflected long-standing internal disagreements in the EU (Meunier 2005: 21–39). While the Commission has the sole right to initiate and conduct trade negotiations, it has much more limited power over domestic legislation concerning services and investment. As a result, most lobbying at the EU level is directed at the Commission, especially regarding technical aspects of agreements and offers made in negotiations. However, industrial associations in the member states also put pressure on national governments. The Council of Ministers of the member states has the power of decision and authorizes the Commission to conduct negotiations in accordance with Article 113 of the Treaties of Rome and Maastricht (renumbered to Article 133 in the Treaty of Amsterdam) by issuing a mandate. This mandate defines the room for maneuver of the Commission in negotiations. Trade interests of the member states, both offensive and defensive in policy parlance, therefore also play out in the setting of the mandate. The EU–Mexico Agreement was mostly negotiated under the rules of the Treaty of Maastricht, but concluded under the Treaty of Amsterdam. According to the latter, member states could grant competence to the Commission on a case-by-case basis for issues beyond tariffs, which they refused to do in the case of investment protection and promotion, as would become clear in the final phase of the negotiations.[8] Eventually, the Commission relied on industry support to try and expand its competence into this domain as well: both the failed EU Constitution and the Treaty of Lisbon contained clauses that opened up the possibility of negotiating investment chapters as part of future agreements.

Following a proposal by the Commission, the details of the Council decisions are prepared by COREPER and adopted by the General Affairs Council of the responsible ministers of the member states.

---

[8] According to the Treaty of Amsterdam Art. 133 §5, the Council may extend the authority of the Commission "to international negotiations on services and intellectual property." The same clauses in the Nice Treaty grant this right permanently, subject to unanimity in the Council and as long as the resulting agreement does not exceed Community competence.

Below this level, the Article 133 Committee of officials from the member states and its sectoral working groups consult with the Commission and interest groups (Meunier and Nicolaïdis 1999). The members of this committee, often with detailed knowledge of the issues, form an important link in conveying member states' aims to the Commission. The mandate adopted by the General Affairs Council is not legally binding, but going beyond its scope risks an agreement not being approved by the Council after its successful negotiation.

The External Economic Relations Committee of the European Parliament (EP) provides information to the EP members, whose assent is required for association agreements (as in the case of Mexico and Chile), but not for the trade agreements embedded in them. Association agreements were originally only intended to prepare countries for EC accession, but they have now come to signify strong economic and political ties. The European Economic and Social Committee, a legacy from the European Coal and Steel Community, has an advisory role in raising issues to the Commission.

In the EU institutions several reports reflected an early concern about the NAFTA negotiations prior to any substantive lobbying by industry groups or firms. The EP External Economic Relations Committee published a report in 1992 that warned of competitive disadvantages for European firms in NAFTA.[9] The report pointed out those industries for which the NAFTA negotiations converged on very restrictive rules of origin of concern to European firms: automobile parts and components producers in all of NAFTA, and producers of fabrics, who would potentially lose market share in Canada under NAFTA's triple transformation rule. A 1993 information note published by the European Commission echoed these concerns, although it argued that broad tariff reductions negotiated in the Uruguay Round promised to limit the preferential benefits of NAFTA for US and Canadian companies. This was much less clear in the services sector, given that the GATS negotiations proceeded slowly. The Commission preferred the multilateralization of NAFTA service commitments under the GATS, but acknowledged that "the absence of such multilateralism could lead to considerable trade diversion in the services sector, to the detriment of Community trade in services and particularly to its potential trade in services with Mexico" (European Commission 1993: 15). At the time,

---

[9] Known as the de Vries report (EP A3-0378/92).

these issues remained abstract. Within a few years, though, problems of European firms were channeled into political action.

Moving towards free trade with Mexico

Shortly after NAFTA came into effect, European firms began to voice concerns. A survey by the delegation of the European Commission in Mexico (1995: 11–13) found that European companies in fields such as telecommunications, automobiles, chemicals, pharmaceuticals, and footwear felt severely disadvantaged by NAFTA. Reacting to this information, the Council adopted a "basic paper" that expressed the readiness to start talks with Latin American countries aiming at "more far-reaching agreements" (Commission of the European Communities 1995). A Commission communication (1995: 13, 17) to the Council and the EP, published on February 8, 1995, urged action in relations with Mexico: "If the EU fails to take appropriate steps, its relations with Mexico run the risk of being eroded by NAFTA ... The available figures on direct investment show that the risk of European operators being marginalized is a very real one." It warned that, "without a new, more advantageous contractual framework for trade, Mexico has considerable scope for protecting its market while increasing its customs tariffs within GATT limits," and requested a mandate to negotiate a new framework agreement with Mexico.

In 1990, the Mexican government's overtures to the EU had been disappointed and Mexico had had to settle for a largely declaratory framework agreement. Nevertheless, the goal of a trade deal with Europe was listed as one of the goals of the five-year national development plan of 1995.[10] Upon learning about the rising concerns in the EU institutions, the government launched several initiatives to move the process along. During visits to Brussels, Mexican delegations to the EU suggested the possibility of an actual free trade agreement. In May 1995, the European Union and the Mexican government signed a Joint Solemn Declaration to establish the foundations of a future "framework" agreement. Using the opportunity of Spain's presidency of the Council during the second half of 1995, the Mexican Minister for Commerce and Industrial Development Herminio Blanco Mendoza, a

[10] See the summary of the 1995–2000 Plan Nacional de Desarrollo at www.
diputados.gob.mx/bibliot/publica/otras/pnd/133nuev.htm.

central figure in the NAFTA negotiations, visited the European Parliament and met with Leon Brittan, Commissioner for Trade, and Manuel Marín, the Spanish Commissioner responsible for relations with Latin America, to pave the way for the move from the joint declaration to an actual trade agreement.

A draft version of a negotiating brief for an agreement with Mexico was submitted to the Council on October 23, 1995. EU member states still differed in their commitment to negotiating an actual FTA with Mexico. In particular the French Minister of Foreign Affairs, Hervé de Charette, mounted strong resistance to a trade accord with Mexico and urged a pause in moves towards agreements that could displace agricultural imports from former European colonies, especially the African, Caribbean, and Pacific Group (ACP) countries and French overseas territories.[11] At the Council meeting in February 1996, the French minister clashed with his counterparts from Spain and the United Kingdom, who supported the negotiation of a free trade agreement in a "single phase" undertaking as proposed by President Ernesto Zedillo during his January visit to several EU capitals.[12] The Italian presidency of the Council finally managed to strike a compromise in May 1996 by proposing a mandate of gradual liberalization and negotiations on a sectoral basis. French resistance could eventually be overcome with the help of two commissioned studies by IRELA, the Madrid-based Institute for European–Latin American Relations, and the European Consultants Organization, that indicated that only about 1.8 percent of Mexican exports to the EU were "sensitive" agricultural products, a share that could be excluded from the agreement without violating WTO rules.

Finally, on June 11, 1997, the EU and Mexico arrived at a framework agreement that established a joint council of the Commission, member states, and the Mexican government that would negotiate on bilateral trade and services liberalization, with the eventual aim of a full-fledged FTA.[13] This agreement was followed by acrimonious arguments in COREPER, in which France threatened to block the framework agreement because of the modification of a clause referring to democracy.

---

[11] *Les Echos* (Paris), February 27, 1996; *El Mundo* (Madrid), February 26, 1996.
[12] *European Report*, February 28, 1996; *European Information Bulletin*, February 27, 1996; *Financial Times*, January 19, 1996.
[13] See Sanahuja (2000) for a detailed account of the path to the 1997 agreement.

The dispute could only be resolved when Mexico agreed to the original version, opening the path to the negotiation of the FTA. In the meantime, between 1995 and 1998, Spain, Belgium, France, Italy, Austria, and Germany negotiated bilateral investment treaties with Mexico to establish a minimum of legal guarantees equal to NAFTA Chapter 11. None of these agreements, however, offered an actual liberalization of Mexico's investment regime. Talks towards a free trade agreement began on July 14, 1998. After nine rounds of negotiations, the agreement was finalized in November 1999 and initialed in December the same year.

Lobbying coalitions and aims

During the protracted process that led to the EU–Mexico FTA, member states and the European Commission came under increasing pressure from lobbyists to counter the competitive disadvantages created by NAFTA. The motto of lobbyists was to achieve "NAFTA parity," an expression coined by Commission officials to describe the same access to the Mexican market as that guaranteed to the United States and Canada. Specific requests reflected the different concerns of exporters who sold to Mexican customers, exporters that were mostly suppliers to European firms, and investors both in services and manufacturing.

The coalitions that emerged closely match those predicted in Chapter 2. Those manufacturing firms that had already invested or planned to invest to use Mexico as an export platform lobbied most strongly for an FTA. Since they were also the most affected by the discriminatory provisions of NAFTA, they specifically sought to counter these parts of the agreement. Services firms aimed for parity in market access, which required liberalized investment in the sector. Of firms with export interests, those in sectors with close links as suppliers to investors actively supported an FTA. By contrast, conventional exporters lobbied less. Furthermore, the negotiating process and outcome corroborate a key claim made in chapter 2: interests convergence primarily on FDI. Conventional exporters were not only less active, but also less successful in achieving their aims, since neither the European Commission nor Mexico accorded them high priority.

On the Mexican side, domestic opposition to the agreement was limited to a few industries. Mexican suppliers of foreign producers, especially auto parts manufacturers, supported the agreement in principle because they would benefit from foreign investment, but they sought to ensure that the country did not become a mere assembly location that imported all parts and components. As in NAFTA, Mexican suppliers of foreign investors therefore preferred strict rules of origin and a slow reduction in tariffs. Outright resistance to the agreement came primarily from small and medium-sized firms that sold processed foods or apparel and feared competition from European imports.

Evidence from the negotiating aims and tactics of EU officials offers further support for hypothesis 4: the liberalization goals directly corresponded to the barriers erected by NAFTA. In the tariff negotiations the EU refused to negotiate on a product-by-product basis and insisted on a deal across the board. The timetable for the tariff phasing was to match NAFTA, with products in three lists: an A list with immediate liberalization, a B list with liberalization by January 1, 2003 – to coincide with NAFTA – and a C list with liberalization by 2007. A deal then had to be struck on which product groups fell into which categories, with an allocation again based on the speed at which NAFTA had liberalized them.[14]

Key advocates: Volkswagen and its suppliers

In the light of Volkswagen's particular interests, the company was clearly the most vocal individual supporter of an FTA. Following its decision to produce the new Beetle and Jetta models exclusively in Mexico for both the US and European markets, as well as all Golfs for the NAFTA market, it had the dual interest of negotiating tariff-free access to the EU and dismantling tariff barriers on parts. Furthermore, Volkswagen sought a larger quota for exporting its luxury cars Audi and VW Passat to Mexico. Volkswagen therefore combined the interests of mass producers and exporters. Just like the US manufacturers who started to use Mexico as an export platform, the company wanted to produce entry-level cars in specialized factories that achieved high volumes of production. Volkswagen lobbied the Commission from 1996 on and became closely involved in 1997 and 1998, with regular correspondence and five personal visits to the Commission by its representatives.[15]

---

[14] Interview with EU official, Brussels, July 2004.
[15] Interviews with interest group representative and EU officials, Brussels, June 2004.

One of the key aims for Volkswagen was to lower the Mexican tariffs on vehicle parts. According to a Volkswagen representative, "even 3 percent tariffs [US tariffs on cars] are difficult with narrow margins, while 15 percent [Mexican tariffs on parts] are outright impractic-able."[16] The Mexican side, under pressure from local parts producers, resisted this issue "in a dramatic battle" almost until the end, fearing that European parts producers preferred exporting to Mexico over further investment there. In a September 1997 letter signed by the ten presidents of the Mexican processing industry association Cámara Nacional de la Industria de Transformación (Canacintra), the Automotive Council, representing primarily parts producers, stressed that its members were still chafing under the difficult adjustment required by NAFTA, in particular the lower domestic content require-ments. The letter also alleged that non-NAFTA producers were import-ing a greater share of parts than the high rule of origin threshold in NAFTA had led them to expect.[17] This assessment was probably accu-rate; in 1998, Volkswagen registered exports of US$33 million and imports of parts under PITEX worth US$22 million, equivalent to a domestic content of less than 30 percent.[18]

To support an outcome in its favor, Volkswagen lobbied the Mexican government directly and promoted the accord in the Mexican media. In an interview with the magazine *El Economista* in March 1999, Thomas Karig, director for government relations at Volkswagen de México, emphasized that during the five years that NAFTA had been in effect, his company's export competitiveness had suffered because of the tariffs and rules of origin imposed on it. In June, shortly before the critical sixth negotiation round, Volkswagen even threatened not to build a planned second factory in Mexico if the agreement failed to deliver the necessary tariff reductions, since the company would then suffer the full impact of the abolition of the PITEX program on January 1, 2001. Bernd Leissner, Volkswagen's chief executive in Mexico, stressed that even though Volkswagen sought to achieve a high regional content quota, key components could not be procured in Mexico alone. Volkswagen's production strategy demanded that in order to achieve economies of

---

[16] Interview, Brussels, June 2004.
[17] *El Financiero* (Mexico City), September 22, 1997.
[18] *El Universal* (Mexico City), October 21, 1999.

scale, some parts were produced in a single factory in Germany for shipping to all its global operations.[19]

The threat of abandoning planned investment was directed at the opposition of the Mexican auto parts manufacturers. Just as in the NAFTA talks, their representatives were based in a nearby hotel room, referred to as "el cuarto al lado," and frequently consulted during the negotiations.[20] The Mexican side proposed a long phase-out period for tariffs on auto parts, initially suggesting a ten-year period. By contrast, the EU side aimed at four years to match the liberalization commitments in NAFTA. Oscar Véjar, the vice-president of the Mexican parts producers group Asociación de la Industria Nacional de Autopartes (INA), criticized the EU demand as a clear attempt to avoid increasing the regional content of European cars produced in Mexico.[21] The Mexican side held out until the sixth round of negotiations in June 1999, when the EU chief negotiator Mendel Goldstein offered a slower reduction in tariffs on other goods. Since the Mexican association of car producers, Mexicar, sided with Volkswagen and emphasized how much employment the company was creating, the Mexican government eventually gave in, agreeing to an immediate elimination of tariffs on 70 percent of all auto parts and the rest by 2007.

Compared with NAFTA, the deal was easier to accept for the Mexican side. Volkswagen was already achieving a higher overall local content quota than US manufacturers. Growing exports from Mexico to Europe promised to compensate Mexican parts producers. However, Volkswagen also managed to press for a special clause that stretched the limits of the agreement: some new Beetle models would be fitted with an engine produced in Hungary, which did not join the EU until May 2004. The origin designation of these engines, from a country itself linked to the EU through an FTA (the Europe Agreements), would "cumulate" with that of products sourced in the Community itself.[22]

In contrast to Volkswagen's conspicuous influence, the organized European auto parts producers association (CLEPA, after its French name Comité de liaison européen des fabricants d'equipements et de

---

[19] *El Economista* (Mexico City), June 17, 1999.
[20] Interview with EU official, Brussels, June 2004.
[21] *El Financiero* (Mexico City), January 20, 1999.
[22] Interview with interest group representative, Brussels, June 2004.

pièces automobiles) was rather ineffective, despite its role as part of Volkswagen's rent chain. While partly due to Volkswagen's pressure for specific tariff offers that matched its suppliers' exports rather than broad reduction of tariffs on car parts, Mexican negotiators also resisted CLEPA's requests strongly.[23] In line with the predictions in table 2.1, suppliers in home and host do not want to share their spoils.

To serve the upper market segment, Volkswagen pushed for a bigger, firm-specific import quota on the basis of their status as a long-term incumbent in Mexico. Other European car manufacturers, in particular Mercedes Benz and BMW, had different aims. Since they only planned to serve the small market segment for luxury cars by exporting, they were mainly interested in an export quota for all firms and eventual tariff-free access to the Mexican market. The European Association of Automobile Manufacturers (ACEA) lobbied on their behalf, trying to balance the interests of Volkswagen and the exporters.[24] ACEA frequently met Commission officials to press its position, although the interests of Volkswagen clearly predominated, since they were represented on both sides of the table. While the Commission tried to get EU automobile producers to compromise, arguing that it "could not well discriminate against some of our own [EU] companies,"[25] the Mexican side preferred Volkswagen's proposal that the Mexican government would allocate the quota. One EU official stated that the negotiators "almost got a sectoral deal in cars for Volkswagen."[26]

European automobile manufacturers also sought to counter the interest of US manufacturers by using rules of origin, turning on its head the scenario that had evolved during the NAFTA negotiations. The Commission insisted on using the standard formula of all EU agreements, on the grounds of simplicity. This coincided with the manufacturers' interests, but proved problematic for Chrysler. The company, which at the time planned to export its PT Cruiser model from Mexico to the EU, only achieved a 30 percent Mexican content quota and lobbied the Commission to count all NAFTA parts as Mexican. While this would have matched Volkswagen's success in pressing its point regarding the Hungarian Beetle engines, the Commission refused and

[23] Interview with interest group representative, Brussels, June 2004.
[24] Interview with interest group representative, Brussels, June 2004.
[25] Interviews with EU officials, Brussels, June and July 2004.
[26] Interview with EU official, Brussels, June 2004.

the Mexican side appeared disinterested.[27] European automotive firms were not above using rules of origin to extend protection against US competitors in the EU–Mexico FTA when it suited their interests.

As a deal in the auto sector appeared to be within reach for the EU and Mexico, US manufacturers decided to mount a rearguard defense to at least slow down what they could not prevent. The president of Ford Mexico, José Manuel Machado, warned the Mexican government in a June 1999 statement that in order to protect the Mexican auto industry and to allow it to develop successfully, the negotiations ought to result in a "gradual opening with the EU that promotes investment in the productive capacity in the auto industry in Mexico and not merely the import of finished vehicles." GM chairman Jack Smith, Ford CEO Jacques A. Nasser, and DaimlerChrysler chairman Jürgen Schrempp sent a letter to Herminio Blanco, urging him to push for a ten-year phase-out of the tariffs on automotive products in the FTA rather than the shorter period requested by the EU, because the Mexican market would otherwise be inundated with European exports. Although DaimlerChrysler was managed from its German headquarters, its interests in North America were determined by Chrysler's investment in Mexico and its competition with VW in the US market, not by the limited export potential for Mercedes cars from the EU. In siding with GM and Ford, it acted as a US manufacturer.

Gerd Klaus, responsible for Volkswagen sales in the United States, dismissed the statement as "obviously not in Mexico's interest," but rather a transparent attempt by the US manufacturers to block their competition from reaping the full benefits of the EU–Mexico FTA. Klaus stressed that on the contrary, the FTA was crucial for laying the foundations for Mexico's continued success in exporting to the US market.[28]

Given its traditionally central role in Mexico's economic development policy, its high share of employment, and its importance as export product, it is not surprising that the auto industry supplied the largest and most vocal group of lobbyists on both sides of the Atlantic. Several manufacturing industries, however, engaged with the Commission almost as frequently, with varying degrees of success.

---

[27] Interview with interest group representative, Brussels, June 2004.
[28] *El Economista* (Mexico City), June 17, 1999.

Lobbying by suppliers: the chemical industry

European exporter interests further up the production chain also lobbied in favor of the agreement. This was particularly true for the
European chemical industry, whose exports to Mexico primarily took
the form of a "remote supplier for European firms," in the words of one
of its representatives. The industry's umbrella organization, CEFIC,
became a staunch supporter of an agreement with Mexico to level the
playing field with the US competition. Between 1996 and 1999, the
organization met on a regular basis with the responsible desk officers in
the Directorate General for Trade of the European Commission (DG
Trade) and emphasized the concerns of its member companies.[29] Early
communications from CEFIC to the Directorate General stressed the
need for an FTA to counter the negative effects of NAFTA. In an April
1996 letter to DG Trade, CEFIC stated that

Considering ... the particular situation created by Mexico's inclusion in the
NAFTA, establishing a bilateral free-trade area should not only revive EU
relations with Mexico but also bring about some compensation towards EU
industry's "third-country" position vs. US and Canadian competitors on the
Mexican market.

When the Commission took up the Mexican offer to negotiate an
agreement, CEFIC was among the most active supporters. CEFIC specifically asked that any tariff reductions by the Mexican side had to
match those negotiated under NAFTA.[30] A March 1999 letter to the
Commission emphasized that

In earlier correspondence regarding this Free Trade Agreement CEFIC has
already pointed at the disadvantages for EU chemical industry resulting from
the NAFTA agreement. While US industry benefits mainly from zero or
reduced import duties ... EU industry is still faced with the negative impact
of Mexico's non-participation in the [WTO] Chemical Tariff Harmonisation
Agreement.

As a result of this pressure the majority of chemical products ended
up in basket A for immediate liberalization, offering better than
NAFTA parity in many instances. Products in basket C were almost

---

[29] Interview with interest group representative; interview with EU official, Brussels,
June 2004.
[30] Interview with interest group representative, Brussels, June 2004.

exclusively less refined chemical products, often derivatives of the petrochemical industry.

By contrast, the Mexican steel industry proved much more influential in the negotiations. EU negotiators went into the talks with the clear aim of NAFTA parity in steel products as well, a request that was refused outright by the steel representatives in the Coordinadora de Organismos Empresariales de Comercio Exterior (COECE), who stressed that European steel producers were to benefit from subsidies in the EU until 2002.[31] Mexican steel producers hoped to delay liberalization by ten years. The Commission negotiating team had charged an experienced senior official of Italian nationality with the "special mission" of persuading the Mexican private-sector representatives during several working dinners that involved the consumption of copious quantities of wine. Although the EU negotiators admitted that they had had "more fun than in any previous trade negotiation,"[32] most steel products remained in category C for liberalization by 2007. Nevertheless, representatives of the National Chamber of Steel Producers (Cámara Nacional de Acero, or Canacero) expressed their disappointment after the conclusion of the steel negotiations. Since the EU had already committed itself in the Uruguay Round to zero tariffs by 2004 on most steel products, Mexico had not gained any preferential access. However, European and Mexican interests converged on strict rules of origin copied directly from NAFTA after a Mexican proposal.[33]

Financial services: from liberalization to securing bastions

In the services sector the key lobbying association was the European Services Forum (ESF). While not originally created to focus on bilateral agreements,[34] the association followed the negotiations closely. In line with the general pattern of service-sector lobbying that also became visible during the NAFTA negotiations, the position papers supplied by ESF requested the same liberalization measures as those sought in the WTO. In monthly meetings with the responsible desk officer at the Commission, the ESF pressed for an opening of the Mexican services

[31] *El Universal* (Mexico City), March 29, 1999; October 1, 1999.
[32] Interview with EU officials, Brussels, June 2004.
[33] *El Universal* (Mexico City), January 13, 2000.
[34] Interview with interest group representative, Brussels, June 2004.

markets.[35] Particularly strong interests targeted the financial sector, where, until 1998, Spanish banks sought to achieve access equal to NAFTA by investing directly or by taking over Mexican banks. BBV and BCH pushed for an agreement primarily by lobbying the Spanish representatives in the Council and COREPER, since services commitments had to be listed and requested by member states. However, the two banks also sought to influence Commission negotiators directly.[36] Requests from the Commission were addressed at both DG Trade and the Directorate General for Financial Services. Although HSBC had interests in Mexico, the bank did not lobby actively. One EU official speculated that the push by the two Spanish banks was already so strong that HSBC opted to "get a free ride."[37] After Mexico lifted all ownership restrictions in 1998 except for the limit of 20 percent market share, the banks left their remaining demands on the table: lifting the market share cap, guarantees on existing liberalization in the form of a stand-still clause, and protection against measures tantamount to expropriation. The ESF expressed its satisfaction with the Mexican measure, but still pressed the Commission to at a minimum obtain a commitment to negotiate further services liberalization in other sectors in the future.

EU services negotiators therefore opted for a deal that abolished the remaining restrictions and then locked in Mexico's commitments. Since Mexico had to adapt its domestic regulatory framework to fulfill the NAFTA schedule for services liberalization, the EU could achieve parity by securing identical commitments for its industries. European negotiators also pressed for clear terms on equal access to maritime transport and its facilities for EU providers. This measure complemented the trade liberalization by clearing the path for European freight companies and was largely undisputed.[38] However, given the contested mandate for services liberalization, the negotiators postponed the negotiation of actual commitments by either side. The European service industry appeared content with a level playing field. Following the lifting of ownership restrictions, Santander acquired a majority interest in

---

[35] Interview with EU official, Brussels, June 2004.
[36] Interview with EU official, Brussels, July 2004. See also *El País* (Madrid), May 5, 1999.
[37] Interview, Brussels, June 2004.
[38] Interview with EU official, Brussels, June 2004.

Serfín, while BBVA bought a controlling stake in Bancomer in June 2000 and majority ownership in June 2002.

The bystanders: labor and agriculture

Despite the EU's entrenched protectionist agricultural policy, relatively little lobbying revolved around market access for agricultural goods, where export interests in very different products predominated. Mexico suggested a slower tariff phasing than the EU and insisted on the exclusion of any product benefiting from EU export subsidies, since these measures had been eliminated under NAFTA.[39]

While agricultural liberalization is the EU's Achilles heel in any trade deal, the Commission often states that a global recognition of geographic origin indications (GI) for traditional European agricultural products is a precondition for greater market opening.[40] Due to its signaling function, perhaps the most important was therefore the May 1997 bilateral agreement negotiated on behalf of European spirits and wine producers. The producers pressed for Mexico's acceptance of EU geographic denominations, but were also willing to accept matching Mexican requests regarding the recognition of tequila as a uniquely Mexican product, banning its production in the EU from bulk agave syrup.[41] Consequently tariffs on wines and spirits were among the first to be eliminated by the EU–Mexico FTA.

EU officials judged that the total agricultural component was neither in violation of WTO Article XXIV, nor threatening to any particular

---

[39] *Europe Daily Bulletin*, March 12, 1999.
[40] The GI system recognizes traditional production techniques and a regional origin as protected, for example banning the marketing of sparkling wine as champagne unless it is produced in the French region of the same name. The EU holds the position that geographic indications cannot be overridden by registered trademarks, although the actual geographic area can be enlarged by administrative fiat of the Institut National des Appellations d'Origine (INAO) in the case of champagne if there is sufficient demand, and has been in the past, as reported in the *Independent*, October 27, 2007.
[41] The *Guardian* reported on May 29, 1997, that the conclusion of the agreement was celebrated in the Mexican ambassador's Brussels residence, featuring samples of sixty different brands of tequila, a Mariachi band, and a hat dance by the ambassador's wife. By contrast, in 2006, US trade negotiators struck a deal that allows the shipment of bulk agave syrup from Mexico to the United States and the production of tequila there, preventing Mexico from enforcing its geographic indications. There were no media reports of celebrations in Mexico.

interest group in the EU, since Mexican exports were only competing in a handful of product categories, and there only with third-country interests.[42]

One of the characteristic features of North–South PTAs is that (with the partial exception of the United States), labor unions have surprisingly little interest in, and even less influence on, actual negotiations or ratification of agreements. The EU–Mexico FTA proved to be no exception. The European Trade Union Confederation (CES) did not issue any statement on negotiations, nor did representatives engage with the Commission on any issues. Only in 2003, after the ratification of the agreement, did CES and the Mexican Confederation of Trade Unions issue a joint statement calling for greater support for social cohesion in the bilateral agreement between the partners. It bears noting, however, that European association agreements always contain clauses similar to NAFTA's side agreement on labor, although these aims are merely declaratory and not legally binding. Members of the European Parliament's Committee on Industry, External Trade, Research and Energy[43] voiced concerns in four recommendations to the EP, criticizing the standstill clause in the services chapter as an undue constraint on Mexico's regulatory freedom. In all cases, however, the EP assented to whatever the Commission had negotiated.

Outcomes: beyond NAFTA parity

The argument so far underscores that firms with interests linked to FDI were the most active in their support of an EU–Mexico FTA. By contrast, supporters of finished goods were less concerned about market access. In services, firms sought to close the gap with their US and Canadian competitors as much as possible. The final outcome of the negotiations directly reflected the interests of these firms.

The treaty establishing a free trade area in goods and regulating government procurement and cooperation and consultation on other matters was signed in March 2000.[44] Following ratification by both parties, the FTA in goods entered into force on July 1, 2000. The EU Commission cited as its achievements similar or better conditions for

---

[42] Interview with EU official, Brussels, June 2004.
[43] Before 2000, the Committee on External Economic Relations.
[44] Formally Decision 2/2000 of the EC–Mexico Joint Council of March 23, 2000.

automotive exports to Mexico than from Canada and the United States by reducing tariffs from 20 to 3.3 percent immediately and eliminating them completely by 2003. In addition, Mexico committed to a quota for the import of vehicles: 14 percent of the Mexican sales of the previous year in units until December 2003, then 15 percent until December 2006.[45] Paragraphs 3.1 and 3.2 granted Mexico the temporary right to allocate up to 11 percent of this quota to incumbent firms in compliance with the 1989 Mexican auto decree and to prefer exporters based on existing trade patterns, which in practice strongly favored Volkswagen. Car parts and components that fall under the Mexican auto decree became tariff-free in 2007. Just like quotas for the import of vehicles, this deal favored the incumbent manufacturer Volkswagen and its parts suppliers over exporters.

Tariffs on agricultural goods levied by either party are only phased out over long periods of up to ten years. The agreement also maintained import quotas by both sides for certain products, but the trade in these products is too limited to be seen as a clear violation of WTO commitments.

Regarding investment, the agreement only refers to the commitments under the OECD and bilateral investment treaties, and points to a future review. In fact, the Commission had negotiated what one source called a "sexy investment chapter better than NAFTA," but dropped it to seal the agreement in services.[46] However, despite the conflict over the mandate, lobbying pressures from the financial sector were apparently strong enough to motivate a special agreement on financial services. Chapter III on financial services contains national treatment and most-favored-nation clauses, a standstill clause, and provisions for liberalization within three years. Notably, Article 23 establishes a special committee that reviews the agreement to allow additional, matching commitments, should either party liberalize its financial services sector further under a regional agreement. This clause offers a commitment to maintain parity even if future preferential liberalization takes place in other deals. Both parties have committed themselves to eliminating all bilateral restrictions in the services sector over a period of no more than ten years. Just as in manufacturing, the treaty guarantees equal access

---

[45] Annex II to Decision Nr. 2/2000 of the EC–Mexico Joint Council of March 23, 2000.
[46] Interviews with EU officials, Brussels, June and July 2004.

Table 4.2. *Foreign ownership of Mexican banks:*
percentage shares of total retail bank assets

1997		2004	
Banamex	24.9	BBVA Bancomer	26.3
Bancomer	21.7	*Banamex*	22.4
Serfín	14.3	Santander-Serfín	14.8
Bital	7.3	Banorte	10.0
Mexicano	6.4	HSBC	9.7
BBV	6.3	*Scotiabank*	5.0
Promex	3.8	Del Bajo	1.2
Banorte	2.9	Azteca	1.1
Banpaís	2.2	Affirme	0.5
Centro	2.2	Ixe	0.4
Citibank	1.5	Banregio	0.3

Source: CNBV 1998, 2004. Bold: European ownership;
bold italic: US ownership; italic: Canadian ownership.

with US and Canadian competitors for European firms, even if Mexico offers improved commitments to its NAFTA partners. The services treaty entered into force on March 1, 2001. By 2004, European and US investors had seized opportunities to acquire the biggest Mexican retail banks. Although no foreign bank managed to dominate the market completely, the data shown in table 4.2 underline the competition between US and European banks. While in 1997 the biggest foreign-owned bank had only 6.4 percent of total retail banking system assets, by 2004 the second- and third-biggest banks were in the hands of BBVA and BSCH, respectively. Citibank took over Banamex in August 2001 in a US$12.5 billion deal, the single biggest transaction in the entry of foreign banks into Mexico. Moreover, there is evidence that the principal foreign-owned banks achieve unusually high returns that suggest lack of competition (Schulz 2006), probably because of the enormous economies of scale that are achievable in retail banking.

Although the services deal was considered a success by EU negotiators, it failed to achieve a key goal in the related field of standards and regulations. This conforms to the expectation of first-mover advantages bestowed by PTAs. Mexican negotiators argued that four years after NAFTA, so much of its trade was with the United States that they could not legislate for the adoption of any European standards. To the dis-satisfaction of EU negotiators, Mexico reserved the right to use NAFTA government procurement rules, although the EU had pressed for its standard clauses.[47]

Within a few months of the conclusion of the FTA, European car manufacturers announced major investments in Mexico. Renault returned to Mexico after a fifteen-year absence with a joint production plant with Nissan, following the merger of the two car manufacturers in April 1999. Volkswagen earmarked US$1 billion for the expansion of Mexican operations, which by then provided a third of the parts imports for its German factories and exported 300 New Beetle models daily to the EU. Peugeot executives visited Mexico in January 2000 to survey sites for future investments.[48]

While EU–Mexican trade is still dwarfed by Mexican trade with the United States, European firms regained market share in the first years after the entry into force of the agreement. European merchandise exports to Mexico expanded by 28.1 percent between July 1999 and June 2003. A considerable share consists of intermediate and capital goods; electrical and power-generating machinery, transport equipment and parts, and chemical products make up 58 percent of exports.[49] The FTA appeared to have leveled the playing field and restored the competitiveness of European firms in Mexico.

Several alternative explanations can be put forth to account for the EU's decision to seek an FTA with Mexico, but different factors suggest that they weighed less on the outcome than the discriminatory effects of NAFTA on European investment in Mexico. Consider whether the EU reached out to Mexico because multilateral liberalization did not make progress. In the case of the EU, at least two arguments stand against this thesis. First, the EU made a turnaround in its policy towards Mexico. During the early 1990s, European investors showed little interest in Mexico. Firms with investments in Mexico were still oriented towards the domestic market. In this situation, even the limited potential of Mexican agricultural exports proved enough of a stumbling block to prevent bilateral negotiations. European firms started to lobby only

---

[47] Interview with EU official, Brussels, June 2004.
[48] *Financial Times*, January 5, 2000.
[49] All figures are from the 2004 statistics available at ec.europa.eu/trade/issues/
bilateral/countries/mexico/index_en.htm.

after the effects of NAFTA on outsiders became evident, at which point their interests outweighed domestic forces. Second, the EU Commission itself perceived the multilateral negotiations as much more important than any bilateral agreements. According to EU officials, Trade Commissioner Lamy made it clear on taking up his post that under his direction no new bilateral negotiations would be initiated before the conclusion of the Doha round.[50] Without pressure by European firms in services and manufacturing, the EU might have negotiated bilateral deals in its immediate region, but would hardly have reached out to Latin America.

A further possibility is that the EU used a PTA as a carrot to support Mexico's democratization, and the threat of a withdrawal of trade preferences as the proverbial stick. Compliance with such conditionality is one of the principal political effects of PTAs (Hafner-Burton 2005), but it is better seen as influencing the design and implementation of an agreement than as the impetus for its formation. Szymanski and Smith (2005) analyze the question of human rights conditionality and the broader political dimensions of the negotiation of the EU–Mexico agreement in detail. The authors argue that France in particular insisted on normative grounds and was prepared to let the negotiations fail. It bears noting that the French objections were only raised after it had lost all allies in its opposition to a trade agreement. Without singling out any government, Commission Vice-President Martín accused members of "double standards" if they insisted on the democratization clause in the case of Mexico, but not of China (Sanahuja 2000: 52). In this particular case, conditionality seems to have worked against a possible agreement.

Finally, EU firms could have responded to trade discrimination against conventional exports in general primarily because Mexico raised its MFN tariffs, as submitted by Dür (2007), rather than the more specific discrimination against trade linked to FDI as argued here. In this regard, the comparison between Volkswagen as a firm with investment in Mexico and exporters such as BMW and DaimlerChrysler is instructive. The latter firms sought a more generous quota for the export of finished cars from Europe to Mexico. However, their lobbying efforts were largely unsuccessful since Mexico had no interest in a market opening by itself with little promise of FDI or job creation. Moreover, DaimlerChrysler even sided with GM and Ford in trying

[50] Interviews with EU officials, Brussels, June 2004.

to slow down the reduction of tariffs that Volkswagen pressed for, suggesting that the German-American firm's position as US investor in Mexico overrode its interests as exporter from Germany. Volkswagen's interests ran counter to those of exporters, since BMW or DaimlerChrysler vehicles from Europe only competed with VW cars in the Mexican market. Without the transnational coalition of a multinational firm with FDI in the developing country – in this case Volkswagen as the only European auto firm – and its local – that is, Mexican – suppliers, an FTA offered no particular advantage over multilateral liberalization and hence resulted in few tariff reductions.

Outside the automotive industry, finished-goods exporters engaged in limited lobbying efforts through EuroCommerce, the association of European chambers of commerce, but they did not make specific demands that differed from their general pro-free trade position taken in multilateral negotiations. Without foreign direct investment and its attendant trade, even the restrictive rules of origin in NAFTA, Mexico's high MFN tariffs, and the – by developing country standards – large market appear to have been insufficient to bring about an FTA on their own because they did not create a broad coalition in the EU in support of an agreement with Mexico.

The previous discussion has shown that the effects of NAFTA on European FDI and trade with Mexico triggered a countermove by the EU, leading to the first expansion of its free trade network across the Atlantic. Yet the EU strategy had an unexpected consequence in itself: it led trade policymakers in Japan to reconsider that country's exclusive focus on the multilateral trade regime, a development that is the subject of the next chapter.

5 | The odd couple: the Japan–Mexico free trade agreement

F OR Japan, the agreement signed with Mexico on September 18, 2004, signified a momentous step in political, if not economic, terms. The FTA is Japan's first agreement with an exporter of agricultural products – pork, citrus fruits, and avocados in the case of Mexico. NAFTA triggered a major shift, highly contested domestically, in Japan's foreign economic policy. Moreover, as described in chapter 7, it led Japan to the active pursuit of bilateral agreements with neighboring countries and beyond. Considering the modest volumes of bilateral trade, the choice of Mexico as partner in the second preferential trade agreement after over four decades of multilateralism is striking. Yet most of this trade is directly tied to FDI by Japanese firms, so that even relatively weak links sufficed to generate the momentum for a defensive PTA.

The coalitions of Japanese firms that supported the FTA correspond to those lobbying for the EU–Mexico FTA, but the case shows important differences in process and liberalization outcomes. Japanese investment in Mexico in general is smaller and narrowly concentrated in fewer industries. Electronics firms were particularly hurt by the abolition of the maquiladora benefits and lobbied actively. Most importantly, without a precedent of preferential trade agreements, Japanese firms first exhausted all possibilities of obtaining tariff relief from Mexico before turning to their own government for help. When the option of negotiating an FTA was put on the table, firms with FDI in Mexico and their suppliers continued to dominate the lobbying in favor of the agreement, although the public discourse in Japan revolved around exports.

The conclusion of the FTA with Japan means that Mexico has established preferential ties to all OECD countries except South Korea, further enhancing its attractiveness as a production site close to the US market. For Mexico, reducing tariffs for the imports of Japanese firms was desirable, but not politically feasible without an FTA. NAFTA Article 303 banned tariff rebates for inputs of goods that would be exported to the United States or Canada. WTO membership implied adherence to the MFN principle. Any tariff relief specifically for Japanese firms would have to be extended to all other countries, including competitors in east Asia, possibly reducing Mexico to the assembly site of foreign parts with little domestic industrial stimulus. In comparison, an FTA would allow tariff reductions on a preferential basis, attract more Japanese FDI, and perhaps even offer improved market access for Mexican exporters. As with many North–South PTAs, this last hope was not fulfilled. The final agreement offers no substantial improvement for Mexican agricultural exporters, even though this outcome was buried in complex tariff and quota formulae. The main political obstacle that nearly led to the breakdown of the negotiations was inevitably a question of pork – literally, Mexican pork exports to Japan, where a small, but well-organized interest group lobbied for sustained protection.

Japanese foreign direct investment in Mexico

Japanese investment in Mexico is small compared with that from the United States and the EU, and is heavily concentrated in the maquiladoras, sectorally in consumer electronics and auto parts, in which Japanese manufacturers have a traditional competitive advantage, and geographically in Baja California and the northeast of Mexico.

Table 5.1 shows the stock of Japanese FDI in Mexico and flow data for services and manufacturing investment. The calculation method for the flow data differs from the standard used by the United States, Germany, and Spain, so that the comparison can only be suggestive. Even at its first peak in 1994, Japan's total investment in Mexico was never more than half the FDI from the EU and never exceeded 9 percent of total FDI in Mexico. Conversely, OECD statistics show that Mexico hosted around 0.8 percent of total Japanese outward FDI throughout the 1990s. The data also show a conspicuous slump in Japanese FDI in 1995–96, but this has to be treated with even greater care: the Japanese source data is missing for those years, so that the values are from the Mexican report to the OECD. However, the values for the other years generally do not differ much.

Japanese firms used their US subsidiaries to set up production facilities in Mexico, benefiting from the Mexican duty-drawbacks and the limited-duty imports under the US tariff headings 806.30 and 807.00. This particular ownership structure prevailed beyond the maquiladora

Table 5.1. *Japanese FDI in Mexico, US$ million*

Year	All sectors Stock	Manufacturing Flows	Services Flows
1990	2,296	188	23
1991	2,447	184	46
1992	2,462	63	5
1993	2,466	22	4
1994	3,095	675	3
1995	887[i]	111	95
1996	956[i]	95	29
1997	1,065	298	3
1998	1,085	73	7
1999	2,199	1,459	24
2000	2,193	–	0
2001	2,367	22	24
2002	2,464	56	23
2003	2,704	106	23
2004	2,645	214	33
2005	3,271	–	–
2006	1,499	–	–

[i] Data from Mexican OECD reports, missing in Japanese source data.
– Missing data.
Source: OECD, Japanese Ministry of Finance (MOF).

sector: of 205 Japanese firms in Mexico in 2002, 135 were wholly or majority-owned by the US subsidiary of the Japanese company (Tōyō Keizai Shuppan 2002). At the time of the NAFTA negotiations Japanese investment in the maquiladoras represented 6 percent of the total number of plants, with about 25,000 employees, of which 55 percent produced electronics components, the rest mostly automotive parts (Koido 1991). Although maquiladora plants also began to export to other countries in the region, most of their products were destined for the US market.[1]

Since the late 1980s, major Japanese companies such as Sony, Sanyo, Sharp, Hitachi, and Matsushita (Panasonic) had produced consumer electronics goods in Mexico, in particular television sets. As a result of

___

[1] *Nikkei Sangyō Shinbun,* July 30, 1991.

such FDI, the share of Mexican exports of the US color television market jumped from 2.6 percent in 1985 to 40 percent in 1989 (Koido 1991: 64). In many cases, labor-intensive production in Mexico was integrated with Japanese-owned factories in the "twin city" across the border in the United States (Ueda 2001: 310–13). However, prior to NAFTA, the maquiladora industry was characterized by minimal local input, with core components exclusively sourced from Japan and other Asian countries. Between 1980 and 1989, the percentage of Mexican inputs in some plants located in Mexico's interior region even fell, from 10 to less than 5 percent, while most border-region maquiladoras never used more than 2 percent domestic parts and raw materials (Wilson 1992: 48–49). Non-NAFTA firms were far from attaining anything close to the level of regional content required by the agreement, making them vulnerable to the discriminatory clauses that US firms had pushed for in the North American negotiations.

Except for Nissan's plant in Cuernavaca and a small assembly operation of Honda motorcycles in Guadalajara set up in 1985, no Japanese vehicle producers were present in Mexico. Nissan had established its subsidiary in Mexico in 1961 and taken up production five years later. Pursuing a strategy similar to Volkswagen in Mexico, the company initially only produced low-priced small cars aimed at the domestic and neighboring Central American markets. Immediately prior to NAFTA's entry into force, Nissan had a domestic market share of 24 percent and exported the required minimum of 30 percent of its Mexican production (Moreno Brid 1996: 19). Like Volkswagen, Nissan Mexico did not operate any production facilities in the maquiladora sector, but used the PITEX duty-drawback scheme to import parts for cars that would eventually be exported to other Latin American countries.

The NAFTA threat

For Japanese firms NAFTA presented problems and opportunities at the same time. Japanese executives and government officials voiced sharp criticism of the likely outcome of discriminatory clauses during the final stages of the NAFTA negotiations, trying to prevent a negative impact on the Mexican operations of Japanese firms. On the ground, coping with NAFTA would have meant greater investments in Mexico, or diverting investment from Asian countries to locations in

Mexico to avoid rising costs. Few Japanese firms chose this route, as described below.

Already, in the early stages of the NAFTA talks, Japanese firms voiced their concerns. Assessing the negotiations in a 1991 interview, the regional managers of several Japanese firms in Mexico referred to NAFTA as an "assault on Japanese firms."[2] Amemiya Shōichi, president of Nissan Mexico, estimated that the cost advantage of US manufacturers over their Japanese competitors would amount to US$500–600 per vehicle because of the required regional content. Kume Yutaka, chairman of the Japanese Automobile Manufacturers Association (JAMA), called NAFTA's rules of origin for cars a "violation of GATT rules" and "contrary to the ideal of global free trade."[3]

The threat of the planned phase-out of the maquiladora benefits also prompted Japanese firms to use existing associations to address the Mexican government directly. In May 1991, membership in the Japanese Chamber of Commerce and Industry (JCCI) in Mexico doubled, to twenty-five firms. Twenty-eight firms, mostly from the electronics industry, used the Japan Maquiladora Association to express their views. Both groups as well as individual firms began a concentrated lobbying campaign to obtain tariff relief. Representatives of Sanyo, Panasonic, and Hitachi met with SECOFI officials in September 1991 to press for an extension of the tariff-rebate system.[4] The Kansai Productivity Centre (Kansai seisansei honbu) sent a delegation led by managers of auto parts maker Marubeni to visit Nissan Mexico, followed by discussions with SECOFI secretary Jaime Serra on how to lessen the impact of NAFTA. Japanese electronics manufacturers also joined the Mexican electronic components producers association and directly lobbied the Mexican government for a reduction of tariffs on electronics, and prompted the Japanese Chamber of Commerce in Mexico to request such reductions from SECOFI.[5]

Officials of the Japanese Ministry of International Trade and Industry (MITI) supported these efforts. In bilateral talks with his Mexican counterpart Pedro Loyola at SECOFI, MITI Minister Watanabe Kōzō stressed that Mexico needed to offer a tariff reduction to firms already

[2] *Ibid.*, July 30, 1991.   [3] *Ibid.*, August 14, 1992.
[4] *Nikkei Bijinesu*, October 28, 1991.
[5] *Nihon Keizai Shinbun*, November 3, 1992. Unless noted, references to this newspaper always refer to the morning edition.

operating in the maquiladoras, and suggested that the liberalization of foreign ownership restrictions in NAFTA had to be extended to other countries as well, if Mexico wanted to keep attracting investment by non-NAFTA firms.[6] A Japanese government panel at the Economic Planning Agency criticized NAFTA's rules of origin in August 1993.[7] Despite these efforts, the Mexican government only managed to delay the termination of the maquiladora benefits until January 2001. SECOFI was squeezed between the desire to attract more FDI to Mexico and the need to retain barriers that pleased local suppliers but risked outweighing Mexico's low labor cost and proximity to the United States. Faced with the choice between procuring more locally or divesting, Japanese firms began to shift their sourcing to North America.

Beachheads in NAFTA and investment diversion

In the consumer electronics industry, the specter of the phase-out of the maquiladora benefits triggered a shift of production from Asian countries to Mexico. Official FDI statistics, however, largely masked the changes on the ground and showed a slight reduction in overall capital stock. Virtually all Japanese firms that restructured their operations in Mexico did so via their subsidiaries in the United States that in turn controlled the production in Mexico.

In many instances the production choices reflected investment diversion rather than the attractions of the Mexican production location: even with the additional cost of transportation, parts from southeast Asia were often about 10 percent cheaper than comparable Mexican components. These cost advantages were eradicated by the combined force of NAFTA's rules of origin and Mexico's MFN tariffs. Cathode-ray tubes for television sets, for example, would now carry a 16 percent duty.[8] NAFTA's rules required that for screens of 14 inches and bigger, only the use of a North American-made cathode-ray tube would confer origin (Solís 2003: 391).

To avoid the higher MFN tariffs and to comply with NAFTA tracing and origin rules, Hitachi shifted the production of television chassis

---

[6] *Ibid.*, September 30, 1992.   [7] Japan Economic Newswire, August 4, 1993.
[8] *Nihon Keizai Shinbun*, December 15, 1998, May 24, 2000; Edgington and Fruin (1994: 256).

from Malaysia to Tijuana because this allowed the products to qualify narrowly as originating in NAFTA. However, in the assessment of Hitachi Mexico's management, such strategies were ultimately limited, since no adequate supplier of microprocessors or transistors existed in North America. Sanyo acknowledged similar difficulties when starting up production of refrigerator compressors in Mexico. Representatives of Kenwood, a company that produced car audio components in Ciudad Juarez, reported their relief at finding a US supplier for heat sinks for amplifiers, allowing a significant cost reduction compared with imports from Japan. Mitsubishi moved all of its production of circuits for large-screen television sets from Asia to Mexico, while Sony switched towards importing cathode-ray tubes to Tijuana from the United States. NEC opened up a factory for computer monitors in Mexicali to supplant exports from Malaysia and China to the United States.[9] Nevertheless, all these firms lobbied the Mexican government in several instances to provide tariff relief, since it proved difficult to establish an adequate Mexican supply base within the short time frame of five years before the abolishment of the maquiladora benefits.[10]

NAFTA not only affected the maquiladora sector. In the auto industry, NAFTA's high-threshold rules of origin and Mexican MFN tariffs presented Japanese firms with a severe problem. Although Mexico would probably have attracted some investment to establish beachheads in NAFTA regardless of the restrictiveness of the rules of origin, important changes in the sourcing and relocation decisions of Japanese firms suggest the diversion of investment.

Despite Nissan's long presence in Mexico and its domestic market orientation, the company was forced to adapt its strategy to the changing circumstances. When NAFTA entered into force, Nissan sourced 50 percent of its parts from within Mexico. However, to raise the regional share to 62.5 percent, it would have to import more parts from the United States. This conflicted with the foreign exchange balancing requirement mandated by the 1989 auto decree, whereby Nissan had to export as much as it imported in value terms.

Nissan began to specialize its North American operations by transferring the production of the Sentra model (except for the engine) from

---

[9] *Nikkei Sangyō Shinbun*, September 5, 1997.
[10] *Nihon Keizai Shinbun*, January 5, 1996; Mendiola (1999: 33).

its US to its Mexican operations, to be exported to US and Canadian markets (United States Department of Commerce 1998: 8). The company invested over US$1 billion in its second, recently built plant in Aguascalientes to achieve greater economies of scale (Moreno Brid 1996: 29) and targeted new export markets, including the sale of 20,000 cars to Chile in reaction to the Mexico–Chile FTA.[11] In 1997, Nissan relocated the production of engines for the Sentra model from Japan to Mexico, and thereby achieved a NAFTA content quota of close to 70 percent by 1999, although the price-to-quality relationship of parts sourced in Mexico and the United States was not always convincing.[12]

Nissan prodded its suppliers to support the changes in production locations. Already, prior to NAFTA's entry into force, many of Nissan's parts providers announced that they would start production in Mexico. Brake manufacturer Nabco announced the building of a factory in July 1993, aiming to start production within two years. Atsugi Yunisia, one of Nissan's closest partners in motor technology, moved the production of engine components from Japan to Mexico. In addition, several suppliers responded to a request by Nissan to enter into joint production arrangements with Mexican parts producers, with the ultimate aim of bolstering their technological capacities. Nissan suppliers Kantei, Yorozu, and Nisshō Iwai switched to local firms in lieu of imports from Japan, increasing the local content in their products from 30–40 to 80 percent.[13] Of thirteen Japanese car parts manufacturers present in Mexico in early 1994, half had established their operations only within the previous two years, following the conclusion of NAFTA. None of these efforts seemed likely to pay off in the short run. In a survey conducted by the Japan External Trade Organization, Nissan's management expressed concern about the state of the Mexican parts industry that did not meet its requirements in terms of quality and efficiency (JETRO 1994: 20).

A second, idiosyncratic factor forced Nissan to abandon its principal orientation towards Mexican and Central American markets: the Mexican currency crisis of 1994 and the resulting devaluation of the

[11] *El Financiero*, October 17, 1995.
[12] *Nikkei Sangyō Shinbun*, March 27, 1997; *Nikkan Kōgyō Shinbun*, March 1, 2000.
[13] *Nikkei Sangyō Shinbun*, September 2, 1992, December 15, 1992, March 8, 1993, April 15, 1993.

peso. In the wake of the crisis, domestic demand in Mexico bottomed out. For US automakers in Mexico, this was no problem: not only were their operations oriented towards export to the home market, but their shipments also became more competitive with a depreciating Mexican currency. Excess production in Mexico could be exported to the United States and Canada, thus balancing out costs within the North American market. This option did not exist for Nissan, which produced no model in Mexico that could be sold in the Japanese home market. Collapsing sales forced the company to lay off 10 percent of its workforce in Mexico, and using Mexico as an export base to the United States presented the only viable outlet, since the traditional markets among Mexico's neighbors, themselves affected by the fallout of the tequila crisis, offered little in terms of short-term growth potential (Walzer 1995).

Nissan's problems reemerged when the French manufacturer Renault took control of the company in 1999. Rather than relying on its network of Japanese-owned suppliers or joint ventures with Mexican manufacturers, the company's restructuring mandated low-cost global sourcing, including from Renault's European suppliers rather than more expensive US-based producers. Nissan planned to increase vehicle production from 200,000 to 330,000 units by 2001. In addition to the Sentra model for the US market, the smaller Renault models Megane and Clio began rolling off production lines in Nissan's factories. In the future, efficiency criteria would have to be paramount – in which case NAFTA's rules of origin would again be a problem.[14]

Although NAFTA raised the costs for newcomers, several Japanese firms decided to expand their operations in Mexico in order to use the country as an export platform. Honda announced in 1994 that it would start assembling cars in Mexico. Toyota began talks with Mexican officials about the same time (Moreno Brid 1996: 26), but did not announce the setting-up of production facilities until 2002, when it opened a plant in Tijuana to produce sport utility vehicles (SUVs) for the whole North American market, aiming for the production on a scale of 30,000 units by 2004. Denso, one of the world's biggest auto parts producers, and the trading house Toyota Tsūshō followed their most important buyer, investing US$6.6 million in a supplier park.[15] Again,

---

[14] *Nikkan Kōgyō Shinbun*, June 17, 2001.
[15] *Ward's Auto World*, September 1, 2003; *Nihon Keizai Shinbun*, September 23, 2002, August 19, 2003.

however, these steps were undertaken via the US-based subsidary, so that official FDI statistics recorded these developments as intra-NAFTA movements.

The investment by firms targeting the US market broadened the potential coalition of supporters of trade liberalization between Japan and Mexico. For Japanese firms, the central goal became to convince the Mexican government to reduce tariffs on the inputs they wanted to import. Initially, these hopes focused on a successor to the maquiladora program that would offer duty free imports without violating NAFTA Article 303.

The PROSEC failure

Japanese firms had to exhaust all options to move Mexico to reduce its tariffs before the proposal for an FTA finally fell on fertile ground in Japan in 1998. With a clear picture of what NAFTA implied for their production, firms organized in the Japan Maquiladora Association, and the JCCI, representing both maquiladora firms and smaller suppliers to Nissan's operations in Mexico, lobbied the Mexican government directly for tariff reductions. The central argument remained that North American manufacturers would be unable to supplant their non-NAFTA counterparts within the short time frame permitted by NAFTA.[16]

The Mexican government found itself under pressure from several sides. Legally, it could not offer tariff reductions for imported parts that would end up in products exported to the United States or Canada. On the other hand, domestic manufacturers lobbied hard to prevent a reduction of MFN tariffs. Japanese manufacturers openly called into question the viability of Mexico as an investment location, although these threats need to be contrasted with only recently expanded Mexican operations.

As the deadline for the abolition of the maquiladora benefits on January 1, 2001, drew near, SECOFI engaged in a dialogue over possible solutions. President Zedillo indicated in an interview with the *Nihon Keizai Shinbun* economic newspaper in February 1997 that the government was planning to offer selected tariff relief for firms that had previously benefited from the maquiladora system. At the

---

[16] *Nihon Keizai Shinbun*, January 5, 1996.

Japan–Mexico Economic Cooperation Symposium in October 1998, Herminio Blanco, Loyola's successor at the helm of SECOFI, announced that the Secretariat planned a sectoral promotion program (Programa de Promoción Sectoral, PROSEC), to be launched in 2000, that would lower barriers for the automotive and electronics industries. Upon request by individual firms, PROSEC reduced tariffs of 5–10 percent on parts imports for the maquiladora sector. Japanese firms had convinced Mexican officials that they could offer tariff-free access on an MFN basis for semiconductors and integrated circuits, because these were not produced in Mexico at all (Byrne 1994). However, other products would carry duties depending on whether they could reasonably be sourced within NAFTA. Blanco explained in March 1999 that the program was responding to the requests of Japanese firms, but admitted that it incorporated a modicum of protection for domestic industries, and recommended that Japanese firms should invest in those industries in Mexico that they deemed unsatisfactory as suppliers. Since many of the potential investors were small and medium-sized Japanese firms, he also suggested the conclusion of a bilateral investment protection agreement that would offer reassurance and a rationalized environment for Japanese FDI.[17]

At the same time, the Mexican government came under pressure from domestic suppliers who feared that Japanese firms might leave Mexico. Organized in the Asociación Nacional de Importadores y Exportadores de la República Mexicana (ANIERM), they lobbied SECOFI to enter into renegotiations of NAFTA Article 303 with the United States and Canada, accusing the secretariat of not implementing the PROSEC decrees in time to cover enough products. Together with Canacintra and Concanaco, the group sent a letter to the Secretariat that outlined a host of problems with PROSEC, among them backtracking by SECOFI on goods that would be tariff-free, sudden changes to proposed tariffs on imports of machinery, and a lack of protection in other sectors that could act as viable Mexican suppliers. At the same time the letter also criticized the fact that blanket reductions to bring Mexico's MFN tariffs in line with those of the United States and Canada were unacceptable because this did not guarantee that the final product would be exported again. In a meeting with Canacintra representatives Blanco rejected the proposal for reopening NAFTA negotiations, since the United States

---

[17] *Nikkan Kōgyō Shinbun*, April 20, 1999.

was unlikely to have changed its position on Article 303.[18] Between the demands of domestic suppliers for protection and maquiladora producers for selective opening, and legal commitments made in NAFTA, PROSEC was the best SECOFI could offer. As a successor to the maquiladora program, the program failed to satisfy the demands of local industry.

Neither did it meet the needs of Japanese firms. In a long list of complaints, one of the lobbying associations of the machinery industry, the Business Council for Trade and Investment Facilitation (bōeki tōshi enkakka bijinesu kyōgikai), complained that SECOFI had announced the list of tariff-free products, to come into effect on January 1, only in late December 2000. Little consultation had taken place with Japanese firms about the list itself. Approval of items was a burdensome process of registration by individual tariff lines. SECOFI had excluded key plastics components completely, despite the requests of Japanese firms. Given such bureaucratic capriciousness, the program seemed to rule out long-term planning, not to mention exploiting the strength of Japanese manufacturing based on just-in-time delivery (JMCTI 2001). At the same time, the development of a broad base of Mexican suppliers to the maquiladora failed to materialize (US GAO 2003: 35, 39). Ultimately, several Japanese policymakers considered that the situation was so severe that they saw the need for a fundamental reorientation of Japan's trade policy.

A regional trade policy option for Japan

Japanese trade policy reflects the "fragmented character of state authority" (Calder 1988: 528) vis-à-vis domestic actors in Japan. External economic policy is conducted by several ministries at the behest of their respective constituencies, with often only the Ministry of Foreign Affairs (MOFA) balancing the various interests. An analysis of Japanese policy outcomes based on interest groups therefore faces particular problems. Mulgan's (1999: xviii) assessment of agricultural lobbying forces holds true for other actors as well: many bodies cannot be clearly delineated as either public or private, operating as auxiliary agencies of government and interest group representatives at the same time, with funding coming from a ministry. But this does not imply that

---

[18] *El Financiero*, November 1, 2000.

they shelter the government from pressure groups or that their primary function is to relay government policy initiatives to the private sector.

Agricultural interests organized in the Japan Agricultural Cooperatives Group (JA Group, formerly known as Nōkyō), acting through its central union Zenchū, link protectionist forces with the ruling Liberal Democratic Party (LDP). They have frequently prevailed in setting policy, often by directly lobbying parliamentarians and the Ministry of Agriculture, Forests and Fisheries (MAFF) (Mulgan 1999: 565–70). The addressees of these efforts are LDP politicians organized in the *nōrin zoku*, or agricultural policy tribe. *Zoku* are groups of members of the Diet (the Japanese parliament) who specialize in a particular policy area, have achieved enough seniority in the LDP to be able to influence policy, and are therefore the principal translators of special interests into political action (Curtis 1999: 53–55). Although the *nōrin zoku*'s influence is much weaker today, since the retirement from politics of a number of LDP heavyweights with strong rural ties, the electoral reform of 1993 brought more balance to the relative weight of rural and urban districts, and more and more farmers have left the traditional cooperatives (Mulgan 2005b), it remains a strong political force in trade negotiations.

Other lobby groups often do not enjoy comparable access to members of the Japanese Diet. Their activities therefore focus on formal representations to advisory councils (*shingikai*) and parliamentary vice-ministers,[19] personal appeals to high-level bureaucrats, the prime minister and cabinet ministers, publications and media contacts. There are, however, *zoku* for most other policy domains as well. Before Japan entered into FTA negotiations, Diet members had traditionally accorded little importance to trade negotiations, since they offered few opportunities for pork-barrel politics. Foreign policy initiatives almost always originated with MOFA, MITI, or the Ministry of Economy, Trade and Industry (METI).[20] More recently, Junichiro Koizumi, prime minister in 2001–06, sought to make the cabinet the locus of decision-making on foreign affairs to bring political practice in line with

[19] Below cabinet level, each ministry is headed by a political appointment, the parliamentary vice-minister, and an administrative vice-minister, the highest civil service rank. Often, successful administrative vice-ministers switch to the political arena and join the LDP after retirement.

[20] In 2000, the Ministry of International Trade and Industry (MITI) was reorganized and renamed the Ministry of Economy, Trade and Industry (METI).

Japan's Westminster-inspired constitution. The debate about the extent of his success is far from over (Estevez-Abe 2006; Krauss and Nyblade 2005), but even the most critical observers concede that Koizumi achieved a more transformative leadership position than most of his predecessors as prime minister (Mulgan 2003). Nevertheless, the center of policymaking is still the ministries. Leadership from the cabinet office should therefore not be seen as independently decisive, but as tipping the balance in favor of one set of interest groups and bureaucrats over another.

In the case of trade policy, governmental organizations such as the JETRO, quasi-non-governmental organizations such as the Japan Institute for Overseas Investment (JOI), and industry associations frequently survey Japanese companies to channel concerns to METI. Nippon Keidanren, the most important industry association, publishes formal requests (*yōsei*).[21] However, many lobbying efforts leave no paper trail and can only be reconstructed on the basis of the information provided by the actors themselves. This fact, combined with the preference of firms to let bureaucrats take the lead in public, has furthered the view of a powerful administrative apparatus sheltered from special interests.[22] METI's capacity to initiate policy changes, however, has long been questioned in other domains, because information asymmetries abound between the small number of bureaucrats compared with numerous, sometimes multinational firms (Okimoto 1989). In terms of trade policy, this implies that bureaucrats often know very little about the specific interests of exporters and investors in foreign markets, unless firms provide the information themselves. Moreover, Japanese elite bureaucrats can still hope for lucrative positions in the private sector upon retirement – known as *amakudari*, or descent from heaven (Curtis 1999: 233–34) – a practice that is likely to make them receptive to industry demands, even if it is a two-way street for bureaucratic and private-sector interests.[23] A few key officials in

---

[21] In May 2002, Keidanren merged with the top employer association Nikkeiren. The new organization is officially called Nippon Keidanren, but is referred to as Keidanren in the following.

[22] This view goes back to the classic work by Johnson (1982: 640). It is extended to trade policy in Ogita (2003).

[23] See Mulgan (2005a) for a thorough analysis of the employment of bureaucrats in the industries they regulated prior to retirement from the civil service.

METI and MOFA must be credited with translating firm company demands into the pursuit of preferential trade agreements. However, this policy only emerged after all other options had been exhausted and the European Union had set an example of an extra-regional, defensive PTA.

During most of the 1990s, Japan's regional trade policy initiatives were limited to the Asia Pacific Economic Cooperation (APEC), an intergovernmental forum intended to liberalize trade and investment around the Pacific Rim. Australia put forth the official proposal, which had originated in a MITI initiative (Berger 1999). While the forum received considerable political and scholarly attention (Beeson and Jayasuriya 1998; English 1999; Gallant and Stubbs 1997; Ravenhill 2000; Terada 1998), its lack of credible commitment mechanisms made trade and investment liberalization difficult to achieve. Although the 1994 APEC summit, held in Bogor, Indonesia, declared the goal of free trade in the region, by 2010 for developed, and 2020 for developing, countries, the proposed unilateral liberalization skirted domestically sensitive sectors. In consequence, the 1994 individual action plans and the 1997 initiative for an early voluntary sector liberalization (EVSL) foundered on a divergence of interests: under domestic pressure, the Japanese government was unable to commit to an opening of its agricultural market, while the United States insisted on reciprocal concessions (Ravenhill 2000). Given this background of resistance to regional initiatives and the limited Japanese FDI in Mexico, few expected an FTA between the two countries to materialize. Motivating the Japanese trade bureaucracy to take action required lobbying by firms over a period of several years.

Concurrent with making investments in Mexico, Japanese firms voiced their concerns over NAFTA to quasi-non-governmental organizations at home. As in the case of the EU–Mexico FTA, the most vocal supporters were firms with investment in Mexico and exporters who supplied them with inputs for their production, including providers of intermediate services such as trade financing. Exporters who sold to Mexican buyers showed much less interest, since the Mexican market in itself was too small to warrant separate lobbying efforts. However, since Japanese farmers feared Mexican imports and had no counterbalancing export interests, protectionist agricultural interests proved to be much stronger than in the EU–Mexico case.

The most detailed report was produced by the Japan Institute for Overseas Investment (1997), a body close to METI. JOI found that

35 percent of Japanese firms in Mexico sourced most of their inputs from Japan, citing a lack of local suppliers and high technological and quality requirements as reasons. Of these firms, a "considerable number" worried about the abolishment of the maquiladora benefits under NAFTA. Automotive and machinery manufacturers were mostly concerned about NAFTA's rules of origin and the low technological standards of Mexican parts producers.

However, the link between investor demands and a possible bilateral trade deal had yet to be made explicit. This responsibility fell upon the Mexican side: during a lunch meeting at the Imperial Hotel in Tokyo in summer 1998, Herminio Blanco informed the JETRO chairman and former MITI vice-minister Hatakeyama Noboru that he had concluded a framework agreement with the EU that would lead to an FTA. He invited Hatakeyama to come to Mexico City to discuss the possibility of a Japan–Mexico FTA. This conversation reportedly convinced Hatakeyama (2003a: 24) that Japan had to pursue bilateral options to maintain its competitiveness, and motivated him to raise the issue with the then prime minister, Obuchi Keizō, and MITI minister Yosano Kaoru. Still, signing an FTA, especially with a Latin American country, represented a major change in Japanese foreign economic policy.[24] Yosano therefore first asked the International Trade Policy Bureau of MITI under its director general Konno Hidehiro to prepare a policy study on a Japanese FTA option that would help to establish a consensus in the ministry. In addition, JETRO undertook a study, based on seven consultative meetings with business representatives between February and December 1999, that emphasized the same factors as those identified by industry lobbyists (JETRO 2004: 4–5):

Mexico's high tariffs are a problem. The unadjusted average tariff in Mexico stands at a high 13.2% (1998) ... As a result, Japanese exports are levied higher tariffs than FTA signatories ... This means that the bond system would not be used for imports of parts and materials that would then be exported to NAFTA regions, starting from the end of 2000 ... Yet the alternative measure [PROSEC] does not offer the same benefits as the previous scheme ... Furthermore, supporting industries such as local auto parts and electronic and electric parts are nonexistent, and transport-related infrastructure is underdeveloped. These factors are raising the cost of local production activities.

---

[24] Interview with former senior MITI official, Tokyo, November 2002.

In 1998 and 1999, President Zedillo and Secretary Blanco spoke on three occasions about the impending changes in the maquiladora system before Japanese business audiences at Keidanren. Using the opportunity, President Zedillo specifically floated the idea of a bilateral FTA between Japan and Mexico.[25]

Once the formal proposal had been made, the potential beneficiaries very quickly voiced their support. Keidanren's Japan–Mexico Economic Committee welcomed the proposal in a study published in April 1999 (Keidanren 1999). The JCCI in Mexico polled its members and found nearly 95 percent in favor of an FTA. The report cited Sanyo Mexico president Matsunaga Masafumi, who suggested that an agreement would give a strong boost for Japanese investment in the challenging post-NAFTA environment. Similar statements came from managers of NEC and Panasonic.[26]

Still, at this point the necessary foundations for a major policy shift remained incomplete. As an interim measure, Keidanren therefore lobbied for the conclusion of an investment agreement along the lines of a bilateral investment treaty. Just as in its trade policy, Japan lagged behind in its efforts at signing international legal agreements to protect and liberalize FDI in important host countries. Only recently had Keidanren put BITs onto its agenda.[27] However, there was little enthusiasm beyond Keidanren for an investment agreement that would not address tariffs, the main problem for Japanese firms, while the Mexican government proved reluctant to offer national treatment and MFN commitments on investment, hoping to keep a bargaining chip for future FTA negotiations. The negotiations over a BIT were rapidly suspended (Solís 2003: 395–96).

Meanwhile, at MOFA the Economic Affairs Bureau under director general Tanaka began to discuss whether and how Japan should negotiate preferential trade agreements.[28] However, unlike MITI, with its close contacts with Japanese multinational firms with considerable

---

[25] *Nihon Keizai Shinbun*, September 15, 1998, October 7, 1998 (evening edition); *Nikkei Sangyō Shinbun*, March 2, 1999.

[26] *Nihon Keizai Shinbun*, October 14, 2000.

[27] Interview with Keidanren manager, Tokyo, December 2002.

[28] METI officials claim to have convinced their MOFA counterparts of the merits of an FTA, as described in Munakata (2001). MOFA officials have disputed this account in my interviews on various occasions. Successful policies tend to have many parents.

overseas investment, MOFA was more concerned about balancing the interests of more protectionist ministries, as well as the implications for Japanese foreign policy in general. Moreover, the Treaty Bureau, responsible for the legal assessment of international commitments and the drafting of many of Japan's international agreements, warned that it would be difficult to make FTAs compliant with GATT Article XXIV unless most agricultural trade was included. This position, while legally strong, proved impossible to maintain in later negotiations.[29] The differences between the two ministries also found their expression in official policy pronouncements. METI's White Papers on foreign trade began over time to reflect the changes in attitudes towards FTAs, from careful appreciation to full support. In comparison, the MOFA *Diplomatic Blue Books* were more cautious, often trailing the METI papers by a year in their positive assessments (Ogita 2002: 5–9).

In order to establish the parameters of a possible agreement, METI Minister Hiranuma Takeo and Mexican Economic Minister Derbez launched a bilateral study group (Nichi Boku kyūdō kenkyūkai) of academics, trade bureaucrats, and business leaders, the latter being representatives of firms with investments in Mexico, such as Sharp and Mitsui-Bussan, a general trading company (*sōgō shōsha*). The study group met seven times between September 2001 and July 2002. In the final report, the Japanese side brought up the aforementioned concerns: an increase in Mexican tariffs for parts and machinery, especially regarding the electronics industry in the maquiladora sector, a loss of competitiveness vis-à-vis firms from NAFTA countries and the EU, the ineffective nature of the PROSEC scheme, and the remaining restrictions on investment in Mexico. The report judged that "since an FTA can be concluded between a small number of countries, it may become an effective measure to promptly solve the present tariff problems under the situation in which Japanese enterprises are subject to serious disadvantages due to Mexico's conclusion of NAFTA and the effectuation of the EU-Mexico FTA" (Japan–Mexico Joint Study Group on the Strengthening of Bilateral Economic Relations 2002: 18). The study group finally connected the various concerns voiced by Japanese firms about their operations in Mexico, their futile attempts to obtain tariff relief, and the failure of the PROSEC initiative as the only legal

---

[29] Interview with MOFA official, Tokyo, March 2003.

option to counter the discriminatory effects of NAFTA: a bilateral free trade agreement between the two countries.

Negotiating free trade between Japan and Mexico

Actual negotiations between Japan and Mexico did not take place until autumn 2002. MITI and MOFA bureaucrats first sought an FTA with Singapore: the city-state did not export agricultural products in significant amounts, allowing a dry run for negotiators and establishing the precedent of a bilateral agreement. One former MITI official described this as a strategy to "first break the ideological opposition to FTAs, then the material resistance [in a later agreement]."[30] In both ministries, support for preferential trade agreements was by no means unanimous. Many senior MOFA and MITI officials had built their careers on expertise in multilateral negotiations and the occasional bilateral talks held with the USTR, although rarely upon Japanese request, and shared a normative commitment to non-discriminatory trade. The limited experience of the Japanese negotiators contrasted with the record of their Mexican counterparts, most of whom had been involved in all twelve FTA deals struck by the Latin American country. A trade agreement with Singapore would likely be politically less contentious than a deal that might expose domestic industries to adjustment pressures, allowing the proponents of PTAs to nurture a consensus position in both bureaucratic agencies before tackling outside political opposition.

Senior bureaucrats in MITI and MOFA also hoped to send a signal of a political commitment to Japan's ASEAN partners by choosing an Asian country as the first partner for a preferential deal. Japan's quick reaction to the Asian financial crisis in the form of the Miyazawa initiative (Hook *et al.* 2002; Katada 2002), they argued, had created a lot of goodwill that contrasted with the critical views of the United States and the IMF. Since future PTAs would likely be with ASEAN countries, the relatively cost-free signal of engagement might smooth the path in later negotiations.[31]

However, the negotiations with Singapore already foreshadowed the problem of liberalizing agricultural trade. Due to the vehement lobbying of agricultural groups, the talks remained stalled for weeks because

[30] Interview with former senior MITI official, Tokyo, December 2002.
[31] Interview with senior MOFA official, Tokyo, March 2003.

of Singapore's exports of goldfish and orchids, creating friction in the Japanese negotiating team and leading to the specific exclusion of these two products in the final agreement.[32] Nevertheless, the MOFA Treaty Bureau managed to hold its line that an FTA had to cover 90 percent of all trade to fulfill GATT Article XXIV's requirement of liberalizing substantially all trade, a position at that point still considered inviolable.[33] Yet this achievement should not be overstated: Japan did not offer any additional market access for agricultural products; Singapore just did not export any besides aquarium carp of the *koi* genus and a few exotic flowers (Solís 2003: 386). If the Japan–Singapore Economic Partnership Agreement (JSEPA) was meant to reassure agricultural groups that they would not be affected by future PTA negotiations, it failed to serve this purpose.

Compared with the relatively smooth passage of the FTA with Singapore, the negotiations between Japan and Mexico, which kicked off on November 18, 2002, in Tokyo, quickly turned into a turbulent political struggle between different ministries, LDP politicians, and lobbying groups. The domestic coalitions that supported or resisted the move towards trade liberalization between the two countries can be divided into three different groups. The principal lobby group in favor of an FTA was Keidanren, acting on behalf of firms with operations in Mexico. Keidanren's role was primarily to muster enough political support to help METI prevail in the inter-ministerial rivalry with MAFF, and to offer a counterweight to the protectionist forces of the rural constituencies of many LDP politicians and the JA Group.

More specialized industry associations did not engage directly with Japanese Diet members, but provided support and input for METI's negotiating efforts. Associations of suppliers transmitted concrete demands to the ministry. Other industry organizations representing exporters of finished goods followed this pattern, but just as in the case of the EU–Mexico FTA, achieved relatively limited improvements in market access.

On the Mexican side, the goals were described by Commerce Secretary Fernando Canales in 2003 as "Better market access for agriculture, [and] more investment, especially in the auto industry – Nissan has just announced an additional $600 million for its Aguascalientes

---

[32] *New York Times*, January 27, 2002.
[33] Interviews with senior MOFA official, Tokyo, March and December 2003.

plant, and Toyota will start to produce pickup trucks in Baja California ... Our hope is to create more jobs for the many young people entering our labour force."[34] These goals precisely matched those of the key lobbying forces in Mexico: the National Council of Agricultural Producers (CNA), the maquiladora industry, and Mexican auto parts producers. The major trade-off would have to be made in the steel industry, where Canacero resisted quick liberalization, just as in the EU–Mexico FTA.

Pork and politics

Unlike with Singapore, Mexico's trade with Japan included a significant share of agricultural products. Pork and citrus fruits alone made up close to 12 percent of exports to Japan between 1998 and 2001, although Mexico's total market share among Japanese pork consumers did not exceed 5 percent. At the outset of the negotiations, President Vicente Fox promised to the CNA that everything would be on the table. The CNA leadership hoped to double Mexico's pork exports to Japan through the agreement, taking market share from their competitors Denmark, Canada, and the United States.[35] Against this background, the statement of MAFF Vice-Minister Kumazawa Hideaki at a May 2001 press conference already foreshadowed the difficulties: he expected a blanket exclusion of agriculture.

While negotiations over manufactured products tariffs proceeded apace, talks over the liberalization of pork imports became a contentious issue by early 2003. Acting on behalf of the 30,000 pork farmers among the JA Group members, the association's chairman, Miyata Isami, appeared to have extracted a concession from MAFF Minister Kamei Yoshiyuki in April 2003 that no increased market access would be offered.[36] MAFF officials repeatedly stated that they could not compromise on the issue of pork, even at the risk of failure of the negotiations with Mexico. Since their position represented the main obstacle to a successful conclusion, Kamei admitted to his worries that the public perceived agriculture as preventing Japan from concluding meaningful FTAs – a perception that was widespread in editorials in Japanese business newspapers at the time. The key to success, according

[34] *El Universal*, July 11, 2003.   [35] *El Universal*, May 27 and July 15, 2003.
[36] *Nihon Nōgyō Shinbun*, April 22, 2003.

to Kamei, was what he referred to as the "Singapore procedure," in effect a complete exclusion of import-competing agriculture from the agreement in exchange for full liberalization of all other trade.[37]

MOFA officials were more guarded in their public pronouncements. Following a meeting with JA Group representatives, MOFA Vice-Ministers Yano and Motegi promised to consider carefully the effect of the FTA on agriculture, but stressed that preferential trade agreements were a world trend, and that Japan could not afford to be a bystander.[38]

The liberalizers: Keidanren and its allies

The strong resistance mounted by the JA Group led to growing worries in Keidanren that the negotiations might fail, not only causing Japanese firms in Mexico to be abandoned but also virtually ruling out the possibility of other FTAs with countries that exported agricultural products. In July 2002, Keidanren representatives met MAFF officials for the first time in three years to convince them of the necessity to compromise on agricultural imports (Yoshimatsu 2005: 271). To follow up, the association sent letters to MAFF, MOFA, METI, and the cabinet secretariat that cited numerous examples of how Japanese firms were affected by NAFTA, including their exclusion from government procurement in Mexico.[39] Most importantly, Keidanren directly targeted the politicians who represented agricultural interests. In June 2003 its chairman, Okuda Hiroshi, met with the LDP secretary-general Yamasaki Taku to discuss policy priorities on Keidanren's resumption of political donations after a ten-year break. At this meeting Keidanren vice-chairman Makihara Minoru emphasized how much weight the association attached to the successful conclusion of the Japan–Mexico FTA. Taro Aso, the then chairman of the LDP policy research council and later Foreign Affairs Minister, promised to select party members for a special FTA research council that would help to establish party support for the agreement.[40]

---

[37] *Ibid.*, April 29, 2003; *Nihon Keizai Shinbun*, May 9, 2003.
[38] *Nihon Nōgyō Shinbun*, May 30, 2003.
[39] *Nikkan Kōgyō Shinbun*, June 17, 2003. I am indebted to Mireya Solís for alerting me to the importance of government procurement.
[40] *Nihon Kōgyō Shinbun*, June 17, 2003.

Keidanren's position was strengthened by a JETRO report on FTAs in Latin America that underscored the fact that Mexico was primarily an entry point to the markets of the region.[41] In addition, Keidanren formed a coalition with the Japan Chamber of Commerce and Industry, the Japan Association of Corporate Executives (*keizai dōyūkai*) and the Japan Foreign Trade Council which issued a joint plea, timed to coincide with a working-level meeting of both sides in Tokyo on August 11–15, 2003, to conclude the FTA with Mexico as soon as possible.[42] Separately, Keidanren published several policy papers that provided concrete information about the issues which would have to be resolved by the negotiations with Mexico. The association stressed the need to be able to import components, machinery, and chemical products from Japan to shorten lead times in starting up production in Mexico. Its joint business council with Mexican executives led efforts on both sides of the Pacific (Keidanren 1999).[43]

Individual companies also intensified their lobbying efforts at ministerial level. Nissan and Toyota demanded strong efforts from METI in several meetings with trade bureaucrats during 2002 and 2003. In particular, Nissan adopted a position similar to that of Volkswagen during the EU–Mexico negotiations. Unlike Volkswagen, however, the company emphasized that it did not want to export to Japan from Mexico, but that it needed an FTA to preserve its relations with Japanese suppliers. Toyota stressed that its investment plans in Mexico could become unprofitable if Mexican tariffs on car parts were not lowered.[44]

Like ACEA, the Japan Automobile Manufacturers Association (JAMA) showed particular interest in the negotiations, but mostly argued on behalf of the export interests. Its president, the chairman of Honda Motor Corporation, Munekuni Yoshihide, lobbied LDP Diet members directly in a meeting on October 3. Munekuni cited the Mexican threat to raise tariffs to 50 percent on imported cars.[45] METI officials, however, gave Nissan's role much greater weight, "since the 20,000 or so cars that Japan exports to Mexico pale in comparison to the hundred thousands

[41] *Nikkan Kōgyō Shinbun*, September 8, 2003.
[42] *Nihon Keizai Shinbun*, August 6, 2003.
[43] See also www.keidanren.or.jp/japanese/policy/2000/016.html. Yoshimatsu (2005) offers further analysis of Keidanren's role in support of the FTA policy.
[44] Interviews with METI officials, January 2003; interview with MOFA official, December 2003.
[45] *Nihon Keizai Shinbun*, October 17, 2003.

Nissan can produce there and sell in the US," which in turn would generate business for Japanese suppliers and machine tools producers.[46] Again, multinational firm interests outweighed those of exporters of finished goods.

This view was supported by the association of the machine tools industry, the Japan Machinery Center for Trade and Investment (JMCTI, Nihon kikai yushutsu kumiai). In comparison to European upstream producers, the Japanese machine tools industry took longer to define its interests. Although broadly supportive of a bilateral deal, JMCTI contracted a detailed study in 2001 of the benefits of a bilateral trade deal to identify which demands ought to be put forward to METI. The study came to the conclusion that an FTA with Mexico could resolve the specific problems created by the NAFTA rules of origin in conjunction with high Mexican MFN tariffs. JMCTI representatives pressed this point in consultations with METI bureaucrats.[47]

In addition, a related association, the Japan Business Council for Trade and Investment Facilitation, published a survey of member companies in October 2002 to identify problems of investors in Mexico that was submitted to METI.[48] Car parts manufacturers noted "a 25 percent tariff that its competitors from the US, EU and other countries Mexico has an FTA with do not have to pay ... We request that an FTA be signed as soon as possible." Machinery firms specifically called for the conclusion of an FTA because they felt that they could not compete given the Mexican tariffs (Hideya 2002: 16).

While these producers found METI bureaucrats receptive to their demands, Japanese steel producers organized in the Japan Iron and Steel Federation (JISF) feared that their interests would be sacrificed in the conclusion of a deal with Mexico. Steel firms formed one of the principal supply industries of the automotive and auto parts manufacturers, but faced tariff peaks of 25 percent on many products. Since the EU–Mexico FTA would abolish duties on steel by 2007, they also worried about being displaced by European competitors.[49] Japanese trading firms added their voices to the growing chorus when the Mexican government announced in spring 2003 that it would only

---

[46] Interviews with METI officials, January 2003.
[47] Interviews with interest group representatives, Tokyo, February 2003.
[48] Interview with interest group representatives, Tokyo, February 2003.
[49] *Tekkō Shinbun*, June 19 and 20, 2003.

accord national treatment in its US$6.1 billion government procure-
ment market to FTA partners (Katada and Solís 2007).

With the positions staked out, the political struggle quickly heated
up. Pork producers from all over Japan united in the Strategic
Association against FTAs (FTA tō taisaku kyōgikai) and invited the
head of the LDP Research Council on Agriculture and prominent
nōrin zoku member Nakagawa Shōichi to their inaugural meeting.
Nōrin zoku members stated categorically that agriculture could not be
sacrificed for business. Nakagawa, a key figure in several party committees, promised that pork would be taken off the table.[50]

The impasse

When Japanese negotiators brought the list of 250 agricultural products, excluding pork and citrus fruits, to the fifth round of talks in
Mexico City in September 2003, immediately before the WTO Cancún
Ministerial, Fernando Canales called the offer "simply unacceptable"
and nearly walked away. Mexican negotiators stated that, given the
circumstances, it was naive to assume that the FTA could be concluded
on the occasion of President Fox's planned visit to Japan in October.
MAFF Minister Kamei retorted that Mexico was asking for too much
and threatened to put the talks on hold unless the other side moved.
After some deliberation, the Japanese side offered to phase out tariffs on
140 agricultural products more quickly, a move that did not persuade
the Mexican negotiators. Compared with this heated exchange, the
meeting between Canales and Hiranuma Takeo of METI took place
in harmony. Both agreed that agricultural liberalization would have to
be exchanged for progress on steel duties.[51]

Without any movement on the issue of pork, the Japanese negotiators
proceeded to the WTO Cancún Ministerial, where the MAFF delegation outnumbered all other ministerial teams. The dramatic failure of
the meeting led many commentators to expect that the global trend
towards FTAs would be given a further boost. Kamei shared this view,
but stressed that he would continue to put emphasis on the WTO as the

[50] *Nihon Nōgyō Shinbun*, July 26 and August 8, 2003; *Nihon Shokuryō Shinbun*,
August 15, 2003.
[51] *Nihon Nōgyō Shinbun*, September 14 and 20, 2003; *El Universal*, September 22
and 24, 2003.

right forum for liberalization.[52] A MAFF official later conceded that the sudden enthusiasm for multilateral rounds in the Ministry was largely due to their glacial pace compared to the intense domestic contest over the FTA.[53] In addition to the official negotiating team, several interest groups and NGOs from Japan had also sent delegations to Cancún, among them inevitably the pork producers, who tried unsuccessfully to arrange a meeting with their Mexican counterparts.

Given the state of the talks, Mexican government officials threatened to take automobiles and parts, fabrics, and light trucks (including pickup models) off the negotiating table if no further concessions were forthcoming – effectively all the products that the auto industry and its suppliers sought to export. In an obviously tactical move, Mexico demanded a rule of origin of 100 percent for metal and steel products from Japan, a requirement that would have given full protection to Mexican manufacturers, since Japan procured all its iron ore from abroad.

The pronouncement made it clear what the trade-off would have to be. The steel lobby JISF pushed for a reopening of the negotiations as soon as possible. JAMA was so disconcerted with the outcome that the vice presidents of Nissan, Toyota, Honda, and Mitsubishi met with Nakagawa Shōichi to demand concrete steps. JAMA chairman Munekuni Yoshihide appeared satisfied after the meeting, in which Nakagawa had promised his full support to the car industry. JCCI chairman Yamaguchi Nobuo suggested that the Japanese government come up with a compensatory mechanism for farmers.[54]

Yet at this point the barrage of lobbying by agricultural groups had not even reached its peak. JA Group representatives broadened their efforts to other groups. Its chairman Miyata paid another visit to MAFF, where Minister Kamei suggested that the JA Group should target other institutions as well. He proposed a broad public campaign, since most consumers were probably unaware that Mexico exported pork to Japan at all. Among the JA Group's new initiatives was an invitation to METI officials to visit a pig farm in Chiba prefecture to inform the industry-focused bureaucrats of the restructuring efforts of

[52] *Nihon Nōgyō Shinbun*, September 11 and 14, 2003.
[53] Interview with MAFF official, Tokyo, December 2003.
[54] *Nikkan Kōgyō Shinbun*, September 18, 2003; *Nihon Nōgyō Shinbun*, September 28, 2003; *El Universal*, October 1, 2003; *Nikkan Jidōsha Shinbun*, October 9, 2003; *Nikkan Kōgyō Shinbun*, October 23, 2003.

Japanese farmers.[55] The JA Group also called in at the LDP headquarters to impress their concerns on the newly elected LDP secretary-
general Abe Shinzō and the party's policy research council chairman
Nukaga Fukushirō, who promised to line up the party behind the
farmers. Finally, the youth wing of the JA Group resorted to the time-
honored practice of staging a sit-in protest in front of METI's
Kasumigaseki building.[56]

It takes a leader

In November 2003, Prime Minister Koizumi returned to power with a
weakened coalition government. In his first address to the National
Diet, Koizumi cited the conclusion of the economic partnership agreement with Mexico as a key goal of the new legislative period. In one of
his signature surprise moves, Koizumi promoted Nakagawa Shōichi,
elected from a farming constituency in Hokkaidō, to the position of
METI minister. The cabinet reshuffle softened METI's stand on agricultural liberalization, but also weakened the *nōrin zoku*, by giving its
most prominent spokesperson responsibilities that ran counter to his
earlier work. Speaking to the *Nihon Keizai Shinbun* at the APEC
summit in October 2003, Koizumi explained the appointment as supporting his goal of economic restructuring that would allow Japan
to negotiate free trade agreements: "Under normal circumstances,
Nakagawa would be at the helm of MAFF and Kamei at METI. But
there is a purpose to the reversed roles. It cannot be that MAFF and
METI only worry about their respective affairs [*nōsuishō, keizaishō no
ryōhō ga jibun no koto bakari wo kangaete ite ha ikenai*]. We need to
think about what kind of structural reforms are necessary to allow
agricultural imports. LDP members with ties to agriculture understand
this point as well."[57]

One of the first moves of MAFF Minister Kamei was to emulate the
MOFA and METI model by creating an FTA task force in the ministry,

---

[55] Speaking under conditions of anonymity, METI officials recounted an episode of
hectic buck-passing in the ministry until suitable volunteers for the visit could be
found. Interview, Tokyo, December 2003.
[56] *Nihon Nōgyō Shinbun*, October 11, 2003.
[57] The then LDP Policy Research Council chairman Nukaga is a member of the
commerce and industry *zoku*, which may have made him less receptive to JA
Group's demands. See Mulgan (2005c: 276).

charged with two assignments: gathering enough information about the partner country to map out a coherent strategy, and coming up with proposals that would allow domestic reform. Both MAFF and METI bureaucrats attributed the stalling of the negotiations to "intelligence failures." Reorganizations also occurred in MOFA's negotiating teams. Within MAFF a consensus was emerging that the ministry did not want to be publicly perceived as the only obstacle for negotiations that would otherwise have been settled long before.[58]

While the bureaucracy began searching for ways out of the impasse, its room for maneuver was more constrained than before the election. At the LDP agricultural liberalization committee meeting on November 20, MPs battered by the recent election results made it clear to the party leadership that they would not tolerate further concessions. Koizumi decided that with little enthusiasm in the party for agricultural reform and clear coordination failure between the different ministries, efforts would have to be concentrated in the chief cabinet office. He sent Deputy Chief Cabinet Secretary Yachi Shōtarō to Mexico to negotiate directly with Derbez, the Mexican Secretary of Foreign Affairs.[59] Upon Yachi's return, Chief Cabinet Secretary Fukuda Yasuo convened a strategic council on agricultural policy with all ministers involved in the FTA negotiations. Several LDP politicians suggested creating a special fund to compensate farmers for their loss of income as a result of the liberalization through FTA, a proposal that was supported by JETRO in a symposium on trade policy options in Tokyo.[60]

On the Mexican side, President Fox declared at a symposium on agriculture that he was prepared to let the deal fail if no further concessions on beef, chicken, pork, orange juice, and pineapple were forthcoming. The CNA's demands converged on a quota of 250,000 tons of pork and the elimination of the "gate price" that Japanese producers were guaranteed.[61] For the negotiators in Mexico time was running out if they wanted to ratify the agreement during the Congress session in

[58] *Asahi Shinbun*, November 14, 2003; *Kagaku Kōgyō Shinbun*, November 21, 2003; Interview with MAFF official, Tokyo, December 2003.
[59] *Nihon Nōgyō Shinbun*, November 21, 2003; *Nihon Keizai Shinbun*, November 21, 2003.
[60] *Kagaku Kōgyō Shinbun*, November 26, 2003; *Nihon Nōgyō Shinbun*, December 4, 2003.
[61] *El Universal*, November 20, 2003; *El Economista* (Mexico City), December 12, 2003.

autumn 2004. In late December 2003, the Mexican government used its MFN tariffs to gain more leverage by raising the applied rate on auto imports to 50 percent, the bound rate under the WTO. With the auto industry's worst fears coming true, JAMA chairman Munekuni stepped up the public campaign, estimating the losses of the Japanese auto industry at US$600 million if no FTA could be concluded, since the investments of the previous years would have been in vain.[62]

By early 2004, the parameters of the actual deal became clear, including side-payments necessary to satisfy enough interest groups to make an agreement viable. As a means of reaching a final agreement, both parties convened a committee of government and industry representatives to identify products that could be liberalized more rapidly because they were not manufactured by Mexican producers. MAFF officials underlined that one of their new policies, a system of direct income support for farmers in its Basic Plan for the Agricultural Industries, Foodstuffs, and Farming Villages (*shokuryō nōgyō nōson kihon keikaku*), backed by Koizumi in his address to the Lower House on January 21, 2004, would make it easier for Japan's farmers to accept a free trade agreement because it decoupled income and sales.[63]

In March 2004, negotiators finally clinched a deal in the 14th round of talks. As was to be expected, the negotiations over auto parts and steel were concluded first, but made conditional by Mexico on final concessions in agriculture that would have to be made at the ministerial level.[64] Japan had offered close to 60 percent of the quota on orange juice demanded by Mexico, but still only 80,000 tons of pork rather than Mexico's 250,000 ton demand. The final deal brought only moderate liberalization of its agricultural market, retaining quotas for oranges and pork. The tariff formula for pork offers access at a rate of 4.3 percent only if it is sold at the equivalent of the price demanded by Japanese farmers; the remainder still faces a 49 percent tariff.[65] Overall, the agreement only liberalizes 86 percent of bilateral trade, and only 40 percent of Mexico's agricultural exports to Japan. A deal could thus only be struck by reneging on the earlier MOFA position that substantially all trade had to be covered. Mexico's schedule offered those

---

[62] *Nihon Keizai Shinbun*, December 20, 2003.
[63] *Nihon Nōgyō Shinbun*, January 22, 2004. See Mulgan (2005c) for further information on the agriculture policy reforms initiated under Koizumi.
[64] *El Universal*, March 4, 2004; *El Economista* (Mexico City), March 9, 2004.
[65] *Tōyō Keizai Weekly*, November 29, 2003.

Japanese auto firms without a presence in Mexico only a marginally enlarged tariff-free export quota equal to 5 percent of the Mexican market, and the elimination of all barriers on metal products within ten years. But, importantly, Mexico turned the de facto benefits PROSEC had offered on specific car parts into tariff elimination commitments under the FTA.[66] The final text was signed by Koizumi and Fox on September 17, 2004, nearly two years after the first round of negotiations.

Among the first to laud the deal was Nissan president Carlos Ghosn, a near-mythical figure in Japan because of his success in turning Nissan around. Nissan's supplier JATCO stressed how beneficial the FTA would be for its new transistor factory in Mexico.[67] JAMA chairman Munekuni praised the FTA as exemplary for future negotiations with southeast Asian partners, an assessment echoed by Keidanren chairman Okuda. A Toyota spokesperson bowed to the negotiators to express the company's gratitude.[68] Japan's firms in Mexico also offered deeds rather than just words: in a JETRO survey, 32 percent announced that they would increase their investments.[69]

Outcomes, comparisons, and alternative accounts

As in the case of the EU–Mexico FTA, the interests of firms with investments in Mexico were given a higher priority by negotiators. Crucial support for a bilateral deal came primarily from intermediate and capital goods producers, who were hurt the most by a loss of competitiveness. Perhaps most strikingly, Japan's labor unions remained completely detached from the political tug-of-war over the FTA with Mexico. In part this may have been simply because of organizational problems, since Japanese trade unions are enterprise-based and the national confederation Rengō has consequently had limited political influence. Moreover, no Japanese jobs were at stake as long as Mexico was primarily an export

---

[66] *Nikkan Jidōsha Shinbun*, March 16, 2004.
[67] *Ibid.*, March 12, 2004; *Nihon Keizai Shinbun*, March 13, 2004. See Tiberghien (2007) for an account of Nissan's restructuring in the context of Japan's economic reforms.
[68] *Nikkei Sangyō Shinbun*, March 18, 2004; *Fuji Sankei Business*, March 29, 2004: 7; *Hokkaidō Shinbun*, September 19, 2004.
[69] *Fuji Sankei Business*, May 11, 2004: 6.

platform to the United States and perhaps later a worthwhile market in its own right.

Did Japan pursue an FTA with Mexico because multilateral liberalization did not make enough progress? While the slow pace of the WTO negotiations certainly contributed to the evolution of Japan's new trade policy, it is unlikely that it was the principal cause. Problems at the WTO cannot explain the choice of Mexico as the partner for Japan's second FTA. Japanese decision-makers first considered the Japan–Mexico FTA in summer 1998, before the failed attempt at starting a WTO Millennium round. Moreover, two Japanese ministries remained strongly committed to the WTO, albeit for different reasons. MAFF preferred the WTO precisely because it was slower in its liberalization of agriculture and because protectionist forces had allies in the EU agricultural sector. Several senior MOFA officials held the view that the WTO was more important than ever, since it could help Japan to enforce China's commitments to trade liberalization.[70] Likewise, METI officials attributed Japan's push for rules on FDI in the Doha round to the need to monitor China better. While Japan pursues FTAs with emerging markets, it remains committed to the multilateral trade regime to guide its relations with major economic powers.[71]

The Japanese move towards an FTA with Mexico invites an alternative interpretation of policy leadership by its bureaucracy rather than the private sector. METI itself claimed in its 2001 White Paper that besides avoiding exclusion from other agreements, Japan's FTAs would advance new trade rules, maintain momentum for multilateral free trade, and promote domestic reform (METI 2001). However, while no business organization specifically requested an FTA until 1998, neither did the ministry's trade bureaucrats. The unexpected proposal for an FTA came from the Mexican side, just as in the case of NAFTA. A look at the process shows that the Mexico FTA was the first to be considered, with the Singapore agreement only a tactical move of bureaucratic politics unsupported by business interests. METI bureaucrats primarily sought an FTA on behalf of their constituents, Japan's multinational firms. Japanese demands in the negotiations matched

---

[70] Interviews with senior MOFA officials, Tokyo, February 2003.
[71] Interview with senior METI official, Tokyo, March 2003. See also the findings of Searight (1999), who argues that multilateralism became more important in Japanese trade relations with the United States.

closely the problems previously cited by firms. Yet as an export market Mexico ranks low in Japanese priorities, as METI officials readily admit. One of the most senior former MITI officials referred to the Japan–Mexico FTA as "purely defensive."[72] Nor were Japanese FTA initiatives launched to promote domestic reform in Japan. When agricultural liberalization stalled the Japan–Mexico negotiations, the chief FTA protagonist Hatakeyama reversed the logic: Japan had to reform itself to be able to pursue bilateral deals (Hatakeyama 2003b). This indicates that business demands and support were crucial for the FTA policy to become viable.[73]

The case studies of the reactions to NAFTA underscore the centrality of foreign direct investment for the proliferation of North–South agreements. Export interests matter most when directly linked to such investment, as in the example of European chemical industry interests in Mexico. Investors who rely on an export platform such as Mexico to serve a third-country market are highly sensitive to cost. In consequence, investor firms and their upstream chain of producers are the most vulnerable to exclusion from a key export platform, and lobby the most for countering agreements. The actions of investors such as Japanese electronics firms, Volkswagen, and Nissan support this account. Table 5.2 shows the predicted outcomes for both sets of negotiations side by side. Japanese services firms did not lobby for the agreement with Mexico for lack of investment interests. Most Japanese banks were still recovering from an almost decade-long struggle with non-performing loans. European telecommunications firms offered unexpectedly little support, perhaps because of the quasi-monopolistic position of TelMex, the conglomerate owned by Mexico's richest man, Carlos Slim. The lobbying by Japan's electronics firms has no parallel in Europe, whose electronics industry has long since lost the battle against Asian competitors.

For conventional exporters of manufactured or agricultural goods in the EU and Japan, a small emerging market like Mexico is of limited importance. For these firms, PTAs appear to offer no specific benefit over multilateral liberalization – in fact, for neither the developed nor the developing country. If they are shut out of these markets because of

---

[72] Interview with former MITI official, Tokyo, November 2002.
[73] See Solís (2003) for a more detailed analysis of why these factors by themselves fail to explain Japan's policy shift.

Table 5.2. *Predictions versus actual lobbying coalitions, EU–Mexico and Japan–Mexico PTAs*

	EU–Mexico		Japan–Mexico	
	EU	Mexico	Japan	Mexico
For	Automotive firms		Automotive firms	
			Electronics firms	
	Suppliers		Suppliers	
	Financial services		*Financial services*	
	Telecommunications			
		Agriculture		Agriculture
Against	Agriculture		Agriculture	
		Auto parts		Auto parts
		Steel		Steel

Italics denote predictions that are not met.

high MFN tariffs, bilateral agreements may be easier to achieve, but offer no intrinsic benefits over multilateral liberalization.

For Mexico, the promise of Japanese foreign direct investment remained the prime motivation for seeking the FTA. While Mexico did not even attempt to pry open the door to the heavily protected European market for agricultural products, the effort to improve market access for exports to Japan was targeted and coordinated across different issues in the negotiations. Although superbly organized and well connected, the protectionist forces in Japan were a small group of pork farmers and were by no means comparable with the powerful rice lobby. Overall, the political influence of farm groups is much diminished. Yet, in the end, the deal converged again on a mutual interest in facilitating FDI. North–South PTAs are no better at breaking the lock agricultural lobbyists have on the trade policy of many developed countries than the WTO, making many of them examples of what Ravenhill (2006: 38) calls "negotiated protectionism."

As elaborated in the next two chapters, neither NAFTA nor the counter-agreements are one-off events. Although the investor interests depend on the specific features of the emerging market country, a competitive dynamic unfolds in a growing number of cases in the Americas and Asia.

6 | *The far side of the world: preferential trade agreements with Chile*

EXICO attracted investment across a range of business activities, much of it drawn to a huge pool of low-cost labor in the proximity of the US market. As the previous three chapters have shown, not only US firms but also their competitors from non-NAFTA countries invested massively in Mexico. The competitive disadvantages created by NAFTA affected a broad coalition of firms in Europe and Japan, creating a powerful constituency in favor of defensive agreements. But was Mexico an outlier, given its high MFN barriers and proximity to the United States? Do smaller markets also trigger a competitive dynamic?

This chapter offers evidence that Mexico was by no means exceptional. Within few years it became evident that NAFTA was only the first in a wave of PTAs between developed and developing countries. Once policymakers recognized this fact, they became increasingly concerned about the competitive effects of PTAs. The previous chapters have argued that bureaucrats in the EU and Japan explicitly considered these effects as relayed to them by firms and lobbyists. This chapter shows that when competitors began pursuing PTAs with developing countries, US policymakers in turn reconsidered bilateral options. Even though the investment interests were limited to services industries in a small country, and despite a number of political obstacles that had prevented Chile's accession to NAFTA itself, the competition over access to invest in services in Chile generated business support for an FTA in both the United States and the EU.

In the services sector, imperfectly competitive market structures help to drive bilateral agreements, even if a host country has comparatively low multilateral barriers to trade and investment. During the second half of the 1990s, this situation arose when Chile attracted significant amounts of services FDI from Spanish companies through concessions from the Chilean government. By acquiring the most desirable takeover targets among Chilean firms, these investors excluded competitors. For

European firms a PTA with Chile therefore primarily promised a locking-in of commitments. These developments spurred their US competitors into action. Early proposals from the Chilean side to accede to NAFTA foundered because of the failure of the Clinton administration to obtain congressional authority to negotiate. When the EU came closer to a deal with Chile, US firms made the case to lawmakers that they needed an FTA to become competitive when entering the Chilean market. Although the debate around the authority to negotiate was clearly a domestic political issue in the United States, the arguments put forth by lobbyists suggest that competitive considerations became increasingly important.

This chapter then considers the belated conclusion of an FTA between Japan and Chile. The proposal, originally floated in 2001, was favored by several actors close to the Japanese government as easier to achieve than the FTA with Mexico, since Chilean products threatened fewer import-competing industries in Japan. Support from business interests, however, was insufficient to generate political momentum. No Japanese firms stood in direct competition with their US and European counterparts or were put at a disadvantage by the FTAs these two actors sought with Chile, undermining the case for an agreement between Japan and the Southern Cone country. The agreement was finally concluded in early 2007, but only after Chile limited its demands for market access.

For the Chilean government, the pursuit of preferential trade agreements with all willing trade partners was a direct continuation of the liberalization undertaken after the democratic transition. Chile's trade policy is perhaps the closest to the ideal of "open regionalism," in that MFN tariffs were reduced concurrently with the negotiation of preferential agreements. Enhanced access to major markets such as the United States and the EU played a bigger role than in other North–South PTAs, since by virtue of location Chile could not aim at becoming an export platform. PTAs offered a chance to increase trade based on Chile's comparative advantage in fresh fruits, delivered off-season to northern countries (Grugel and Hout 1999). Nevertheless, the economic counselor of the Chilean representation in Brussels, Roberto Paiva, clearly stated that tariff matters were secondary in the negotiations with the EU: the principal benefit would be an increase in foreign direct investment.[1]

---

[1] *El Mercurio* (Santiago de Chile), November 8, 2000.

Foreign direct investment in Chile

Just like Mexico, Chile has sought actively to promote itself as an investment location since the country's democratic transition in 1990, and to expand its exports by signing free trade deals with developed countries. Unlike most of its Latin American neighbors, however, Chile carried with it hardly any legacy of import-substitution industrialization. Under the military regime from 1973 to 1989, the country's economy was transformed and oriented towards international markets. The liberalization of imports proceeded apace, following the prescriptions of a group of *técnicos*, economists trained at the University of Chicago (Teichman 2001). Import tariffs were reduced to a flat rate of 11 percent, with the exception of a brief period between 1982 and 1984, when Chile struggled with the debt crisis that engulfed most of the Third World.

As a result of these policies Chile diversified its exports away from an almost exclusive dependence on copper, from a share in exports of close to 80 percent in 1973 to around 45 percent during the 1990s (Meller 1996: 275, cited in Grugel and Hout 1999: 62). Rather than growing manufacturing exports, however, diversification meant an increase in overseas sales of other primary goods such as wine, fruit, vegetables, and fish. Chile lacks any significant manufacturing base, whether foreign-owned or domestic. At the same time, the relatively small market of 15 million people, with a per capita income of only US$5,000 (in purchasing power terms) in 1995, shows the limited importance of Chile as an export market. In the second half of the 1990s, however, the country became an important location for foreign direct investment, heavily concentrated in the services sector, from Europe and the United States. In comparison with other emerging markets, Chile has been enormously successful in attracting FDI. In relation to its GDP, Chile hosts more FDI than the other three big Latin American economies, as shown in table 6.1.

The Chilean military regime had liberalized foreign investment in 1974 by enacting Decree Law 600 (DL 600), enshrining non-discrimination and access to virtually all productive activities, while still reserving the right of the government Foreign Investment Committee to screen investment. Investing firms sign a contract with the Chilean government that guarantees access to the necessary foreign exchange and optionally locks in an effective tax rate of 42 percent

Table 6.1. *FDI as a percentage of GDP, major Latin American economies*

Year	Chile	Argentina	Brazil	Mexico
1985	14.1	7.4	11.5	10.2
1986	14.4	6.0	10.4	16.4
1987	14.9	6.1	10.7	17.0
1988	16.3	5.4	9.7	14.6
1989	17.7	9.1	7.6	13.4
1990	33.2	6.2	8.0	8.5
1991	30.6	6.1	9.5	9.8
1992	27.0	7.1	10.2	9.8
1993	27.3	7.8	8.0	10.1
1994	27.2	8.7	6.8	7.9
1995	21.6	10.8	5.9	14.4
1996	32.5	12.3	6.2	14.1
1997	41.8	14.3	7.6	13.9
1998	47.4	16.0	10.4	15.1
1999	59.6	21.8	16.5	16.2
2000	60.7	23.8	17.2	16.7
2001	65.9	25.6	24.0	22.5
2002	65.1	37.2	22.3	24.3
2003	65.0	27.1	25.8	26.5

Source: World Bank, World Development Indicators Online 2008.

(UNCTAD 2004b). In practice, Chile's economy has been open to foreign investment since the mid-1970s.

Most FDI simply reacted to natural resource endowments and comparative advantage. Chile is blessed with the world's biggest deposits of copper ore, most of which can be mined close to the surface, as well as precious metals and natural gas resources. Consequently, mining attracted the lion's share of FDI, most of which came from the United States and Canada. Yet, from the mid-1990s on, investors from the European Union began investing in Chilean services companies on a broad basis. The vast majority of these acquisitions were undertaken by Spanish companies: of the cumulative FDI from the European Union, about 80 percent is from Spain. Since the late 1990s, Spanish investment has represented the second-biggest stock of FDI in the country, closing the gap with the United States, as shown in table 6.2 (ECLAC 2001: 106). The concentration of

Table 6.2. *Percentage shares of individual countries in Chile's FDI stock*

	1989	1992	1995	1996	1998	2001	2003
Canada	9.77	12.62	18.29	16.83	17.31	15.03	15.02
France	1.86	1.95	1.55	1.57	1.79	2.58	2.51
Germany	1.32	1.16	1.10	0.81	1.06	0.97	0.92
Japan	2.82	4.25	3.29	3.24	3.72	3.37	3.24
Spain	10.59	7.46	5.14	6.31	11.64	19.08	18.11
UK	8.14	9.27	6.92	6.74	8.27	7.34	9.75
US	43.87	37.63	39.95	41.67	34.17	30.37	29.73
Others	0.22	0.26	0.24	0.23	0.22	0.21	0.21

Source: Comité de Inversiones Extranjeras de Chile, www.cinver.cl.

these flows into services is evident in table 6.3. The figures also suggest that Spanish investors committed considerable amounts of additional capital to Chile once the EU–Chile agreement was in place.

Spanish investors focused on three industries: financial services, energy, and telecommunications. In all three, their massive entry resulted in commanding shares in market and ownership that put competitors from other countries, in particular US firms that attempted to enter markets later, at a disadvantage.

The most striking wave of acquisitions took place in the banking sector. The same two Spanish banks that invested broadly in Mexico – BBVA and BSCH – also bought major stakes in Chilean banks. Both banks faced a dilemma in the EU market, where a lack of candidates for a takeover limited the opportunities for growth. Santander, one of the banks that later merged with BSCH, began its expansion with the establishment of Banco Santander-Chile in 1978. Santander's acquisition of Banco Osorno y la Unión in 1996 turned it into one of Chile's principal banking institutions. In 1998, it raised the stake in Santander-Chile's holding company Santangroup to 98 percent (ECLAC 2002: 125). Following the merger of BSC and Santander in Spain, the new bank acquired a 43 percent share of Banco Santiago from a Chilean group, a stake that had been increased to 79 percent by 2002. As a result, BSCH's subsidiaries had a combined market share of close to 25 percent in 2002. Its Spanish competitor BBVA bought Banco Hipotecaria de Fomento, now BBVA Banco BHIF, in 1998, giving it an 8 percent market share by loans granted (Calderón and Casilda 1999: 24).

Table 6.3. *FDI inflows to Chile by sector, US$ million*

	Germany		United States		Japan		Spain	
	Manufacturing	Services	Manufacturing	Services	Manufacturing	Services	Manufacturing	Services
1990	2.0	3.7	18.7	436.2	10.8	68.0	6.1	72.5
1991	3.2	21.1	33.0	496.3	75.0	94.4	0.5	110.4
1992	11.4	21.6	-7.4	494.4	11.2	104.6	0.5	16.0
1993	7.2	14.6	206.6	767.9	6.4	97.7	1.1	232.9
1994	8.1	10.4	124.0	1,313.2	3.1	68.7	2.9	44.2
1995	4.0	117.1	95.8	2,198.8	16.0	34.9	5.1	114.9
1996	12.0	-26.7	350.2	4,177.1	11.2	169.1	2.8	1,036.4
1997	13.9	39.1	204.9	1,586.4	11.0	175.3	3.9	3,157.5
1998	11.9	284.8	222.8	2,188.6	8.9	390.2	1.7	1,855.1
1999	9.9	129.2	368.0	1,895.3	18.5	263.1	92.7	9,347.3
2000	3.7	15.8	89.3	1,452.6	8.2	73.8	0.9	1,284.8
2001	3.4	105.3	490.0	3,016.3	25.1	145.7	4.0	750.1
2002	0.2	14.8	65.0	882.0	13.7	56.7	0.3	475.9
2003	0.0	21.8	80.1	618.9	2.4	30.1	5.1	296.6
2004	0.0	32.5	44.0	178.2	0.0	16.8	74.8	6,803.5
2005	0.0	39.0	3.3	-38.6	0.0	43.7	1.3	365.0

Source: Comité de Inversiones Extranjeras de Chile, www.cinver.cl.

The rapid expansion contributed to the importance of Latin America in these banks' portfolios: by 1999, BSCH had 29 percent of its assets in the region; BBVA had 21.1 percent of its invested capital in Latin America (Calderón and Casilda 2000: 77). Both banks used their subsidiaries to expand into the countries of Mercosur, the customs union of Argentina, Brazil, Paraguay, and Uruguay, testimony to Chile's role as entry point to the rest of the Southern Cone (Calderón and Casilda 1999: 32).

In addition, both BSCH's and BBVA's subsidiaries are active in the pension fund market. Chile's registered pension plans, AFPs, are limited to 20 percent foreign investments, and can only be managed by subsidiaries of foreign banks, not by branch operations.[2] This regulatory element and the dominant position of the two Spanish banks facilitated their access to this market: BBVA holds 51 percent of the biggest Chilean fund, AFP Provida, and BSCH holds 100 percent of the fourth-biggest fund, AFP Summa Bansander. The concentration of market control in the hands of these two banks worried Chilean regulators, who first contemplated legislative proposals that would have limited market shares to 20 percent per bank, then proposed a veto clause for future takeovers (ECLAC 2000: 128–29), and finally sought an injunction against BSCH in the Chilean Supreme Court.[3] Eventually the Chilean central bank and BSCH came to an agreement that the Spanish firm would reduce its stakes in one of the two local banks it controlled (Manger 2008). Nevertheless, the position of these two banks prevented viable competition. In addition, both banks hold minority stakes in other Spanish enterprises that are active in the region (Calderón and Casilda 2000: 76). Such investment focused mostly on the telecommunications and energy industries.

Just like other service industries, energy companies had been privatized much earlier in Chile than in other Latin American countries. With the first steps in liberalization taking place in neighboring countries, Chilean firms successfully branched out into these markets. By acquiring a Chilean energy provider, foreign investors therefore gained access

---

[2] Circumventing a theoretical regulatory "firewall" between pension funds and banks, foreign banks initially acquired AFPs via their home country rather than Chilean operations.

[3] DowJones Newswire, March 14, 2000.

not only to local but also to regional markets, and to important know-how about the business opportunities in these countries (ECLAC 2001). Most important among these investors is Endesa, a Spanish electricity provider, Chile's biggest foreign firm on the basis of sales. Outbidding the US firm Duke Energy in May 1999, Endesa acquired a 60 percent stake in Endesa Chile. Through its Chilean subsidiary Endesa also holds shares in energy companies in Argentina, Brazil, and Peru. Other foreign firms that made major acquisitions in the Chilean energy sector were TotalFinalElf (France), AES and Pennsylvania Power & Light (United States), and HydroQuebec (Canada). Almost 80 percent of the accumulated investment in the sector occurred between 1996 and 1999 (Rozas Balbontín 2001: 72–84).

In the telecommunications sector two firms came to dominate the market. In 1990, Telefónica de España bought local telephone operator CTC Chile, gaining an almost 85 percent market share (ECLAC 2000: 121–22), and took a 20 percent stake in the smaller, long-distance provider Entel Chile. Telefónica expanded into Chile for reasons similar to the Spanish banks: only fully privatized in 1997, it had limited opportunities in European markets dominated by the global giants Vodafone and Deutsche Telekom, but had a competitive advantage when entering Latin American markets, based on familiar language, legal, and cultural backgrounds. Competing US firms chose not to enter the market at the time, with the exception of Bell South, which built up a mobile phone network in Chile, but it later withdrew from the market and sold its subsidiary to Telefónica.

In a way similar to the regulatory process in most developed countries, Chilean authorities limited the number of licenses for mobile telephony. This had the unintended effect of benefiting established, European operators. EU firms preferred the European GSM standard and planned the introduction of their own "third generation" technology (W-CDMA), while US firms hoped to establish the CDMA2000 standard that had already been successfully introduced in Japan. Entering the market with a different standard would raise costs because existing networks would have to be refitted, and worked against competition because consumers could not use the same telephones when switching providers. Regulatory authorities were therefore inclined to prescribe the adoption of common standards as precondition for licenses (ECLAC 2000: 181). This issue would later reappear in the FTA negotiations between the United States and Chile.

In all three industries European firms established dominant positions through the acquisition of Chilean firms. No trade or investment agreement was necessary, since the Chilean government freely handed out the necessary concessions in accordance with DL 600. Concurrently, it made less far-reaching commitments under the GATS that omitted key areas of commercial banking, including the provision of loans and taking of deposits. Foreign investors could obtain a concession and often did so in practice, but the government was under no legal obligation and maintained an economic needs test.

European firms used the expansion room provided by regulators to the fullest, enjoying highly profitable operations that left enough margin to lower prices and thus potentially deter the entry of competitors. Table 6.4 shows the profit margins of banks, together with a comparison of similar financial institutions in other markets. Although bank profitability offers only an indirect measure of how competitive markets are (Claessens and Laeven 2004, 2005), the comparisons indicate that Chilean banks have consistently had higher profit margins than institutions in other countries – including those in protected, developed country markets such as Canada and developing country markets such as Mexico. At a minimum, the figures explain the incentives to secure Chile as an investment location. The data also suggest that BSCH and BBVA had a sufficient margin to price competitors out of the market if they had chosen to do so.

The picture is not much different in telecommunications and energy generation, as shown in table 6.5. Throughout the 1990s the two industries were highly profitable for foreign investors, often more so than the parent companies in Europe. Until the turn of the millennium, CTC achieved margins comparable with TELMEX, generally seen as a failed case of liberalization. Endesa Chile achieved high margins until the Chilean government strengthened energy regulations in 1999 (Manger 2008).

The dominant market share of these European-owned firms and the remaining regulatory barriers impeded the entry of competitors. US firms paid relatively little attention to the Chilean investment location at the time. This lack of business interest contributed to the delay of a project that would have opened the Chilean service sector further, possibly enabling new firms to enter the market: the negotiation of Chile's accession to NAFTA, or a bilateral agreement with comparable commitments.

Table 6.4. *International comparison of bank profit margins, expressed as a percentage*

				Chilean banks			
	BSCH	Santiago	O'Higgins	Santander	Osorno y la Unión	Crédito	Edwards	Bhif
1994		15.71	30.97	21.31	26.89	21.31	12.25	13.47
1995		18.94	30.58	21.91	27.49	25.20	30.60	16.23
1996		23.32		25.78		23.84	26.71	28.76
1997		32.89		17.91		23.85	25.44	26.03
1998		32.30		21.48		21.58	17.43	0.46
1999		22.99		24.60		15.85	-5.94	10.68
2000		34.90		32.80		22.08	2.65	16.13
2001		40.76		34.30		27.62	6.96	13.41
2002	27.60					27.93		17.70
2003	36.01							

	Chilean banks		International comparisons				
	Bice	Internacional	RBC (Canada)	Deutsche (Germany)	BBVA (Spain)	Banamex (Mexico)	Banorte (Mexico)
1994	45.42	2.34	15.82	11.92		6.66	23.7
1995	40.88	3.25	17.24		17.7	3.03	12.6

1996	42.45	21.90	18.01	10.81	17.69	1.31	13.76
1997	33.54	24.58	18.03	8.44	15.04	14.99	26.49
1998	4.26	13.74	18.08	1.75	17.00	27.17	22.61
1999	40.72	8.07	16.21	6.64	19.17	23.38	14.49
2000	29.14	12.35	18.41	39.74	17.77	29.14	20.63
2001	47.83	13.79	14.53	0.59	19.54	0.49	15.8
2002	43.30	18.55	15.81	1.62	19.56	–0.34	16.8
2003			17.46	6.77			

End of time series denote mergers and acquisitions activity; see text for details.

Source: Smith Barney Citigroup, Mergent Online, and Investext Plus, various years.

Table 6.5. *International comparison of energy and telecoms profit margins, expressed as percentage*

| | Chilean telecoms | | International comparisons | | | |
	CTC	Entel	Vodafone (UK)	Deutsche Telekom	Telefonos de Mexico	Telefonica de Argentina
1994	24.37	19.09	28.83	1.93	26.91	18.22
1995	25.86	8.69	20.60	19.75	22.33	16.76
1996	27.80	3.90	22.14	14.14	22.01	13.99
1997	26.32	7.01	20.80	15.61	21.16	15.83
1998	17.19	−4.33	16.95	14.64	20.96	14.88
1999	−5.93	7.41	18.95	11.09	25.64	13.42
2000	−13.47	5.25	6.19	13.78	25.84	9.49
2001	0.46	4.82	−65.07	3.45	21.17	8.04
2002	−2.05	5.11	−70.72	−32.24	17.34	−113.16
2003	1.25	8.22	−32.33	8.75	19.21	14.73
2004	44.34	6.84	−26.86	12.28	20.05	−0.26

| | Chilean energy providers | | | International comparisons | | |
	Endesa Chile	Chilectrica	Compania General de Electrica	Endesa (Spain)	Tractebel (Belgium)	Edenor (Argentina)
1994	50.97	13.95	15.07		9.56	
1995	43.25	20.64	17.84	17.94	9.64	6.11
1996	29.18	25.86	20.54	15.20	9.99	8.55
1997	18.31	29.15	19.98	14.37	9.51	11.83
1998	5.57	32.33	22.88	18.83	9.27	9.41
1999	−20.53	26.75	16.23	9.57	16.38	9.99
2000	12.26	21.18	12.39	12.71	8.81	9.97
2001	6.9	19.74	10.20			10.64
2002	−0.99	−7.79	6.54			−55.16
2003	8.49	12.06	6.55			22.33
2004	8.11	16.01		12.15		

End of time series denote mergers and acquisitions activity; see text for details.
Source: Mergent Online.

A road not taken: Chile's accession to NAFTA

Demonstrating its commitment to hemispheric liberalization, Chile originally planned to become a member of NAFTA under the treaty's accession clause shortly after the agreement came into effect. At the Summit of the Americas in Miami in 1994, the three NAFTA members officially invited Chile to join. Negotiating accession, however, proved impossible, since the Clinton administration and the US Congress failed to come to an agreement over the conditions under which the President would be granted fast-track authority.

The 1988 Omnibus Trade Act had granted President George Bush Sr. and President Clinton the power to negotiate the Uruguay Round and NAFTA. The expiration of its 1991 extension coincided with the negotiations for Chile's NAFTA accession. Building on the NAFTA precedent, USTR Kantor announced in February 1995 that the Clinton administration would negotiate agreements on labor and the environment in future preferential trade agreements, including the use of trade remedy laws to ensure compliance.[4] This proposal met with immediate resistance from Republicans in the House of Representatives, who refused to grant the President fast-track authority if trade agreements were to become a vehicle for environmental goals, and warned that Chile's accession to NAFTA would be delayed at least until after the 1996 US presidential election.[5]

Despite these difficulties the Chilean government signaled its willingness to begin negotiations. Working-level talks kicked off in July 1995 in Mexico City. However, it shortly became apparent that the United States would be unable to commit to what it negotiated. Although the House Ways and Means Committee offered the compromise of granting fast-track to negotiate labor and environmental clauses with Chile only, Senate Republicans under Bob Dole resisted this effort, possibly in view of the upcoming presidential campaign. Unable to come to a resolution, the House of Representatives abandoned the effort to reach a compromise in January 1996.[6]

In reaction, both Mexico and Canada decided to negotiate separate FTAs with Chile. Canada signed an agreement in November 1996; Mexico and Chile upgraded their 1990 FTA to include chapters on

---

[4] *Inside US Trade*, February 9, 1995.   [5] *Ibid.*, May 12, 1995.
[6] *Ibid.*, December 13, 1995, January 5, 1996.

services and investment with a new treaty, signed in October 1998. However, the Chilean government deliberately avoided any explicit commitments in financial services in these agreements. Neither country could promise much FDI in the sector, but including a financial services chapter would have set a minimum of liberalization that the United States and the EU would probably try to take as a starting point in the negotiations with Chile in order to push for more (Sáez 2006).

The Chilean government considered it highly unlikely that fast-track would be granted to the reelected Clinton administration. In March 1997, it announced that it would negotiate with the United States as part of the Free Trade Area of the Americas (FTAA)[7] process if and when the US president would be in a position to do so,[8] and officially abandoned its efforts to join NAFTA in August 1999.[9] For the remainder of Clinton's time in office, he failed to obtain fast-track authority to negotiate bilateral trade agreements.

Throughout the debate, most US industries remained uninvolved in the debate, offering little support for a push to achieve fast-track. Whether because of an accurate reading of the polarized political situation or limited interest in the Chilean market, an invitation for the submission of statements to the USTR on the proposed accession to NAFTA elicited few responses. A partial exception was the services sector. The telecommunications firm AT&T urged US negotiators to press for a further opening of the Chilean telecommunications market and lower tariffs on related products. In this case of rent chain formation, the link between service firms as investors and suppliers of telecommunications products as followers reversed the scenario of FDI in Mexico described in chapter 3. Rather than services following manufacturing to provide trade financing and insurance, the rent chain of AT&T consisted of producers of equipment who would only be likely to sell into the Chilean market if AT&T invested there. The company's 1995 letter to the USTR referred directly to competitive considerations:

Concessions under the NAFTA would have the advantage of being limited to the closed circle of NAFTA member countries ... Chilean concessions may be

---

[7] The FTAA promised the creation of a hemisphere-wide PTA, but was eventually put on ice with the shift to left-wing governments in key countries. See Wise and Studer (2007) for an evaluation of the progress and prospects of the initiative.
[8] *Inside US Trade*, March 21, 1997.
[9] *Diario Financiero* (Santiago de Chile), August 11, 1999.

easier to achieve in the accession negotiations and they could also provide a competitive advantage to firms in this hemisphere to the extent that the GATS negotiations do not achieve similarly favorable results.

AT&T also asked that Chile be pressed to drop its investment review mechanism under DL 600, and that NAFTA Chapter 11 be harnessed to secure an open investment environment in Chile.[10] During a hearing before the International Trade Commission, the American Chamber of Commerce in Chile supported the further liberalization of the telecommunications sector and demanded the opening of the financial services industry via negotiations for NAFTA accession, since the de facto moratorium on new banking licenses had effectively shut US banks out of the Chilean market.[11]

Such competitive considerations would later reappear in the negotiations of the United States–Chile FTA. For the time being, though, they were too limited to trigger a concerted lobbying effort by US service industries. This position would soon change when the EU began to negotiate an FTA with Chile.

The EU–Chile FTA

While the negotiations between the United States and Chile stalled, the EU moved quickly to establish ties with the Southern Cone. Due to their strong investment interests, Spanish firms became the principal supporters of free trade agreements with both Chile and the Mercosur countries. Unlike the Clinton administration, the European Commission could thus rely on significant domestic support in negotiating the EU–Chile FTA. Chile and the EU had only had two major disputes at the WTO – over the Chilean price bands for agriculture and tariffs on certain liquors – that Chile had lost. In both cases the United States had brought the same complaints against Chile to WTO panels. Already in 1995, 82 percent of Chilean exports entered the EU tariff-free, while the remainder carried an average tariff of only 2.4 percent.

The Commission proceeded along similar lines as during the negotiation of the EU–Mexico FTA: building on a 1990 political agreement between Chile and the EU, signed principally to express support for Chile's democratic transition, the EU concluded a "framework

[10] *Inside US Trade*, April 21, 1995.   [11] *Ibid.*, July 21, 1995.

agreement for cooperation" in 1996. The agreement followed a European Commission recommendation of 1995 in expressing a commitment to negotiate a free trade agreement. In July 1998, the Commission submitted its draft mandate to the Council. The formal start of negotiations was announced at the June 1999 EU–Latin America summit in Rio de Janeiro. As Chile had begun association talks with Mercosur, the Commission mandate originally called for parallel negotiations with both Chile and the Mercosur countries. The initiation of negotiations with Mercosur was itself reportedly triggered by concerns in European capitals about the FTAA process and its implications for EU firms.[12]

Negotiating issues

Pre-negotiation talks in three working groups (trade in goods and related matters, services and investment, and government procurement and competition rules) began in November 1999. Unlike in the EU–Mexico FTA, the most important EU interests lay in the service sector. Given this emphasis and the precedent of the EU–Mexico FTA, EU member states were willing to grant the Commission a mandate to negotiate service commitments on their behalf. For the same reason, however, the Commission was tied to a positive list approach, rather than a NAFTA-style schedule for liberalization with excluded sectors.[13]

More problematic was the mandate to move in lockstep with both Chile and Mercosur. Under French pressure, EU member states limited possible concessions to Mercosur by stating categorically that agricultural liberalization could only be discussed when linked to progress in the multilateral trade round.[14] As a result, the negotiations quickly slowed down to the same pace as the WTO round. The French presidency of the EU during the second half of 2000 also reinforced the link between the negotiations with Chile and Mercosur.[15] To prevent this outcome the Chilean government decided on a diplomatic offensive to convince the EU to separate the talks, as part of which Foreign Minister Soledad Alvear visited several European capitals in October 2000. Following the request of the Chilean government, the Commission

[12] *Bridges Weekly*, July 5, 1999, December 8, 1999.
[13] Interview with EU official, Brussels, June 2004.
[14] *Bridges Weekly*, April 18, 2000.
[15] Davis (2003) shows that GATT/WTO negotiations that coincide with a French EU presidency are consistently less successful at agricultural liberalization.

proposed to the Council to separate the talks, with the aim of concluding an FTA with Chile before the WTO round. After some wrangling, the Council approved the proposal, winning the support of the European Parliament in March 2001, based on a resolution brought by two Spanish parliamentarians.[16]

An easy ride: market access

Following this decision the FTA was negotiated during ten separate rounds between April 2000 and June 2002. The coalitions emerging in the EU resembled those of the negotiations with Mexico: France initially opposed an FTA with Chile because of its agricultural export potential. Chile not only exported fruit that would displace imports from ACP countries, but also wines and spirits that competed directly with French products. While the Commission expected that negotiations could be concluded within a short time frame of less than a year, French representatives suggested they were aiming for at least five years – a goal that led senior negotiators to question whether the EU would begin negotiating in good faith[17] and motivated them to make a bold opening gambit. During the first round of talks in Vilamoura, Portugal, the Chilean negotiators stressed that they expected the Free Trade Area of the Americas to be signed off by then – a tactic that led the Commission negotiators to reiterate their commitment to a rapid conclusion.[18]

During a visit by President Lagos to France in April and to Spain and Germany in late May 2001 to drum up support in the respective business communities, it became clear that tariffs for non-agricultural products would be completely eliminated in three stages.[19] Industry representatives in Brussels and Santiago expressed their satisfaction. EU Commission officials felt vindicated in their decision to separate the talks with Chile from those with the Mercosur countries.[20]

Even in agricultural products, the negotiations went smoothly. Market access for fruits and juices, Chile's main agricultural exports

---

[16] *Latin America Weekly Report*, No. 46, 545; *El Mercurio* (Santiago de Chile), September 21, 2000; *Estrategia* (Santiago de Chile), March 1, 2001.

[17] Interview with Chilean negotiator, Santiago de Chile, July 2007.

[18] *El Mercurio* (Santiago de Chile), April 11, 2000.

[19] *Financial Times*, May 31, 2001; *El País* (Madrid), June 4, 2001.

[20] *Diario Financiero* (Santiago de Chile), May 28, 2001; interview with EU officials, Brussels, June 2004.

to the EU, proved to be uncomplicated. Since the growing seasons of Europe and Chile are complementary, French resistance in the Council was quickly overcome by the push of Spain and, to a much lesser extent, Germany. More difficult for the Chilean side was the demand to comply fully with the geographical indications for wines and spirits used in the EU. Here, Chile could not count on the support of Spain to balance out French requests, leading the Chilean side to concede on this issue.

The most difficult problem in the talks tied fisheries subsidies, maritime services, rules of origin for fish products, and access to the EU market for Chilean fishmeal into a complex that was dubbed "the swordfish issue." Chile and the EU were locked in disputes at the WTO over the question of fishing rights next to Chile's exclusive economic zone, where European vessels were alleged to overfish sword fish, a migratory species. The EU refused to grant Chile better access for fishmeal if Chile persisted in the pursuit of the issue, and demanded access to Chilean ports for European fishing boats. Chile insisted on its long-held position that fishing rights were exclusively for Chilean vessels, the only ones who would be allowed to unload in national ports. The issue dragged into the final negotiating rounds. Eventually, the Chilean side gave up almost all its demands, accepted the full opening of its ports, 100 percent foreign ownership of Chilean vessels (up from 49 percent), and the unloading of EU vessels. The EU offered very little in return, including no reduction of duties on cod, which made up a quarter of Chilean fisheries products to the EU.[21] The most heavily subsidized EU fishing industries were those based in Spain and Portugal, where cod played a crucial role in cuisine and politics.

Why did Chile make such major concessions? Asymmetry is part of the answer, but not all of it. With its relatively open markets, Chile had few bargaining chips to give away. Most importantly, Chilean negotiators focused on services, where their interests converged with those of the EU.

Demands of European firms

European negotiating goals centered primarily on the locking-in of Chilean commitments to keep open its services markets. In part, this

---

[21] *El Mercurio* (Santiago de Chile), February 28, 2002; *Diario Financiero* (Santiago de Chile), September 20, 2001.

reflected the relatively liberal Chilean regulatory framework. At the same time, several European firms were concerned that a further opening of the Chilean market could do little to improve their competitive position and might invite others to try to enter the market.

A principal goal in financial services was to get the Chilean government to lift the 20 percent ceiling on foreign content in registered pension plans. Since almost all banks were already in foreign hands, the Chilean resistance to financial market opening originated more in a concern about the loss of regulatory competence than protectionism. Moreover, high-ranking officials of the Ministerio de la Hacienda (Finance) expected that European demands would primarily reflect the interests of European firms, and personally preferred unilateral opening measures to bilateral deals (Sáez 2006: 20–21).

From the Chilean point of view the concession would have counteracted a central aim of the FTA by potentially exacerbating capital outflows rather than attracting investment.[22] Still, neither of the two Spanish banks with direct interests lobbied hard for a change in the way in which the Chilean central bank granted concessions to foreign firms. This led to a situation in which Commission negotiators, who wanted to use the Chile FTA to set an example of far-reaching commitments for future Mercosur negotiations, at times went beyond private-sector concerns.[23] Likewise, there were no European demands for the lifting of the subsidiary establishment rather than branching requirement. This requirement again played into the hands of the Spanish incumbents: under Chilean law, subsidiaries of foreign banks are limited in their lending activity by the reserve requirement in relation to local capital, rather than the much larger international capital of the parent bank (Sáez 2006: 19). Given the strong position of the Spanish banks, such a requirement served as a barrier to entry against competitors. Perhaps most strikingly, the EU did not push for a most-favored-nation clause in the financial services chapters, since no European financial services firm would have gained from such a Chilean concession.

Among telecommunications firms, Telefónica had come into conflict with regulators because of its control of 85 percent of the local telephony market via its share in Telefónica CTC Chile. Already, in 1990,

[22] *Latin America Weekly Report*, No. 46, 545.
[23] Interviews with EU official, interest group representative, Brussels, June 2004.

CTC had been ordered by the Anti-Monopoly Commission and, following an appeal, by the Supreme Court to divest its stake in the long-distance provider Entel. In 1999, the Chilean government passed Decree 187 to regulate rates in "non-competitive activities" for a five-year period. Telefónica reacted by threatening legal action in Chile and announcing a freeze on investment, forcing regulatory authorities to revise the rate decree to meet its demands (Manger 2008). Following this experience, Telefónica individually urged the Commission to "approach a NAFTA standard" in its investment clauses to prevent a reoccurrence.[24] Further opening, however, was of little interest to Telefónica. In the words of one source, "Telefónica had little to gain by inviting US operators, because its main business is not in long-distance operations. [They] mainly tried to prevent undue regulatory activism by the Chileans." A Chilean negotiator from the Ministry of Foreign Affairs recalled his surprise when his team realized that the EU did not require a binding commitment in local telephony[25] – Telefónica simply would not have benefited. The firm instead encouraged high-level clauses that would match BITs with regard to expropriation, regulatory takings, and transparency that would be advanced through lobbying by the European Services Forum and the European Telecommunications Network Operators' Association. This contrasted with the firm's close involvement in the Mercosur-European Union Business Forum, since Mercosur markets offered much more room for expansion.[26] Given their dominant market position, European firms were less interested in a further liberalization beyond the GATS. The manufacturing sector supported the negotiating endeavor while making few specific demands,[27] especially since Chile had unilaterally reduced its MFN tariff to a uniform rate of 6 percent. Volkswagen was the only firm that intervened individually to ensure that Chile lifted its ban on diesel engines in passenger cars.[28]

The compromise formula dovetailed with European firm interests. According to Chile's commitments, registered pension funds could still only be offered by firms established in Chile, which in effect strongly favored the two main Spanish banks once the regulatory firewalls

---

[24] Interview with interest group representative, Brussels, June 2004.
[25] Interview with Chilean Ministry of Foreign Affairs official, Santiago, July 2007.
[26] Interview with interest group representative, Brussels, June 2004.
[27] Interview with interest group representative, Brussels, June 2004.
[28] Interview with interest group representative, Brussels, June 2004.

between the two services fell. These no longer need a special authorization: from March 2005 on, only the individual plans have to be approved by the regulatory authorities. Chile also committed to the opening of postal services and marine transportation, the only important service industries that had remained closed. Since the service and investment chapters of the FTA guarantee national and most-favored-nation treatment, European operators would be granted at the least the same conditions as any preferential agreement signed by Chile. For the dominant European firms, this was sufficient. As argued in chapter 2, both regulatory frameworks and the structure of service markets can penalize late entry. US competitors, in comparison, still faced difficulties when entering the market. The opportunity to gain better access presented itself when Chile reconsidered its position on an FTA with the United States.

Playing catch-up: the United States–Chile FTA

Although negotiations between the United States and Chile began only a few months after the first rounds of EU–Chile talks, the United States–Chile FTA proved more difficult to conclude. In August 1999, the Chilean foreign minister proposed to explore the possibility of a Chile–United States bilateral agreement, leaving the question of fast-track authority for later stages of the negotiation. Following discussions between officials of both parties at the sidelines of the APEC meeting in Santiago de Chile in September 1999, the two sides did not reach agreement until November 2000, when Presidents Clinton and Lagos announced the start of negotiations.[29] The agreement was negotiated during 14 rounds between December 2000 and December 2002. Like the EU, US interests primarily focused on the service sector, often targeting the same industries, although specific demands reflected the market position of US firms.

In Chile the start of negotiations was received with guarded optimism by key lobby groups. The National Society of Agricultural Producers (SNA), the association of traditional, hacienda-based farmers, even announced that it gave priority to an agreement with the United States over an integration into Mercosur because of the potential of the US export market, the second most important destination for Chilean

[29] *Inside US Trade*, November 29, 2000.

products after the EU. The choice would have to be made, as the Mercosur member stated that Chile's accession negotiations would be given a "pause for reflection." In practice, an FTA with the United States ruled out Mercosur membership unless the FTAA were to subsume the agreement.[30] At the same time, the SNA worried that the negotiations would force the government to abolish the price bands for wheat and other key hacienda products and expose the sector to subsidized US exports. Several senators close to the SNA stated that they would try their best to block the agreement if it threatened to hurt the sector.[31]

Among competitive exporters, wine and fruit producers hoped for the greatest gains. Their associations, Decofrut and Viñas de Chile, also shared the hope of gaining exemptions from US safeguard clauses, although Canada and Mexico had tried and failed. More realistic commentators in the Chilean press expected a dispute-settlement mechanism along the lines of NAFTA as the best possible outcome.[32]

Chile's most important industry association, the Confederación de la Producción y del Comercio (CPC), although supportive of the negotiations, warned that the PTA would be much less desirable if the price of ratification was a substantive agreement on labor and the environment that could be used to protect US industry from imports. These worries were alleviated by a statement by President Lagos in a press conference with his US counterpart, in which he made it clear that Chile would not be interested in negotiating an FTA with labor and environmental standards backed up by trade sanctions.[33]

Although Chilean exporters hoped for tariff reductions and protection from US trade laws, the biggest gains were not likely to occur in the primary sector, given the resistance of Californian peach, grape, and apricot growers, winegrowers from the US west coast states, and salmon fishers from Alaska. By contrast, interests dovetailed almost completely on foreign direct investment. CPC president Riesco stated that the main benefit for Chile would not be market access, but FDI from the United States. The official in charge of the negotiations at the Hacienda, Raúl Saéz, echoed these views: one of the main purposes of

---

[30] *Estrategia* (Santiago de Chile), December 6, 7, and 11, 2000.
[31] *Diario Financiero* (Santiago de Chile), March 7, 2002.
[32] *Ibid.*, January 4, 2001.   [33] *El Mercurio* (Santiago de Chile), May 10, 2001.

the agreement would be to encourage investment in financial services from the United States to create more competition in the Chilean market and establish the country as the financial hub of Latin America.[34] The Chamber of Commerce of Santiago even published a joint letter with the US Coalition of Service Industries (CSI) that expressed their full agreement on these goals.

US firms' demands

In both the telecommunications and the financial services industry, US firms sought to use the FTA with Chile belatedly to gain access to markets. Firm demands centered on the two issues identified in the analytical framework of this study: market structures that excluded competitors, and regulatory barriers such as standards and licensing procedures.

In March 2001, the CSI and the American Chamber of Commerce in Chile called upon US negotiators to enable US telecommunications providers to compete in the Chilean market. As part of a deal, the Chilean authorities would have to be banned from using regulatory means to exclude firms from markets, for example by limiting the number of licenses if the number of operators was deemed sufficient by regulators. Likewise, competitors in the fixed-line business – that is, US telephony providers – pressed for a legal right to use and lease lines of Telefónica CTC. This would have required a commitment beyond what Chile had offered in the GATS, where the telephony service remained unbound.[35]

Commitments beyond the GATS also became the focus of financial services negotiations, again reflecting the relative position of US firms vis-à-vis their European competitors. Since Chile had not offered additional liberalization measures in the 1997 Financial Services Agreement, entering the Chilean retail market in banking required either subsidiaries or joint ventures, but not mere branches of foreign-based banks. Since the acquisitions by European banks and the Canadian Scotiabank had left no desirable takeover targets in Chile, entering the market would have required considerable investment to set up a subsidiary.

---

[34] *Diario Financiero* (Santiago de Chile), August 14, 2001.
[35] *Inside US Trade*, March 26, 2001, June 1, 2001, January 11, 2002.

Consequently, in a letter sent to USTR Zoellick in December 2001, the CSI asked for a commitment to allow branches.[36]

Matching an EU request, the Investment Company Institute, as representative of the mutual fund industry, demanded that the 20 percent ceiling on foreign content in registered pension plans be lifted, and that US brokers be allowed to offer such plans in Chile. In a March 1, 2002, letter to the US Treasury Secretary, the association sought to ensure that capital could be withdrawn if necessary. Between 1991 and 1998, Chile had applied a rule requiring investments to stay in the country for a minimum of one year (the policy of *encaje*), with a reserve requirement between 10 and 30 percent to be deposited with a bank. Rightly or wrongly credited with helping Chile to avoid the contagion of various financial crises,[37] these capital controls were no longer applied. Yet because US firms had fewer direct investments in the service sector and would likely be limited to minority stakes, they would have been particularly affected by a reimposition, motivating them to seek strong commitments (Hornbeck 2003).

Important demands by services industries were therefore clearly motivated by the benefits the FTA would entail vis-à-vis their European competitors. Given the divisions emerging in the US Congress over trade policy, President Bush would have to obtain fast-track authority. In the lobbying process to support this goal, arguments about the competitive effects of FTAs would assume prominence.

The trade promotion authority debate

The fact that US firms' competitiveness declined without FTAs was not lost on lobbyists and political decision-makers, leading to a March 2001 hearing of the Subcommittee on Trade of the House Ways and Means Committee entitled "Free Trade Deals: Is the United States Losing Ground as its Trading Partners Move Ahead?" (US Congress, House of Representatives 2001). Lobbyists pressed committee members to grant the president fast-track, now referred to as trade promotion authority (TPA), to allow the United States to catch up. Business Roundtable president Sam Maury argued that

---

[36] *Ibid.*, December 4, 2001.
[37] See Edwards (1999) for an overview over the policy and an empirical evaluation of its success.

[B]ecause these FTAs increasingly cover trade and services, they often place our service industries at a competitive disadvantage against their foreign rivals [and] establish product standards that favor our foreign competitors. Their product becomes the standard while the US product becomes non-standard. These FTAs grant our foreign competitors investment opportunities that US investors lack ... Without Trade Promotion Authority, our trading partners will be reluctant to engage in comprehensive and time-intensive negotiations with the United States and will turn to other nations to negotiate deals that exclude the United States. (US Congress, House of Representatives 2001)

John T. McCarter, vice chairman of the board of directors of the Council of the Americas and CEO of GE Latin America, argued for the need to conclude an FTA with Chile in order to compete successfully with German and Japanese companies in the field of power generation. With the exception of a small number of import-competing agricultural groups who opposed free trade in general and a single academic, Daniel Tarullo of Georgetown University, all parties present at the hearing stated their support for granting TPA to enable the US president to pursue more FTAs.

Despite such support, it was clear that the United States would not cede any more ground in an agreement with Chile than it had done with other partners. In May 2001, sixty-one senators signed a letter to President Bush in which they emphasized that US laws on anti-dumping were not at the disposition of the negotiators. Moreover, the president would have to obtain trade promotion authority. This proved to be a difficult affair. The first version of the bill only passed with the narrowest of majorities – 215–214 – in the House of Representatives in November 2001. The Senate version (66–30) offered more support to American workers affected by trade, leading to the compromise bill H.R. 3009: The Trade Act of 2002, again passed with only a razor-thin margin of 215–212 at 3:30 A.M. on July 27, 2002, with four out of five representatives from Oregon and thirty out of fifty-two from California (including two Republicans) opposing the bill. The final conference committee version was approved in a 64–34 roll call vote in the Senate on August 2, 2002, paving the way for the conclusion of the negotiations in November 2002.

With such narrow support for the agreement in Congress, ratification seemed by no means guaranteed, triggering a second lobbying effort that emphasized the competitive disadvantages for US firms in the absence of a preferential trade agreement. The National Association of Manufacturers pushed for more bilateral agreements in a statement submitted to the Subcommittee on Commerce, Trade, and Consumer Protection of the House Committee on Energy and Commerce: "Competition is very keen between U.S. and European firms, and every day that they have duty-free access to Chile while we don't is just one more day when we are simply giving American business to European firms."[38] During a hearing before the Subcommittee on Trade, the president of Qualcomm, one of the leading providers of mobile telecommunications technology, argued that the United States–Chile FTA contained important pro-competitive and transparency clauses including (nonbinding) provisions calling on the Chilean government to ensure that operators had the flexibility to use a technology of their own choice. The "technology neutrality" question represented the competition over the establishment of standards as part of an FTA. Again, the lobbying coalition showed the existence of a clear rent chain: centered on service firms as principal investors, it was broadened by their suppliers, in this case telecommunications equipment manufacturers.

More broadly, the American Chamber of Commerce in Chile argued that an FTA with Chile was crucial because in sectors such as power generation, financial services, telecommunications, and transport, the country served as a testing ground for regional investments (US House of Representatives 2003). Finally, in his response to the Senate approval of TPA H.R. 3009, USTR Zoellick issued a statement on August 1, 2002, noting that "the United States had fallen behind other countries that had been aggressively negotiating trade agreements … however, that passage of the trade legislation would offer … a boost to the U.S. and global market."

However, several key Chilean concessions made the agreement palatable to a more protectionist Congress. Chile had conceded all points of contention – a ban on the *encaje* policy, US standards of intellectual property rights, a tenth of the quota for milk products originally envisaged (3,500 instead of 35,000 hectoliters). With wine, salmon, and fresh fruits the only products for which market access was substantially enhanced, support in the House (270–156) and the Senate (65–32) proved to be stronger than expected.

---

[38] *Inside US Trade*, May 8, 2003.

Outcomes: parity between the United States and the EU

Despite differences in legal cultures, treaty "templates," and domestic institutional characteristics, the FTAs with Chile negotiated by the United States and the EU are strikingly similar. In part, this again reflects the legal expression of the "nesting" of international regimes (Aggarwal 1998) – that is, the need to make international agreements compatible. Accordingly, much of the language in service agreements draws on the GATS. Nevertheless, the United States obtained several commitments from Chile that reflected the competitive position and demands by its service sector outlined above.

Importantly, the United States–Chile FTA eliminates the right of Chilean authorities to limit the number of financial services providers through licenses, quotas, or an economic needs test.[39] Likewise, it allows cross-border supply of mutual funds from 2005 on, and provides for mutual fund management by US institutions, although they still have to be incorporated in Chile.[40] Along similar lines, the United States obtained commitments that leveled the playing field for its telecommunications firms. The agreement contains an obligation to ensure that "major providers" (which in practice only applies to Telefónica de Chile) do not exclude competitors from their network.[41] Likewise, it guarantees the "technology neutrality" demanded by US telecommunications providers, calling on parties "not [to] prevent suppliers of public telecommunications services from having the flexibility to choose the technologies that they use to supply their services, including commercial mobile wireless services."[42]

By contrast, the commitments in the EU–Chile FTA still allow the Chilean government to regulate market access, but subject to both national and MFN treatment. In practice this implies that EU firms are guaranteed the same access as US firms. However, in specific areas the EU pressed for and obtained commitments that matched the United States–Chile FTA: Chile offered the same rights to provide mutual funds through cross-border service from the same point in time as US firms.[43] According to the laudatory official assessment by the European Commission,

---

[39] Article 12.4.   [40] Annex 12.9, Sections B and C.
[41] Article 13.4, Section 3.   [42] Article 13.14.   [43] Annex VIII.

Coverage of financial services by both Parties is extremely significant and it represents the highest liberalisation commitments ever achieved in a bilateral trade agreement, both in terms of market access commitments and of the framework of rules to be applied by the Parties ... This is the most open investment regime ever granted by Chile to any third country.[44]

A recent legal evaluation notes that the United States–Chile FTA (and hence by extension the agreement with the EU) established numerous precedents for liberalization beyond the GATS (Secretaría General de la Comunidad Andina 2003). In particular the efforts by the United States reflected the demands from service firms that spur on the competitive logic of FTAs.

Epilogue: trading fish for cars

In contrast to the active pursuit of agreements by the United States and the EU, Japan declined an initial offer from Chile to start negotiations. Japanese investment in the Southern Cone has focused almost exclusively on trade-related services such as financing, where an FTA would offer only limited benefits. Despite strong lobbying by the Chilean side and important advocates close to the Japanese government, in the absence of concrete competitive benefits to investing industries and their suppliers, bilateral agreements are not the most urgent.

The official Chilean proposal for an FTA resulted from a visit by Foreign Minister Valdes to Tokyo in November 1999. Following a pattern similar to other Japanese FTAs, the Japanese government first commissioned a report by a tripartite study group, led by JETRO officials and including representatives of the Japan Mining Industry Association and the Japan Chamber of Commerce and Industry. The report acknowledged that Chilean exports to Japan consisted mainly of copper, copper products that entered the country tariff-free, and products such as farmed salmon, and called for the rapid conclusion of an FTA (JETRO 2001). Likewise, former MITI vice-minister and JETRO chairman Hatakeyama, who had been instrumental in starting the process towards the Japan–Mexico FTA, strongly advocated the agreement in the press.[45] Chilean business representatives presented their case at various fora in Japan and pointed out the competitive

---

[44] Accessed May 16, 2005.   [45] *Japan Times*, June 8, 2001; July 12, 2002.

advantages EU and US firms would achieve through FTAs, but found little resonance. Japanese firms did not see enough benefit in an FTA with a country with already very low MFN tariffs. On the Chilean side, the officials at the Ministry of Foreign Affairs were relieved to be able to prioritize the negotiations with the United States and the EU that already stretched the capacity of the Directorate of Economic Relations to its limits.[46]

Once the agreements with the EU and the United States were concluded, Chilean President Lagos undertook a second attempt at a visit to Japan in February 2003 to propose an FTA, but earned a polite rejection. According to the official communiqué, Koizumi responded that "developments in FTA negotiations with other countries and negotiations by the World Trade Organization would have to be taken into consideration and that although such an FTA could not be realized soon, Japan would like to respond to this matter as a medium- and long-term issue."[47] Only in November 2004 did Japan and Chile agree, on the sidelines of an APEC meeting in Santiago, to install a second, higher-ranking tripartite commission to study the mutual benefits of an FTA.[48]

The offer was finally taken up by the Japanese side in November 2005, when the parties agreed to start negotiations in February the following year. One Japanese foreign affairs official described the initiative as "low cost, low benefit."[49] The accord itself was negotiated in the record time of seven months. No substantial differences emerged; Chile was willing to grant the exclusion of rice, wheat, and sugar from the agreement, given that even in the absence of any tariff, its producers would not be particularly competitive in the Japanese market vis-à-vis respectively US, Canadian, and Australian farmers. In a unique pattern, a Japanese firm with FDI in Chile became a liberalizing force: Nissui Suisan had invested in Chilean salmon farms that in 2005 generated sales worth US$100 million, and planned to export to Japan in the medium term in response to exploding prices in the home market. As a result, Japan agreed to abolish its 3.5 percent tariff on salmon. The agreement also restored parity in market access for cars, where Japanese

---

[46] *Diario Financierio*, June 8, 2001.
[47] www.mofa.go.jp/region/latin/chile/pv0302/overview.html
[48] *Japan Times*, November 23, 2004. Without any apparent intention of irony, the Japanese government also stated that it was ready to cooperate on arithmetic education as part of bilateral technical cooperation.
[49] Interview with MOFA official, Tokyo, December 2005.

exporters feared competition from South Korea, which had concluded an FTA with Chile in 2003 – but only at the margin, given that exports from Japan to Chile only totaled US$740 million in 2005. Yet despite the weak trade links, Japan committed only to liberalizing slightly over 90 percent of its imports from Chile over twelve years, with the longest time frame reserved for abolishing the tariffs on wine.[50]

Bilateralism comes into its own

In the cases of the EU–Chile and United States–Chile FTAs, the competitiveness concerns of interest groups assumed considerable importance. While some EU officials saw the negotiations with Chile as a chance to set "an example of a really good FTA" in legal terms prior to negotiating with Mercosur,[51] European firms were active in lobbying in the limited areas where the FTA could enhance their competitiveness. Most importantly, interest group demands had helped to move the United States–Chile FTA negotiations forward almost a decade after NAFTA accession was first considered by government officials of both parties. The renewed focus on Chile and consideration of a bilateral FTA, as opposed to requests in the GATS or the FTAA negotiations, underscore the pressure exerted on policymakers not to be left behind, even though a multilateral or at least broader regional deal that creates fewer transaction costs for exporters is theoretically possible. Table 6.6 assesses the predicted lobbying coalitions in both negotiations. The lack of lobbying by European telecommunications and financial services firms resulted from a commanding position that would not benefit from further liberalization – in effect, the "Chilean" services firms were already in European hands and acted liked import-competing domestic capital. On the Chilean side, the fishing industry did not support the EU–Chile FTA, an anomaly caused by the specter of competition with a heavily subsidized industry in the European Union.

When drawing the case of the Japan–Chile FTA initiative into the comparison, the limits of competitive pressures are evident. Government policymakers primarily worry about the trade and investment benefits

---

[50] *Nihon Nōgyō Shinbun*, November 20, 2005; *Nihon Keizai Shinbun*, September 21, 2006. Readers who have tried Japanese wine (from grapes, not from rice) will understand the industry's calls for protection.
[51] Interview with EU officials, Brussels, June 2004.

Table 6.6. *Predictions versus actual lobbying coalitions, EU–Chile and United States–Chile PTAs*

	EU–Chile		US–Chile	
	EU	Chile	US	Chile
For	Manufacturing exporters (as rent chain of services) *Financial services*		Manufacturing exporters (as rent chain of services) Financial services (including cross-border supply)	
	Energy *Telecommunications*		Energy	
		Agriculture		Agriculture
Against	Agriculture		Agriculture	
		Fisheries		
		Domestic manufacturing		Domestic manufacturing

Italics denote predictions that are not met.

PTAs bestow on firms. These competitive pressures were much weaker in the case of Chile. Japanese service-sector companies have not engaged in the same full-scale investment in emerging markets as manufacturing companies. Consequently, they are not affected by the competitive benefits the EU–Chile or United States–Chile FTA might grant. Manufacturing firms neither had major investments in Chile, nor appeared concerned about the diversion of Chilean imports from Japan – although the latter factor should not be overstated, since Chile also had much lower MFN tariff barriers than other emerging market countries. Yet once countries set out on the course of North–South PTAs, staying at the sidelines becomes more costly than adding a further negotiation to the list. In sum, the cases presented in this chapter show that the proliferation of free trade agreements between developed and developing countries is further accelerated by foreign direct investment in services.

7 | Japan's NAFTA route: preferential trade agreements with Malaysia and Thailand

B
EGINNING in the mid-1990s, several Latin American countries embarked on policies of preferential trade with regional neighbors, the EU, and the United States. Through the effect on flows of FDI and trade, the influence of these PTAs extended beyond the region. Chapters 4 and 5 have shown how two important agreements were directly prompted by the discriminatory effects of NAFTA. Today, PTAs are a global phenomenon. Even countries in Asia-Pacific, the last region to hold out, have now fully embraced preferential trade agreements.

Japan, drawing on the experience of trade discrimination caused by NAFTA and the successful leveling of the playing field through the Japan–Mexico FTA, has emerged as one of the principal promoters of this development. NAFTA, as the first North–South PTA, set an example of how to facilitate the use of a developing country as export platform while raising costs for competitors. In this chapter, I argue that the Japan–Thailand and Japan–Malaysia FTAs, each officially referred to as an "economic partnership agreement" (EPA), have followed the same model, although several important differences in initial conditions and liberalization outcomes emerge.

In southeast Asia, the "contagion" of the Asian financial crisis forced countries to try to attract more FDI rather than volatile portfolio investment. The crisis thus boosted a process of investment liberalization that had got off to a slow start in the early 1990s, and gave further impetus to the development of the ASEAN Free Trade Area (AFTA) and the ASEAN Investment Area (AIA). It rapidly altered the environment for Japanese firms with existing operations in Asia that had been set up under restrictive host country policies. Considering the central role played by the automotive industry, the parallels with the origin of business support for NAFTA are striking. In Mexico, changes in host country policies motivated US firms to use the southern partner as an export platform to the home market. Although a trade agreement was not necessary to stimulate the vertical integration of manufacturing across the Rio Grande, it offered various benefits, among them the inclusion of discriminatory clauses against non-NAFTA firms.

In the case of Thailand, Japanese automotive firms strongly supported a PTA because they were reorienting production towards exports, the Asian financial crisis having changed the environment for Japanese multinational corporations in southeast Asia. In an unprecedented development, Japanese firms began to ship parts and complete vehicles from Thailand back to the home market. Reflecting these changes, the PTA initiatives advanced by METI and MOFA provided backing for firm strategies similar to those of US manufacturers in Mexico. Whereas Japanese firms had in the past primarily produced vehicles for protected local markets in the ASEAN countries, all major firms have started to expand and retool their operations in Thailand for overseas sales.

Japanese firms did not primarily seek a PTA to prevent US firms from threatening the Japanese home market, since US manufacturing products were largely unsuccessful with Japanese consumers. However, Japanese negotiators sought high rules-of-origin thresholds for industries fearing imports from Thailand that used inputs from third countries, although in general the ROOs demanded by Japanese negotiators were much less strict than those in NAFTA or the PTAs negotiated by the EU. To implement a vertically specialized production strategy, Japanese automakers pressed for the liberalization of import tariffs on high-end vehicles for which production in Thailand and Malaysia was likely to be less efficient, and for specialized parts and components that they preferred to source in Japan. To this end, they lobbied hard to obtain the most rapid tariff elimination for high-value goods, especially luxury cars with large engines. At the same time, Japanese firms had defensive interests. They voiced concerns about the better treatment accorded to foreign investors from other countries, citing in particular the 1968 United States–Thailand Treaty of Amity and Economic Relations, an accord that provides US firms with rights comparable with those of domestic Thai investors.

A comparison of the cases of Thailand and Malaysia as investment hosts also throws into relief the competition between foreign multinational firms. For both countries, Japan remains their most important commercial partner, and both have in the past focused on the automobile industry to create a manufacturing base. In the early 1980s,

Malaysia embarked on a government-sponsored project to develop a domestic car industry with the Proton and Perodua brands, originally based on a joint venture with the Japanese makers Mitsubishi and Daihatsu. The company began to design vehicles independently by the late 1990s, with small numbers of exports to New Zealand, Australia, the United Kingdom, and the Middle East. In contrast, Thailand, much like Mexico, sought to attract a variety of foreign producers and to nurture a technological base that built up from suppliers and parts producers. During the negotiations of the Japan–Thailand EPA, non-Japanese manufacturers played a key role in pressing the Thai side not to give in to demands that would have eroded their competitive position. Rapid tariff reductions would have enabled Japanese manufacturers to sell luxury cars exported from Japan at a lower price than their primarily European competitors. This element was completely absent in Malaysia, but the host country remained much more protective of its domestic car industry.

The negotiations also differed in that Thai agricultural exporters tried to gain access to the Japanese market for their products, even though they were mostly unsuccessful. Rice and sugar, two products of which Thailand is among the most efficient producers in the world, were completely excluded from the final deal. By contrast, Malaysia does not have a comparable agricultural export industry, resulting in much less contentious negotiations. Ultimately, liberalization again converged on those goods relevant for the multinational firms that had invested in Thailand and Malaysia and that therefore pressed hard for the deals.

Liberalization of services played a negligible role in both agreements. The lack of lobbying efforts by Japanese service industry firms and the strong resistance to the opening of investment regimes by both host countries resulted in outcomes that did not go beyond the commitments made in the WTO. This suggests that at least in these two cases, the oft-cited argument that preferential trade agreements can proceed into domains which multilateral negotiations have not reached – including comprehensive investment liberalization – does not hold. Japanese firms have offered little support for these demands in the past.[1] Most of the changes in the investment regimes of southeast Asian host countries

---

[1] Partly as a result, Japan has not signed many bilateral investment treaties.

Table 7.1. FDI stock by source in Thailand and Malaysia, US$ million

Year	Thailand			Malaysia		
	EU	US	Japan	EU	US	Japan
1990	–	2,194	5,419	–	1,796	3,961
1991	1,385	2,398	6,191	4,158	2,100	4,869
1992	1,755	3,003	6,813	4,761	1,847	5,573
1993	1,971	3,330	7,314	5,515	2,234	6,353
1994	2,307	3,972	7,960	6,077	3,488	7,044
1995	2,929	4,651	16,782	5,942	4,601	6,126
1996	4,102	5,328	16,782	6,632	6,034	6,126
1997	3,936	4,540	5,997	6,604	6,844	4,934
1998	3,479	5,399	5,906	5,338	5,835	4,585
1999	4,315	5,620	4,711	7,987	6,358	3,692
2000	5,244	5,824	4,767	8,928	7,910	4,004
2001	4,780	6,031	5,954	10,903	7,313	4,204
2002	7,110	7,468	6,012	6,300	6,821	3,765
2003	9,555	6,495	7,207	7,257	6,657	3,730
2004	9,076	6,968	9,078	9,201	7,441	3,737
2005	9,707	7,729	10,505	8,918	9,028	3,737
2006	10,312	6,959	12,543	9,900	10,544	6,562

– Missing data.
Source: Eurostat, OECD.

took place in the aftermath of the Asian financial crisis that fundamentally transformed the parameters of foreign investment in the region.

The changing character of FDI in southeast Asia

Although foreign direct investment played an important role in Thailand's and Malaysia's recent economic development, both countries originally imposed strict requirements on manufacturing investment and limited FDI in the services sector. Table 7.1 shows that both countries hosted almost equal capital stock from the EU, the United States, and Japan. Japanese firms invested comparatively more in Thailand and less in Malaysia, but their commitment to the former proved to be highly sensitive to the 1997 financial crisis. The data on FDI inflows by sector from Japan to Thailand and Malaysia shown in

Table 7.2. *FDI inflows from Japan to Thailand and Malaysia,*
US$ million

	Malaysia		Thailand	
Year	Manufacturing	Services	Manufacturing	Services
1990	725	157	884	46
1991	737	242	717	16
1992	555	195	355	352
1993	772	127	493	159
1994	632	198	632	95
1995	555	83	1,115	163
1996	457	132	1,026	289
1997	484	262	144	366
1998	393	104	816	533
1999	461	64	618	206
2000	209	27	609	14
2001	174	84	645	74
2002	54	12	41	39
2003	18	245	459	117
2004	82	31	512	173

Source: Japanese Ministry of Finance (MOF).

table 7.2 underlines the predominance of manufacturing investment, but also indicates that FDI flows declined from their peak in the 1990s.

Prior to the crisis, Japanese manufacturing in southeast Asia was oriented towards regional markets, with about 60 percent targeting regional sales (Japan Bank for International Cooperation 2003; Kitamura 2003: 22). In the automobile industry, Japanese investment began in the 1970s under tightly constrained conditions. While producing cars in joint ventures with local companies, the characteristic structure of Japanese multilateral corporations led them to replicate their vertical production or *keiretsu* networks in the region. Consequently, as Japanese car manufacturers invested in southeast Asia, they pressed their Japanese suppliers to follow and start up subsidiary operations.

Host country governments, trying to spur on the development of their domestic industrial base and to improve human capital, mandated ever-higher local content quotas (Doner 1991: 40–63; Humphrey and Oeter 2000: 59–60), making it difficult to achieve efficient production scales and driving up prices for domestic sales as a result. The initial reaction of Japanese firms was to try to protect the regional markets against entrants from Europe and the United States (Doner 1991: 76, 80). In order to achieve economies of scale to the extent possible in the protected market, Japanese manufacturers built regional production networks around host country policies, whereby locally produced parts could be sourced tariff-free within ASEAN under certain conditions (Yoshimatsu 1999, 2002). The original framework, referred to as brand-to-brand complementarity (BBC), followed a proposal by Mitsubishi to allow parts procured in other ASEAN countries to be counted towards fulfilling local content requirements in the country of final assembly, provided imports and exports were "complementary." The practical purpose also related to the balancing of foreign currency transactions. In an implicit bargain, these schemes also acted as a barrier to the entry of competitors (Doner 1997: 112), because the small market size required large, "commanding" shares to be efficient, and production networks throughout the major ASEAN countries. As a result, by 1992, Japanese affiliates accounted for 94 percent of production in Thailand (Hatch and Yamamura 1996: 37). In the major ASEAN countries, combined imports, local assembly by Japanese firms, and joint ventures accounted for 70–95 percent of all auto sales (Noble 2002; Shimokawa 2004; Takeuchi 1993).

The successor to the BBC, the ASEAN Industrial Cooperation (AICO) scheme, would have provided for free trade in parts and components among the ASEAN members upon permission by member country governments. Despite applications by Japanese manufacturers, no company actually operated under AICO, since only the Thai government supplied permits. Malaysia and Indonesia refused to grant permission and insisted upon balancing of imports and exports, compromising the essential purpose of the system (Shimokawa 2004: 153).

In comparison, the electronics sector in southeast Asia has been much more open to foreign investment without onerous restrictions (Shimokawa 2004: 141). It has also long been characterized by a much stronger presence of US firms and production networks. Yet, whereas US firms initially sought local low-cost suppliers in Asia to produce for reexport to other advanced markets, Japanese investment was primarily aimed at serving nascent regional markets, and only secondarily at exports (Borrus 1999: 220). Moreover, compared with their direct competitors, Japanese electronics multilateral corporations still source much more input from their home country, leading to ratios of 85–90 percent of trade within the firm or with close affiliates (Arimura 2002; Ernst 2000: 83; Guerrieri 2000).

From protectionism to export orientation

Until the mid-1990s, the dominant position of Japanese firms and the character of FDI in Thailand and Malaysia therefore provided little incentive for closer economic integration with Japan itself. Japanese investment in the auto industry was primarily tariff-jumping and oriented towards host country markets, and put a low emphasis on exports. Yet in the wake of the Asian financial crisis, the conditions for Japanese investment changed. Slumping demand and trade liberalization began to affect Japanese production networks, while South Korean and Western firms began to make inroads into previously uncontested markets (Noble 2002: 124). In the ASEAN Five,[2] non-Japanese firms increased their share of the passenger car market from 5–10 percent to 25–30 percent compared with the early 1990s, prompting some of them to make new investments that competed with Japanese incumbents (Dunne 2001). Ford started up production in 1998; GM and BMW followed in 2000. The non-Japanese firms also complained to host governments about newly announced policies such as the AICO scheme that they perceived as favoring Japanese firms, motivating further liberalization measures by host governments (Yoshimatsu 2002: 139).

Restructuring in Thailand

In the immediate aftermath of the crisis, host country governments liberalized the investment environment in order to attract more FDI. Thailand made bold steps towards liberalization of the investment regime, partly as a requirement of the IMF support package during the Asian financial crisis.[3] The Thai government eliminated the 30 percent export requirement necessary to qualify for an exemption

[2] Indonesia, Malaysia, Thailand, Philippines, and Singapore.
[3] The respective letters of intent were sent to the IMF by the Thai government on May 26 and August 25, 1998. See www.imf.org/external/np/loi/052698.htm and www.imf.org/external/np/loi/082598.htm.

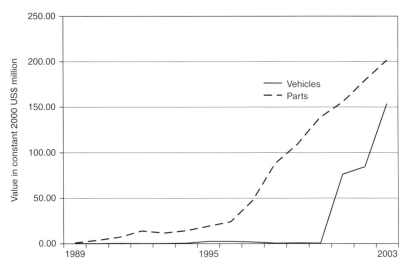

Figure 7.1. Exports of automotive products from Thailand to Japan, 1988–2003.
Source: UN Comtrade Database.

from import duties on goods used in local manufacturing (UNCTAD 1998: 342). Although, legally speaking, most industries still faced a 49 percent ceiling for foreign ownership, in practice a variety of special investment promotion schemes and administrative discretion opened most manufacturing activities to 100 percent foreign participation. Services remained closed, even the 49 percent ceiling in financial services being at the discretion of the central bank (Sally 2007: 3–6).

Although Japanese operations in the region faced a stiff wind of competition, the depreciation of the Thai baht created the prospect of a highly cost-competitive production. Japanese automotive firms reacted quickly. Already, before the crisis, the expansion of automotive parts production for export to Japan had accelerated. Firms began a rapid process of centralization and restructuring of their operations in Thailand to achieve high-capacity utilization rates.[4] In an unprecedented development, Japanese manufacturers began to ship finished cars to the home market. The striking trend becomes apparent in figure 7.1. While no separate data on the exports of Japanese auto and auto

---

[4] *Kagaku Kōgyō Nippō*, September 8, 2003; *Nikkei Bijinesu Daily*, February 12, 2004.

parts manufacturers from Thailand to Japan are available, it is safe to assume that virtually all are shipments by Japanese-owned producers, given the notorious lack of success of foreign brands in Japan. Exports of parts and complete vehicles grew exponentially within a short time, although it should be noted that the overall volume is still low.

Besides taking up the production of passenger cars for the Japanese market, all major manufacturers developed and started to implement plans to use Thailand as an export platform for other markets.[5] Concurrent with the start of PTA negotiations with Thailand, Japanese firms announced plans for significant investments in the country. Toyota confirmed the production of the Hilux model as "IMV–International Multipurpose Vehicle," a light pickup truck. Half the projected 280,000 units were destined for exports to markets in Europe as well as important developing countries. Suppliers closely affiliated with the group, such as Aisin Seiki (brakes), Aichi Steel (engine and transmission parts), NSK (bearings), and Denso (electronics) prepared to increase production quickly. Initial plans proved to be too conservative, motivating Toyota to increase production capacity from 140,000 to 260,000 units per year. Nissan presented plans to expand production capacity in Thailand by over 50 percent. Honda considered building a second plant for its small, environmentally friendly car model marketed as "Life" in Japan because its current factory operated at full capacity. Even struggling automaker Mitsubishi announced a capacity expansion of 30 percent because of the rising demand for pickup trucks in Europe.[6] In total, Toyota announced US$1.5 billion, Nissan US$678 million, Mitsubishi US$257 million, and Honda US$55 million in new investments in their vehicle and engine production subsidiaries in Thailand between 2003 and 2005.[7]

Japanese electronics firms, having replicated the production network strategy of the automobile sector, were affected by the same forces when host countries began to liberalize their markets, although many of the new entrants were in fact local companies from South Korea, Singapore, and Malaysia (Borrus 1999: 224). Similar developments affected the upstream component of Japanese investment in the

---

[5] *Nikkan Jidōsha Nyūsu*, March 22, 2003.
[6] *Nihon Keizai Shinbun*, May 7, July 3, August 8, 24, and 25, December 6, 2004; *Nikkei Bijinesu Daily*, February 12 and August 8, 2004.
[7] Figures from the Bank of Thailand's official statistics, available at www2.bot.or. th/statistics/.

chemical industry.[8] Although many firms also produced in China, Japanese multinationals were not willing to abandon southeast Asia as a production base, likely because they sought to hedge against instability in China and because operations in the ASEAN countries tended to be more profitable.[9]

Restructuring in Malaysia

Malaysia managed to weather the Asian financial crisis better than its immediate neighbors, partly because of a policy of capital controls implemented immediately after the crisis hit, but also because the country had a more favorable balance of long-term to short-term loans (Nesadurai 2000). Malaysia also imposed high tariffs on cars and parts and a luxury vehicle duty that mirrored Thailand's import barriers. Finished vehicle tariffs ranged from 140 to 300 percent, while completely knockdown kits carried a 40–80 percent duty (Athukorala 2005: 23). However, the purpose of the tariffs was different. One of the central planks of Malaysia's industrial policy was a domestic automobile program that resulted in the creation of the two producers Proton (Perusahaan Otomobil Nasional) and Perodua (Perusahaan Otomobil Kedua). The two national car producers together captured most of the market during the 1990s, when their models were still closer to then-current technological standards. By 2004, however, Proton's market share had dropped to 44 percent, or about 155,000 units, even though its family saloon car sold for only slightly over half the price of a Toyota or Honda model of the same class, and despite an excise tax of half that applied to imported vehicles. The decline can partly be attributed to quality issues – according to the automotive consultancy JD Powers, Proton vehicles had the most faults of any for sale in Malaysia. Unsurprisingly, the maker sold a mere 8,000 cars overseas in 2003.[10] Mitsubishi ended its involvement with Proton in March 2004. Perodua hoped to fare better by taking the opposite route, selling a 41 percent stake to Daihatsu, itself a Toyota subsidiary, in order to gain better access to modern technology, but its market share also fell, to 30 from

---

[8] *Nikkan Kōgyō Shinbun*, May 26, 2000.
[9] JETRO survey, cited in *Mainichi Economist*, July 15, 2003.
[10] *The Economist*, August 5, 2004.

35 percent.[11] Nevertheless, this still implied a dominance of domestically produced vehicles, especially in the mass market.

In terms of exports, however, the automotive industry plays a minor role in Malaysia compared with electrical and electronics products, which account for over 50 percent of shipments abroad. Foreign producers, again mostly Japanese, outnumbered domestic firms by a factor of three to one. Although more important in terms of foreign trade, the liberalization of electronics manufacturing did not have the same political implications as tariff reductions for the auto industry. While the latter was itself the pet project of the former prime minister, Mahathir, who even remained an advisor to Proton after his retirement in 2003, the former experienced a second boom after the turn of the millennium.[12]

Perhaps the most important factor that affected all the ASEAN states, but in particular Malaysia, was the emergence of China as a direct competitor. Eichengreen and Tong (2007; 2006) show that countries in Asia that compete with China in the production of light consumer goods (such as Malaysia) have suffered most directly by attracting less FDI, although the effect is not uniform. Thailand, by virtue of producing and exporting components, has fared better than other countries.

Preferential trade in ASEAN – or beyond?

For both countries, preferential trade agreements presented a means to attract more investment in general and to prevent or at least slow the diversion of FDI to China. Among the first measures announced after the crisis was a deepening of the ASEAN Free Trade Area and the creation of an ASEAN Investment Area. Free trade between ASEAN countries had been one of the longest-standing goals of the association, but it had frequently run into problems because the members were competing in the same export markets. Again, neither mutual tariff reductions in the AFTA nor the open investment regime in the AIA were fully implemented. Malaysia in particular reneged on its commitments to liberalize trade in cars and parts (Kiyota 2006: 218), prompting a rethinking by the Thai government of the potential for regional economic integration in ASEAN. At the same time, ASEAN cooperation in the WTO became increasingly fractious (Sally and Sen 2005: 111).

---

[11] *Automotive Forecast Asia & Australasia*, December 2005: 61.
[12] *Electronic Engineering Times*, Manhasset, NY, April 26, 2004, 36.

With the AFTA process slowing down precisely in the area in which Thai policymakers wanted to boost production, a search for additional markets and means to attract FDI became necessary. Already, under the Chuan government (1997–2001), talks with Australia, South Korea, and several other countries were initiated. Under the following Thaksin cabinets (2001–06), the scope was broadened to include China, India, the United States, several developing countries, and, most importantly, Japan. During Thaksin's first visit to Japan in November 2001, Koizumi agreed to launch a joint research project on the feasibility of a bilateral agreement (Nagai 2003).

A policy of preferential trade agreements with major markets dovetailed with the interests of Japanese firms in the new environment. The changes in the operations of Japanese firms in Thailand had already been relayed to MITI bureaucrats, who in 1999 began a formal study of how to offer government support for firms in a changed environment.[13] Companies interested in supplying Japanese factories abroad with machinery also expressed their interest in a PTA with Thailand in consultations with METI. Following discussions in the International Trade Policy Bureau as well as the regional bureaus, MITI/METI began to develop plans for a PTA with Thailand.[14]

Initially, Japanese support for a PTA was ambivalent, with METI plans wavering between a preference for negotiations with all ASEAN members and PTAs with individual countries. However, the rapid conclusion of the China–ASEAN Free Trade Agreement, although clearly seen as driven by politics rather than economics,[15] galvanized the supporters, especially in MOFA, to pursue agreements with Thailand and Malaysia as the most important host countries for Japanese investments in ASEAN. Faced with strongly protectionist agricultural groups spurred into action by the negotiations with Mexico, the success of the PTA policy depended on support by Japanese firms with investments in the partner countries and their chain of suppliers – the central constituency in favor of a free trade agreement.

---

[13] *Nikkan Kōgyō Shinbun*, March 22, 1999.
[14] Interview with METI officials, Tokyo, December 2002.
[15] Interview with former senior MITI official, Tokyo, March 2003.

Getting to the negotiating table

One of the most important effects of the experience of the Japan–Mexico FTA was the better organization of all interest groups and the bureaucracy in Japan. Unfortunately for Thai export interests, this did not mean that liberalizing protected Japanese markets for agricultural products would be easier to achieve. On the Thai side, optimism and a willingness to send positive signals were abundant. When Keidanren intervened in Bangkok during a tariff conflict over temporary increases in duties on electrical appliances, the government responded by immediately lowering the tariffs again.[16]

In a similar positive spirit the first informal talks of government officials were held between September 2002 and May 2003, aimed at identifying what elements of the Japan–Singapore EPA could be adapted in order to begin negotiating with a template treaty. Using the JSEPA model in negotiations with individual countries appealed in particular to the elite jurists at MOFA, because it was more likely to produce harmonized rules that could later be merged into a regional Japan–ASEAN partnership.

Meanwhile, opposition to the agreement began to stir in Japan. Now forewarned that the Japan–Mexico FTA was not an isolated measure to counter the effects of NAFTA, but rather a comprehensive strategy of trade agreements pushed by METI and MOFA, officials at the Ministry of Agriculture, Forests, and Fisheries set out their position that future PTAs would have to proceed even more cautiously in terms of liberalization. The JA Group sent a mission to Bangkok to make it clear to the government that it would resist any demands for the opening of the Japanese market for rice, one of the best-protected farming sectors in the world. Together with LDP politicians of the *nōrin zoku*, MAFF managed to create such a strong impression on the Thai government that it agreed to delay negotiations originally scheduled to start in June 2003, after the visit of the Thai Prime Minister to Japan.

During their meeting, Prime Ministers Thaksin and Koizumi agreed to the by now standard procedure of establishing a task force with representatives from governments, academia, and the private sector. The group highlighted potential difficulties in the liberalization of agriculture in its final report. The document also marked an early use of the

---

[16] *The Nation*, February 9, 2002.

term "multifunctionality" of agriculture that MAFF had adopted from the EU to suggest that farming was not merely an "industry like any other," but crucial in maintaining employment and social cohesion in rural regions. It also noted ominously that the sensitive goods mentioned in the report were only indicative, as Japan would have to negotiate over several hundred different goods currently restricted by tariff-rate quotas.[17]

MAFF officials also publicly discussed the possibility of seeking a blanket exclusion for rice as a precondition for a PTA with Thailand, and to resist liberalization of boneless chicken, fisheries products, and refined sugar; this last was a concession to domestic refiners. Like other developed countries, Japan generally taxes imports of processed materials more highly than raw inputs, and accordingly allowed imports of sugar molasses from Thailand in large quantities. Other proposals included a strengthening of domestic support payments for affected farmers. Immediately before the start of actual negotiations, the JA Group published a statement titled "Fundamental Considerations for the FTAs with South Korea, Thailand, the Philippines and Indonesia," in which the same four product groups were identified as non-negotiable.[18]

Since in preliminary talks Thailand had suggested putting labor mobility on the agenda, MAFF and the JA Group also gained an ally that helped to restrict the Japanese side's negotiating space. The Thai government hoped to negotiate temporary work permits for nurses, massage therapists, and chefs. Opposition to this demand came from the Japanese Nursing Association (*kango kyōkai*) and their responsible ministry, that of Health, Labor, and Welfare (MHLW), although the issue seemed less contentious than in the negotiations with the Philippines, whose government had made labor mobility central to the talks.[19]

To counter the protectionist groups, several industries organized a concerted lobbying effort with strategies similar to those employed to

---

[17] The tariff-rate quota system originated in the Uruguay Round Agreement on Agriculture. Imports within the quota enter at a lower (in-quota) tariff rate, while a higher (out-of-quota) tariff rate is used for imports above the concessionary access level.

[18] *Nihon Keizai Shinbun*, June 9, 2003; *Nikkei Weekly*, December 15, 2003; *Nihon Nōgyō Shinbun*, February 11, 2004.

[19] *Nihon Nōgyō Shinbun*, March 25, 2004.

support the negotiations with Mexico. Individual firms and occasional Keidanren missions focused on relations with the Thai government, while Keidanren as an association acted as vanguard in the public battle in Japan, starting with a November 2003 policy statement that requested the pursuit of FTAs with the advanced ASEAN countries.[20] During the following months, the association began to push relentlessly for a speedy conclusion of a PTA. Keidanren and individual industry associations also supplied METI with highly detailed demands, warning that US firms were outcompeting Japanese companies in terms of using Thailand as a production base because of the better investment conditions afforded to US firms under the United States–Thailand Treaty of Commerce and Navigation.[21] Concern about the risk of foundering negotiations was also voiced by representatives of the textile industry, a sector with significant overseas production in southeast Asia.[22] When the actual negotiations started, industry associations shifted to more detailed demands.

Negotiating the Japan–Thailand EPA

Negotiations began in February 2004 in Bangkok and spanned a total of ten rounds. The Thai government opened the talks with a gambit that, in addition to sending nurses to Japan, Japanese patients could also come to Thailand, with Japan's public health insurance covering the bill. This was refused outright by the MHLW, whose only apparent aim in the negotiations was to represent the interests of Japanese medical and nursing associations against foreign competition, despite a public discourse around an aging society and a growing need for professional care for the elderly. Initial Japanese proposals focused on improving the Thai investment environment for Japanese firms by guaranteeing national treatment.[23]

Thailand's offers on duties, excluding only thirty-eight different product categories, were much more aggressive than the Japanese counter-proposals that suggested leaving 350 different products out of the negotiations, almost all of them agricultural exports. From the first to the seventh round, in March 2005, both sides expended most of their

---

[20] See www.keidanren.or.jp/japanese/policy/2003/114.html.
[21] *Nihon Keizai Shinbun*, April 18 and May 12, 2004.
[22] *Ibid.*, June 9, 2003.   [23] Nikkei News Service, February 17, 2004.

time and energy on identifying common ground. Tariff rates for electrical and electronic products were easy to agree on; Japan imposed no tariffs to begin with, while Thailand was eager to attract more FDI into an industry in which it had few domestic suppliers. During the final three rounds, the negotiations revolved around the core topics: rules of origin, agricultural liberalization, and Thai import tariffs on luxury vehicles, car parts, and high-grade steel products as inputs for the automotive industry. The public discussion in Thailand surrounding the talks was characterized by tensions between local businesses and the government, especially Thaksin himself, who appeared ready to make sizable concessions to the Japanese in order to conclude the deal. Thaksin also clashed with the bureaucracy, which was used to more discretion in the handling of its affairs, as in other recent trade negotiations that were initiated by the prime minister's office. The foremost instruction was to move quickly in the talks, even if this meant skimping preparation and attention to detail (Sally 2007: 14), an approach that rankled with the diplomats and some domestic interests.

The limits of liberalization: agriculture and movement of labor

When Koizumi made LDP politician Shimamura Yoshinobu the Minister of Agriculture, Forests, and Fisheries in August 2004, Thai newspapers briefly speculated that the agricultural lobby in Japan would be weakened, as Shimamura represented an urban Tokyo district and had no personal ties with the farming industry. These hopes were quickly disappointed. From the start of the negotiations MAFF officials stalled the opening of the home market for the goods that would have brought the greatest economic benefits for Japanese consumers and Thai exporters. Japan offered to increase the tariff-rate quotas for flour from 70,000 to 200,000 tons and for sugar molasses to 4,000 tons in the third year and 5,000 tons in the fifth, while lowering tariffs from ¥15.3 to ¥7.65 per kilogram, and to cut tariffs on frozen, boneless chicken from 12 to 8.5 percent over five years. Even with this relatively minor reduction, the MAFF delegation refused to face the Japanese chicken producers and instead left it to the co-chair of the negotiations, Suzuki Yoichi from MOFA, to convey the bad news.[24] However, MAFF

---

[24] Interview with MOFA official, Boston, June 2008.

negotiators did not concede any improvement in market access for refined sugar,[25] but after some prodding offered tariff-free access for prawns.

Most importantly, Japanese negotiators sought and obtained the blanket exclusion of rice from the negotiations. After the Japanese side blocked repeated attempts even to discuss the issue, Thaksin intervened in March 2005 and instructed his officials to take the matter off the table. The Thai negotiators were dismayed, having spent much energy on trying to convince MAFF to offer concessions on the grounds that Thai Jasmine rice and japonica grains were different products – as one Thai negotiator stated, "you cannot make sushi with Jasmine rice." The same instructions also moved sugar and tapioca starch to a subject for renegotiation after five years.[26] Instead, Japan offered cooperation on a project, "Kitchen to the World," that promoted Thai cuisine abroad.

The main concession was to give ground on a Thai demand for labor mobility: Japan would allow Thai chefs with five rather than ten years of experience to work legally in Japan.[27] Spa workers and massage therapists and other occupations (for which formal qualifications were more difficult to ascertain in the eyes of the Japanese government) and nurses were left for future talks.

Aside from concerns about mobility for these professions, labor unions in Japan proved to be completely passive and did not even issue any statements. Since labor in Japan is organized along company-specific lines, it is unsurprising that it did not mount any broad resistance. Companies that sold parts or machinery to Japanese buyers for their investment in Thailand could be expected to benefit. For unions in larger multinational firms such as Toyota, the prospect of a trade agreement was mixed. On the one hand, it promised greater sales of luxury models, but, on the other, it might lead to the outsourcing of the production of low-end models. In part, the passivity of labor may just reflect its comparative weakness, long the subject of debate among scholars of Japanese political economics (Kume 1998; Pempel and Tsunekawa 1979). Perhaps more importantly, most Japanese overseas investment may have been perceived as the growth of the company

---

[25] *The Nation*, April 6, 2005.
[26] *Bangkok Post*, March 26, 2005; *The Nation*, May 12, 2005.
[27] *Fuji Sankei Bijinesu*, August 2, 2005.

rather than the replacement of Japanese workers, especially since Japanese multinational firms remained reluctant to lay off their core workforce. Either way, no Japanese labor organization outside the health services industry became politically active in lobbying against the FTAs with southeast Asian partners, including Thailand.

Rules of origin

The general template of Japanese free trade agreements called for moderately strict rules of origin, often with a minimum of 40 percent of qualifying originating goods and a tariff header change. The specific instances where the demands deviated from this standard therefore stand out as efforts to protect the Japanese market against imports. In the negotiations with Thailand, three industries asked for particularly strict rules of origin. The auto industry mirrored some of the US demands during the NAFTA negotiations, reflecting concerns that foreign manufacturers could use Thailand as a base to export to Japan. At the same time, any rule of origin requirement would have to provide for full regional cumulation, allowing parts from other ASEAN countries to be used in vehicles that would be exported to Japan.

The Thai government's position was almost identical to the views expressed by Mexico during the NAFTA talks. On the one hand, it wanted to support its local parts producers, requiring a higher threshold to be imposed in the rule of origin. On the other hand, a restrictive rule would deter investment by non-Japanese companies. Although the question of ROOs for the automobile industry was not settled until the last round of the negotiations, the outcome was more liberal in its effect than NAFTA's rules, with a standard 40 percent requirement – likely because Japanese firms were ultimately less concerned about the penetration of their home market, and because investment by European firms in Thailand was much smaller than in the Mexican case.

The question of rules of origin for the textile industry was much more difficult. The Japanese textile industry differs from its counterparts in the United States and Europe in that it engages directly in significant overseas production. In almost all other developed countries, "sunset industries" such as textiles and apparel are by now split into firms that design and develop at home but procure their clothes from suppliers at arm's length, based in developing countries, and a declining industry of inefficient producers. Examples of the former are H&M in Sweden and

Gap in the United States. The latter holds true for many textile firms in southern US states and producers in Italy that do not own established luxury brands.

In contrast to these firms, the Japanese textile industry has benefited from strong government support for overseas investment, in particular in southeast Asian countries (Solís 2004). In most cases, these operations are directly owned subsidiaries, although in recent years the Japanese fashion brand Uniqlo has adopted the H&M model by sourcing apparel from Chinese-owned suppliers. The interests of these firms aligned with Japanese fabric producers, among them high-tech firms such as Teijin and Toray, which also had substantial investments in the ASEAN countries. In total, seventy Japanese firms operated in Thailand at various stages in the apparel industry and exported 90 percent of their production back to Japan.[28] The overseas production turned the Japanese textile industry into a strong supporter of the EPA, provided it could secure a rule of origin that excluded non-Japanese competitors.

On behalf of these firms and the producers organized in the Japan Textile Industry Federation (Nihon sen-i sangyō renmei), Japanese negotiators asked for a fabric-forward rule (in contrast to the yarn-forward rule in NAFTA). The effect was that the Thai industry was split between fabric producers, who favored the Japanese approach, and the apparel industry, that sourced more than 60 percent of its inputs from other countries. With Thai fabric producers switching sides and joining the rent chain of Japanese firms, the negotiations quickly settled on the Japanese proposal.[29]

In an unusual application of the measure, rules of origin were also used to extend protection for the Japanese fishing industry, which faced direct competition from its Thai counterpart. Japanese negotiators (again from MAFF, only this time from its fisheries bureau) demanded that for tuna to qualify as originating in Thailand, it would have to be caught by vessels that were 100 percent Thai-owned and with a 95 percent Thai crew, and in Thai or Japanese waters. In practice, the last two conditions would have excluded any Thai tuna from Japanese markets. Only during the last round of the negotiations did MAFF offer more flexible rules, although it did not go further than a requirement for the vessels to sail under an ASEAN flag.[30]

---

[28] *Bangkok Post*, May 19, 2005.   [29] *Ibid.*, June 17, 2005.
[30] *The Nation*, August 12, 2005, February 10, 2006.

Luxury vehicles, car parts, and steel

The most dramatic struggle in the negotiations revolved around the automotive industry and its direct suppliers. While the Thai government sought to prevent the reduction of duties on auto parts in order to protect its domestic manufacturers, the Japanese negotiating team was under pressure by Japanese car companies and their Japan-based suppliers, who had already raised very specific demands. Prior to the negotiations, the Japan Business Council for Trade and Investment Facilitation had submitted a policy paper to METI (Hideya 2003) that pointed out the issue of intermediate and capital goods tariffs:

[Regarding electronics parts, ball bearings and rubber products] it is requested that a further cut in tariff rates be undertaken … focusing on those materials that cannot be produced in Thailand. Furthermore, tariffs on cutting tools ought to be reduced rapidly … On auto parts, the duty ranges from 5 to 42 percent, necessitating a significant reduction. (Hideya 2003: 8)

These demands were also conveyed to the Thai government by the Keidanren chairman Okuda, then president of Toyota Motors, who toured the ASEAN countries to muster business support for free trade agreements.[31] Meanwhile, the chairmen of the Japan Automobile Manufacturers Association and the Japan Auto Parts Industrial Association (JAPIA) met with the LDP policy research council chairman Nukaga and the METI minister Nakagawa to emphasize that the liberalization of auto parts and vehicles was the centerpiece of the agreement. If it were necessary to conclude the deal, they hoped that the government would make the right trade-offs and admit more nurses from Thailand to the Japanese labor market, a point to which Nakagawa agreed.[32]

Supplied with these industry requests, METI negotiators pressed their Thai counterparts to offer sweeping tariff reductions on components. The Thai side started out with the completely opposite position of a full exclusion, but quickly moved on to separate the discussions over goods that were not yet produced in Thailand, where they offered a more rapid tariff reduction, and those over parts in which the domestic producers had an interest.

Similar pressure came from Japanese steel firms that supplied the automotive industry. Like the parts producers, Thai steel producers at

[31] *Nihon Keizai Shinbun*, November 1, 2004.
[32] *Nikkan Jidōsha Shinbun*, April 16, 2005; *Kagaku Kōgyō Nippon*, April 27, 2004.

first asked to be completely exempt from any tariff reductions. Thailand's Minister of Commerce, Thanong, attempted to strike a compromise by suggesting a ten-year phase-out for the tariffs, but offered to eliminate immediately tariffs on hot-rolled steel, that was not produced in Thailand at all. The proposal did not satisfy the Japanese negotiating team, and was slammed by the Thai Chamber of Commerce (TCC) and the Federation of Thai Industries (FTI). The secretary-general of the FTI's steel division, Pibulsak Athabavornpisan, warned at a press conference that more than 100,000 jobs could be at risk if the market were swamped with Japanese imports, considering that already close to 40 percent of the steel products used in the Thai auto industry originated there. The chief of JETRO's Bangkok office countered that the tariffs were counterproductive because they only served to deter investment in the auto industry.[33]

Behind the issue of steel tariff liberalization stood the politically well-connected Sahaviriya Group, the oldest steel producer in Thailand. After reemerging from bankruptcy after the Asian financial crisis, the company had just received generous tax credits for a new plant that would make it the only Thai producer of hot-rolled steel. Without the rents generated by the protected steel production to subsidize the new investment, the company saw it as not viable. The FTI's steel division emphasized the case as evidence that Thai producers would be unable to upgrade their technology unless some protection was sustained.[34]

Both issues were linked by Thai negotiators to the central Japanese demand for the elimination of the luxury vehicle duty of 80 percent, levied on cars with an engine displacement of more than 3 liters. The primary beneficiary of this measure would have been Toyota's luxury brand Lexus and Nissan's high-end models. If prices were to be reduced substantially, from 5 million to 3 million baht (or from US$126,000 to $76,000), most of the gains in the market would have come at the expense of European and US manufacturers.

Faced with clear and present danger to their sales in Thailand, European manufacturers went on the offensive. After receiving alarming messages before his departure on a tour of the ASEAN countries, the EU trade commissioner, Peter Mandelson, called in front of Thai journalists for caution in the Japan–Thailand negotiations and warned that the operations of EU automakers in Thailand could be undermined if

---

[33] *The Nation*, March 22, March 31, April 5, 2005.   [34] *Ibid.*, April 22, 2005.

the luxury tax was abolished. The presidents of the Thai subsidiaries
or importers of General Motors, DaimlerChrysler, Land Rover,
BMW, Volvo, Ford, Jaguar, and Audi sent letters to the Deputy Prime
Minister Somkid, Foreign Minister Kantathi, Industry Minister Watana,
Commerce Minister Thanong, and Deputy Permanent Secretary Pisan
of the Foreign Ministry, who was heading the Thai delegation in the
talks with Japan. The letters stated that future investments by these
companies would be in question if the protective tariffs were to be
eliminated for Japanese imports only. Ford vice president Bieguhn predicted a severe imbalance in vehicle trade between Japan and Thailand.
Finally, in July 2005, the German ambassador to Thailand sent a letter
to Thaksin asking him to keep the interests of non-Japanese manufacturers in Thailand in mind when negotiating with the Japanese side.[35] For
the final deal it proved to be crucial that the European and US manufacturers found allies in the Thai Auto-Parts Manufacturers Association
(TAPMA).

Tying the knot

The final phase of the negotiations saw intense lobbying by automotive
firms and parts producers, as well as a more heated tone in the domestic
discussion in Thailand. Thaksin briefly intervened again in the negotiations, to propose a deal of steel for agriculture, to the consternation of
the negotiators, who felt that they had explored these possibilities to
their limits.[36] His alleged readiness to make concessions was sharply
criticized by the Senate Committee on Foreign Relations, which called
on labor unions and local business to ally to prevent Thaksin from
"selling off a slice of the country." When asked about his views on the
Senate report during a press conference before meeting METI minister
Nakagawa, Thaksin retorted that he would not support companies
trying to maintain "the status quo as cartel businesses ... calling for
help from the government when they collapse into non-performing
loans."[37]

JAMA sent a detailed letter to Somkid in which it outlined the way in
which the investment plans of Japanese firms would ensure that

---

[35] *Ibid.*, July 30, 2005.
[36] *Ibid.*, May 25, 2005; interview with MOFA official, Tokyo, December 2005.
[37] *Bangkok Post*, May 11, 2005.

Thailand would benefit greatly, and that tariff reductions were crucial for these aims to be fulfilled.[38] The breakthrough occurred on August 3, 2005. METI negotiators realized that the resistance of the united front of the TAPMA and the non-Japanese vehicle producers was unlikely to fall apart. To close the deal, they settled for a gradual phasing-out of tariffs on car parts by 2013 and a stepwise reduction of the luxury car duty by 5 percent a year until 2010, with subsequent renegotiation. Imports of small cars would not be liberalized at all. TAPMA also managed to retain restrictions on investment in parts producers that would have to remain majority-owned by Thai nationals if they produced parts for locally sold vehicles. European manufacturers expressed their satisfaction with a deal that exposed them to little competition, since their vehicles were assembled locally, although still subject to an excise tax of 40 percent.[39]

Why did non-Japanese producers gain so much influence despite the barrage of Japanese demands and lobbying? The outcome is surprising when one considers that Japanese manufacturing firms provided three times as much direct employment as the combined total of German and US firms in Thailand – 340,000 compared with 93,000.[40] In the absence of investment by non-Japanese producers, Thai producers might have resisted, but it is unlikely that they would have obtained the same concessions, especially considering the promise of more FDI from Japan. Still, the presence of non-Japanese firms changed this situation.

The most important factor was the threat by European and US firms to revise their plans for future investment. In addition, the European and US makers procured a greater share of components from Thai-owned or at least Thai-managed suppliers, especially those not affiliated with Japanese companies.[41] Although Japanese firms sourced between 50 and 80 percent in Thailand, most of the parts came from Japanese-owned firms. Moreover, Japanese firms produced the highest value added components. Wholly Thai-owned firms provided only 1 percent of inputs on a value basis (Lecler 2002: 809). In an evaluation after the talks had been concluded, the TAPMA honorary president Pramot stated that it did not make sense to invite in European manufacturers

---

[38] *Nikkei Sangyō Shinbun*, June 17, 2005.   [39] *The Nation*, August 4, 2005.
[40] OECD Statistics on Measuring Globalisation, Online Database – The Role of Multinationals in OECD Economies: Manufacturing, ISIC Rev. 3, 2007 edn.
[41] *Bangkok Post*, July 21, 2006.

and then open the market for Japanese exporters.[42] However, even if the luxury vehicle tax was only slowly phased out, Japanese manufacturers obtained the more important concession of liberalization of duties on parts, which allowed them to continue with the vertical specialization of their operations. Mass-market, small-engined vehicles and low-technology components would be exported from Thailand back to Japan, while high-end vehicles would slowly enjoy better access to the Thai market. Ultimately, this proved to be more important to the deal than the relatively small Thai market for luxury vehicles.

In the steel industry, Thailand conceded a generous tariff-rate quota for hot-rolled steel, but only in exchange for a commitment to explore technical cooperation and a possible investment in Sahaviriya Group, giving the Thai firm a better chance to upgrade its technology to produce higher value added products. With only technical details of some rules of origin outstanding, it seemed that the deal could be signed by both prime ministers within a few months.

Post-negotiation troubles

The first obstacle to the signing arose when Koizumi called a snap election to the Japanese Diet to overcome the resistance of members of his own party to postal privatization, delaying by several months any parliamentary discussion of the agreement. Meanwhile, the Thaksin government slid into political troubles that would end only with its forced removal in September 2006. In January 2006, a political scandal exploded when the Singaporean state-run holding company Temasek acquired Shin Corporation, the telecommunications conglomerate officially owned by Thaksin's wife and children, for a record US$1.88 billion. By exploiting a provision that exempted individuals, the transaction took place without the payment of a single baht in capital gains tax. Facing a public uproar, Thaksin dissolved parliament and scheduled elections for April 2006, won by his Thai Rak Thai party by a landslide because of a boycott by the major opposition parties. Immediately after the election Thaksin announced that he would only act as a caretaker prime minister until the assembly elected his successor. The crisis culminated in the coup d'état of September 19, 2006, and Thaksin's removal from office.

[42] *Ibid.*

Neither the Japanese government nor Thai domestic interest groups in favor of the agreement minded that a military-installed government would ratify the agreement. The Thai government reassured the Japanese side that since the text of the EPA had been finalized, there would be no problem in putting it to a vote in the new (selected rather than elected) national assembly. However, perhaps to shore up its legitimacy and to signify that the Thaksin government's policies would be scrutinized, the government allowed the civil society movement FTA Watch to analyze the text prior to a public hearing. The non-governmental organization noted with alarm that among many concessions the previous government had agreed to reduce tariffs on certain toxic wastes. Fearing a reopening of the talks, the Japanese government immediately agreed to add a one-page annex to the agreement reaffirming both countries' commitment to the Convention on the Control of Transboundary Movements of Hazardous Wastes. With the promise of the inclusion of this rider, the cabinet approved the PTA and obtained majority support on February 16, 2007. The agreement was finally signed on April 3, 2007.[43]

The Japan–Malaysia EPA

Before the negotiations between Malaysia and Japan, it would not have been unreasonable to expect the talks to be as contentious as the Japan–Thailand EPA. Notwithstanding prime minister Mahathir Mohamed's often professed admiration for Japan, the Malaysian government had openly criticized the attempts by neighboring Thailand and Singapore to seek individual bilateral trade agreements with partners outside ASEAN. In part, this reflected worries about the cohesion of the association, but these trade deals also ran counter to Mahathir's vision of an east Asian grouping that excluded the United States (Athukorala 2005: 32). In key aspects Malaysia's trade policy resembled that of Thailand, from the luxury vehicle tax to tariffs on car parts and steel products, the latter only raised to bound levels in 2002, in some instances reaching 50 percent (Suzuki 2003: 291). Yet despite these factors, the negotiations proceeded much more smoothly than those between Thailand and Japan.

---

[43] *Ibid.*, February 16, 2007; *The Nation*, February 22, 2007; Thai News Service, April 4, 2007.

Several factors facilitated reaching an agreement. Japan remained Malaysia's most important market and source of foreign direct investment both before and after the Asian financial crisis. If any immediate neighbors were to gain preferential access, it was likely to affect Malaysia's ability to attract foreign direct investment and to export at competitive prices, and would only have exacerbated the difficulties of competing with China. In addition, Mahathir retired in 2003 after twenty-two years as prime minister, allowing the government to pursue preferential agreements without the baggage of earlier commitments. However, even without Mahathir Malaysia remained a much less democratic state than Thailand. Politics remains dominated by the Barisan Nasional coalition and its strongest component, the United Malays National Organization (UMNO). The Malaysian government had fewer problems with expressions of domestic dissent, and could rely on a docile, self-censoring press.[44] Most importantly, Malaysia did not seek better market access for goods that would have run into the opposition of MAFF and its domestic constituents.

The negotiations took place at the same time as the talks with Thailand, starting in January 2004 and ending with their successful conclusion in May 2005. One of the earliest signals that an agreement would be feasible was that the report of the joint study group on the prospects of the PTA had identified very few areas of genuine disagreement. The only sensitive export good was plywood. The Japanese side mentioned the decline in the forestry industry in Japan, but also cited concerns about unsustainable logging practices in Malaysia as a reason for why exports of plywood would have to be limited, although the argument was not extended to timber or other wood products.

Using the report as a base, the negotiating teams agreed to remove rice, wheat, several dairy products, beef, and pork from the current agreement, instead scheduling them for renegotiation. Japan offered tariff-free status for tropical fruits, prawns, jellyfish,[45] reduced the tariff on margarine (made from palm oil), and finally added a quota for bananas. Both countries also committed themselves to preventing illegal

---

[44] For the same reason, the account of the negotiations presented here relies primarily on interviews with Japanese policymakers and press sources.

[45] See Hsieh *et al.* (2001) for a proposal to introduce jellyfish to the Western palate as a low-cost, low-calorie food product.

logging.[46] This left manufacturing tariffs as the central item on the agenda.

In terms of bilateral trade and investment, the most important industry was electronics. Much of Malaysia's quick economic rebound after the Asian financial crisis was fueled by exports of a variety of consumer electronics. It was also one of the least contentious issues in the negotiations. The Malaysian government unilaterally announced in April 2004 that it would allow 100 percent foreign ownership in the industry. Here, the Malaysian government also had very little room for maneuver, should it have wanted to restrict imports of certain parts, because of the competitive pressure created by the Chinese electronics industry, that attracted a growing proportion of global FDI in the electronics industry, largely at the expense of ASEAN countries (Xing and Wan 2006).

With agriculture and labor mobility presenting no obstacles, the negotiations could mostly be handled by the METI minister Nakagawa and his counterpart Rafidah Aziz of the Malaysian MITI. The two struck the final deal on May 22, 2005. Malaysia would continue to protect its domestic car industry until 2015, but would liberalize import tariffs for bigger cars with an engine displacement of over 2 liters that did not compete with Proton and Perodua. Steel tariffs were scheduled for elimination over a ten-year period. Malaysia also retained exceptions to national treatment for the steel industry, but offered a gradual liberalization of import tariffs. Strikingly, the government also liberalized car parts imports, with reductions to 0–5 percent by 2008 and complete free trade by 2010, equivalent to the commitments made vis-à-vis its ASEAN partners. Although the Malaysian supply firms (referred to as "vendors") objected to this, they almost exclusively sold to the still-protected domestic manufacturers, and were in any case much smaller in number than in Thailand – fewer than 300 compared with over 1,000 in 2002 (Lecler 2002: 802). Having to weigh the interests of suppliers against those of Proton and Perodua, which needed access to advanced components in order to upgrade their models, the government decided to favor the vehicle manufacturers, a principled extension of Malaysia's pre-EPA "cascading" tariff structure that taxed finished goods much higher than inputs (Athukorala 2005: 24). This also

[46] See Dauvergne (1997) for the role of Japanese companies in the degradation of the southeast Asian rain forest.

coincided with the interests of Daihatsu and indirectly Toyota, as a minority shareholder in Perodua. The final deal was signed in December 2005, making it Japan's third preferential trade agreement, after Singapore and Mexico.

Overall, the improvement in bilateral access for trade and investment was minimal beyond the 86 percent tariff-free access to Japanese markets that Malaysia had enjoyed previously. Neither investment nor services were liberalized beyond GATS commitments. Why did Japanese auto and steel producers accept this relatively weak deal? Although the Japanese steel industry lobbied through the Japanese Chamber of Commerce and Industry in Malaysia,[47] the stakes were clearly not as high as in the agreement with Thailand. Most importantly, however, the agreement offered the chance to lock in existing benefits. One METI official conceded that he had not seen much chance for a liberalization of the protected automobile sector anyway, given the direct ties of the two Malaysian firms to high-ranking politicians.[48] Since Japan imposed no tariffs on electronics, the interests of both parties fully converged: foreign-owned firms used the developing country as an export platform.

Outcomes – in the region and beyond

Despite historical, cultural, and institutional differences between Latin America and southeast Asia, countries in both regions have reacted to severe financial crises in similar ways. Trying to avoid short-term debt and portfolio capital, Thailand and Malaysia have both chosen preferential trade agreements in order to attract more foreign direct investment. The emergence of China as a competitor for manufacturing investment has only strengthened this trend. Yet the Asian financial crisis also laid the foundations for a second Asian export miracle by forcing countries to let go of pegs to the dollar, maintained to prop up domestic financial institutions. The rapid depreciation of the baht brought about a contraction of demand, but at the same time made Thai exports highly competitive. The ringgit did not fall as much because of the renewed peg, but the depreciation was enough to reduce the export prices of Malaysian-made electronics by 30 percent.

---

[47] *Nikkan Sangyō Shinbun*, October 28, 2004.
[48] Interview, Tokyo, December 2005.

Table 7.3. *Predictions versus actual lobbying coalitions, Thailand and Malaysia*

	Japan–Thailand		Japan–Malaysia	
	Japan	Thailand	Japan	Malaysia
For	Japanese automobile firms		Japanese automobile firms	
	Textiles and fabric producers		Japanese electronics firms	
	Services		*Services*	
	Auto parts and steel	*Auto parts and steel*	Auto parts and steel	
		Agriculture		Agriculture
Against	Leathermaking			Domestic auto makers
	Fisheries			
	Agriculture		Agriculture	

Italics denote predictions that are not met.

These forces affected Thailand more than Malaysia, but Thailand's choices in turn motivated its neighbor to negotiate preferential agreements. Malaysia's electronics industry also experienced a boom, but its domestically oriented and heavily protected auto industry, with limited foreign participation, did not enjoy the same success. Consequently, the industry remained opposed to liberalization in the Japan–Malaysia PTA.

For Japanese firms the crisis was therefore an opportunity as much as a problem. In particular with regard to the Thai automotive industry, these firms reoriented production from regional sales to exports to the home market. For the strategic decision, the currency effect was more important than the need to achieve greater economies of scale. Table 7.3 shows the coalitions in home and host country in both cases. Industries that did not lobby are not represented.[49] The predictions for an offensive PTA are borne out, with two notable exceptions. Services played no role at all, since Japanese firms did not lobby and the Thai and

---

[49] I could not obtain any information about the views of labor in Malaysia, so no position is shown in the table.

Malaysian governments avoided any commitments to opening the sector. More importantly, Thai parts manufacturers and steel producers slowed down the liberalization, while Malaysia's domestic auto industry managed to slow down tariff reductions. The latter is easily explained by the fact that Proton and Perodua are import-competing-, import-substitution-era firms that have not managed to achieve export success. The position of Thai parts suppliers and steel producers is similar to that of the Mexican industry, except that the position of the Thai manufacturers was greatly strengthened by forming a coalition with European and US manufacturers who were more important buyers than their Japanese competitors.

When multinational firms lobbied to use the country as an export platform, as in the case of the auto and textile industries in Thailand, the suppliers of these firms acted as rent chains, as evident in the support of the Japanese steel and auto parts industry and Japanese fabric producers. Their lobbying for specific rules of origin also served to split the industry in Thailand, and directly reflected their links to other companies beyond the preferential agreement. Japanese firms only sought very strict rules of origin in extremely protectionist sectors such as fisheries and textiles. It is possible that the plans of Japanese automotive firms to integrate their operations across ASEAN also forestalled any interest in ROOs as strict as those in NAFTA. Unlike in the EU–Mexico FTA, no categorization of the different manufacturers as firms that produced overseas and those that only exported became apparent in the negotiations with Thailand, possibly because all firms were committed to local production, and because their investments broadly corresponded to their relative size in Japan and commensurate political influence. In the PTA with Malaysia, a split between Toyota as producer and the other Japanese firms as exporters could have been expected, but did not become evident. A likely explanation is that in contrast to Mexico, Malaysia did not give a privileged quota for high-end models from firms that also produced in the country, but discriminated equally against all foreign firms. Accordingly, all Japanese firms had similar interests in tariff reductions for luxury vehicles.

Overall, Japan made minuscule concessions in the Japan–Thailand EPA on import barriers for agricultural products, and none for the goods in which Thailand was a competitive exporter. If the Japan–Thailand EPA had been aimed at supplanting the slow liberalization at the multilateral level, then we would have seen greater trade-offs between agricultural market access in Japan and tariffs on industrial products and market opening in services in Thailand. The actual outcome was much more one-sided. The quota enlargement for the import of sugar molasses and prawns did not endanger Japanese producers at home. Only the reduction of the tariff on chicken represented a concession, although Japan effectively limited exports by requesting a certification of Thai factories because of concerns regarding bird flu. In addition to the particular obstinacy of Japan's MAFF and its agricultural constituency, it again becomes clear that the convergence of interests of North and South on foreign direct investment does not create opportunities for trade-offs that would lead to tariff reductions on inter-industry trade. The Japan–Malaysia EPA granted even less additional market access, but Malaysia also had fewer agricultural export interests. Nevertheless, for Thailand and Malaysia the agreements appear to have paid off in terms of foreign direct investment. While the data available at the time of writing do not yet permit a detailed quantitative analysis, the trend is suggestive: FDI flows to Thailand and Malaysia grew 30 percent year-on-year in 2006 according to OECD statistics. Project applications and approvals in Malaysia during the first six months of 2007 increased eightfold over the previous year.[50]

If the agreements with Thailand and Malaysia are cases of offensive agreements, this time pursued by Japan, then we would expect reactions from direct competitors: the EU, the United States, and eventually South Korea. Obviously, the most direct reaction occurred when the non-Japanese vehicle manufacturers in Thailand allied with Thai parts producers. Both groups would have been import-competing, in line with hypothesis 3. However, the reactions following the actual conclusion of the PTAs suggest that foreign manufacturers appeared dissatisfied with merely slowing down the tariff reductions for their Japanese competitors. The United States had already been pursuing preferential trade agreements with both southeast Asian countries at the same time as Japan. These agreements, however, will be much more difficult to conclude, since central US interests lie in the liberalization of services (Sally 2007: 19–24). The EU reacted by promoting a countermove to these efforts. In its 2006 document "Global Europe: Competing in the World," the Commission pointed out that, while the WTO

[50] Jiji Press English News Service, May 21, 2007.

negotiations were stalled, "several of our main trading partners and priority targets have been negotiating FTAs with our competitors (e.g. ASEAN members with Japan or Korea with the United States). The EU would be putting itself at a disadvantage if we did not seek to improve investment conditions in our bilateral negotiations" (Commission of the European Communities 2006: 14). Once preferential trade agreements begin to supplant multilateralism, competitive pressures force more and more countries to negotiate North–South PTAs.

8 | Conclusions and implications

T RADE liberalization is a powerful force for increasing the wealth of nations. As an avenue to development, the reintegration of developing countries into the global economy heralds profound changes in North–South relations. The increasing popularity of North–South PTAs, a crucial dimension of this reintegration, is one of the most striking developments in the international trade regime since the end of the Cold War. This study began by asking why these agreements have proliferated so rapidly since the early 1990s.

Most existing explanations tend to lump all preferential trade agreements into the same category. Moreover, much of the public discourse about PTAs focuses on the opening of markets. Yet for developed economies preferential trade agreements with developing countries offer only limited opportunities for exports. What is more, these PTAs often exclude significant shares of trade from liberalization or delay the reduction of tariffs for long periods, precisely in those areas where the participating countries are the most competitive. Other studies argue that the proliferation of North–South PTAs resembles a beauty contest, in which developing countries with the most liberal trade policies are rewarded with access to developed country markets. But these explanations offer little account of the interests of rich countries in signing on to these deals.

Finally, many scholars and practitioners claim that deadlock in the WTO has created the impetus to pursue PTAs. While stalling multilateral negotiations have surely convinced countries of the need to find alternative venues, this explanation can only be a partial account. Most of the PTAs analyzed in this study were well under way before the Doha round ran aground, but were negotiated after the GATT had been elevated to the status of a full-blown international organization with the conclusion of the Uruguay Round. Considering the timing of many North–South PTAs, the slow progress of the WTO appears to be either a contributing factor or, at times, even a post hoc justification for a strategy previously decided upon. Once PTAs begin to proliferate, the slowing of WTO rounds may become a self-fulfilling prophecy, as countries hold on to their MFN barriers as bargaining chips for PTA negotiations.

Moreover, a focus on system-level effects cannot explain the particular pattern or the characteristic features of North–South PTAs. Why do major economic powers choose at times small, distant countries as partners? Why do different developed countries in succession sign PTAs with the same developing country? Why do they often incorporate very restrictive rules to define the origin of goods, when they are supposed to liberalize trade? Why do they tend to phase out the tariffs for certain goods quickly, while others, including many finished goods and agricultural products, remain excluded?

To answer these questions, this study has argued that North–South PTAs are driven by foreign direct investment and its attendant trade, rather than by the search for export markets. This holds in manufacturing, where developing countries capture a growing share of global production, as in services, where foreign direct investment or a "commercial presence," in GATS parlance, is often required. The principal actors in the negotiations of these agreements are multinational firms that undertake direct investment, their home governments, representing their interests in negotiations, and developing country governments seeking to attract FDI, at times in the face of domestic resistance. The main conclusion of this work is that North–South PTAs are driven by three different dynamics.

First, PTAs facilitate the integration of production between developed and developing countries. Increasingly, trade in manufactured goods between developed and developing countries is vertically differentiated trade in the same industry. Mass-market goods are produced in developing countries and exported, while high-end products are designed and manufactured in developed countries, consumed at home, and shipped abroad to developing countries, in smaller quantities but with higher values. For firms engaged in this kind of trade and investment, PTAs reduce tariffs on the goods they want to ship back and forth. Yet such targeted liberalization comes with the price of considerable protectionism. The fact that developing countries have lower wage levels implies that multinational firms from third countries can likewise invest there and export to the market of the developed country. To raise the costs for these outsiders, North–South PTAs therefore require strict rules of origin.

Second, in the service sector PTAs function as investment liberalization agreements. In many service industries, market structures create
first-mover advantages. At times these advantages are reinforced by the
regulatory practices of host governments, which limit market access to a
few firms. At the behest of service sector firms, home country governments use PTAs to secure such first-mover advantages.

Third, bilateral agreements between developed and developing countries create an endogenous dynamic. Frequently, multinational firms
cannot afford to eschew desirable export platforms and promising
service sector markets, especially if their competitors invest there. If,
by means of a PTA, these competitors gain preferential access to such
countries, then firms have to respond. They therefore press their own
governments to sign defensive agreements. Developing countries will
have to seek PTAs in order to remain attractive for foreign investors.
This endogenous dynamic is a key force of the explosive growth in
North–South PTAs.

These three benefits, this study has argued, drive the recent proliferation of North–South PTAs. This chapter summarizes the most important findings and discusses some implications. Table 8.1 provides an
overview of the findings discussed in the next three sections.

Findings: offensive agreements

The North American Free Trade Agreement was the cumulation of the
efforts of successive Mexican governments to liberalize Mexico's economy and attract more foreign direct investment. In reaction to these
policies, US manufacturing firms began to move production south of the
border, where they benefited from lower labor costs than at home. The
free trade agreement between Mexico and its northern partners facilitated the relocation of production by reducing tariffs on the goods
shipped back and forth, and by locking the Mexican government into
a commitment to sustain an open trade and investment regime. But
without discriminatory measures, NAFTA would have given the same
opportunity to firms from Europe and Japan. Drawn to Mexico because
of its economic reforms, low wages, and proximity to the US market,
these firms had made significant investments that turned the country
into a platform for exports to the north.

The case of the NAFTA negotiations has shown that rules of origin
assume prominence in North–South PTAs. US manufacturing firms

Table 8.1. *Overview of empirical findings*

Hypothesis	NAFTA	EU–Mexico	Japan–Mexico
1a: Rules of origin	Auto firms demand stricter ROOs than electronics		
1b: Intermediate goods	Parts producers from US and Mexico call for strict rules	Parts producers from EU call for strict rules	
1c: MFN rebates	Maquiladoras phased out		
2a: First-mover advantages in services	Banks lobby in favor	Banks lobby in favor	
2b: Services and standards		Commission asks for neutrality in standards	
3: Import-competing	Opposed	Opposed	Opposed
4: Defensive	NA	Volkswagen, suppliers call for defensive PTA	Electronics firms, Nissan, suppliers call for defensive PTA
Alternative hypothesis: exports rather than FDI	Auto firms with FDI dominate	Auto firms with FDI dominate, exporters are less successful	Auto, electronics firms dominate talks, exporters are less successful

Table 8.1. (*cont.*)

Hypothesis	NAFTA	EU–Mexico	Japan–Mexico	
	EU–Chile	US–Chile	Japan–Thailand	Japan–Malaysia
1a: Rules of origin	*No manufacturing interests in Chile*	*No manufacturing interests in Chile*	Textile firms demand strict rules of origin, but more flexible than in NAFTA	
1b: Intermediate goods			Japanese suppliers in favor	Japanese suppliers in favor
1c: MFN rebates				
2a: First-mover advantages in services	Banks, telecoms, energy, other services	Banks, telecoms, energy, other services	*No services interests in Thailand*	*No services interests in Malaysia*
2b: Services and standards	Telecoms firms call for technology neutrality	Services lobbyists cite standards issue in hearings		
3: Import-competing	Opposed	Opposed	Opposed	Opposed
4: Defensive		Financial services, telecoms call for defensive PTA	European automakers call for defensive PTA	
Alternative hypothesis: exports rather than FDI		Auto firms with FDI dominate, including EU and US firms	Electronics firms with FDI dominate	

Italics denote predictions that are not met.

lobbied strongly for restrictive rules of origin if they had production facilities in Mexico, or if they were part of the North American rent chain of US multinationals. For many US firms, NAFTA was not a precondition for the continental integration of their operations. Rather, the agreement allowed them to go the last mile by using Mexico as an export platform for the home market, while raising the costs for European and Japanese competitors.

Most prominent among the supporters of NAFTA was the automotive industry. Automobiles and auto parts made up the biggest share of US firms' exports back to the home market. The operations of US automotive firms are textbook examples of vertical integration: high-volume, low-margin parts and entry-level cars are produced in Mexico, while the capital-intensive development and production of luxury cars remain in the United States. Such investment created relatively high-paying jobs in Mexico, assuring US auto firms' influence on both sides of the negotiating table beyond what finished goods exporters from the United States and Mexico could hope to attain.

The degree of restrictiveness of the rules of origin that firms demanded depended on their supply networks. In line with hypothesis 1a, firms that sourced globally rather than regionally, for example in the US computer industry, favored an open regime. By contrast, automotive firms used primarily North American components and pressed for strict rules of origin. Since these rules extended protection up the production rent chain, their suppliers supported these demands, as predicted in hypothesis 1b. Even among automotive firms differences emerged, depending on the degree of regional sourcing, with GM demanding less restrictive rules because of a higher foreign content in some of its operations. Unsurprisingly, import-competing firms in the United States as well as labor demanded the strictest rules of origin in addition to putting up broader resistance to NAFTA, matching the prediction of hypothesis 3. For these actors, however, any liberalization would have been problematic, whether bilateral or multilateral.

In determining its position regarding these rules of origin, the Mexican government was sandwiched between two competing goals. On the one hand, stricter rules of origin would act as a deterrent to outside investment that would have used Mexico as a beachhead. While the Mexican government sought this investment, the US side wanted to exclude it as much as possible. On the other hand, Mexican domestic suppliers would benefit from strict rules of origin because they would induce a switch towards intermediate goods from within NAFTA. In the end, the latter position prevailed, as the positions of the US automotive firms and Mexican parts producers converged. Furthermore, this outcome may have contributed to Mexico's raising of MFN barriers after NAFTA came into force.

By themselves, rules of origin are already an administrative burden on firms, but they exert their full force when they interact with host country tariffs. Accordingly, US firms sought to prevent Mexico from rebating its most-favored-nation tariffs for firms from non-NAFTA countries, offering support for hypothesis 1c: the maquiladora system of export-processing zones had to be phased out. NAFTA enabled US firms to produce anywhere in Mexico with the same benefits created by the maquiladoras, while severely restricting the ability of non-NAFTA firms to do so.

In addition to multinational manufacturing firms that integrate their production vertically, service-sector firms become key supporters of North–South PTAs. Many of these firms follow manufacturing firms and offer services such as export financing. Others hope to serve the partner country's market through a commercial presence that puts them close to their consumers. The case study of NAFTA showed that, in particular, banks and insurance companies from the southern United States, sectors with considerable economies of scale, supported the agreement as a business opportunity as predicted by hypothesis 2a. Other US financial services firms used the agreement to gain access to a new market. The weakly capitalized Mexican banks were attractive takeover targets, allowing US banks to acquire a retail branch network at a low cost.

For these service-sector firms, a bilateral agreement was an opportunity for expansion. However, while US service firms did not yet cite the potential benefits of preferential liberalization as motivation as they did in the case of the United States–Chile PTA, NAFTA did create first-mover advantages for US firms. Mexico negotiated the opening of important service industries under NAFTA and subsequently adapted its domestic regulation in many aspects, but only granted non-NAFTA firms similar conditions after a delay of several years, as predicted by hypothesis 2c. The case provides very limited evidence for hypothesis 2b. US firms did not explicitly press for standards and regulations that would have favored their own investment over competitors, but as first-movers, their standards would by default become templates for Mexico's future regulation.

Findings: defensive agreements

If developing countries attract beachhead FDI after they sign a first PTA with a developed country, then non-member firms that invest have a strong incentive to lobby for tariff reductions. Lower tariffs take away much of the force of strict rules of origin because, even if the required regional content quota is not met, only reduced host country and low developed country tariffs have to be paid. Non-member firms thus primarily look for parity with the firms of the first partner. In a slow, piecemeal fashion, offensive and defensive PTAs will therefore whittle away the remaining tariff barriers of the developing country – although only for those goods of interest to these firms. Service liberalization as part of a PTA levels the playing field by lifting restrictions on foreign participation and limiting the regulatory competence of host states. This study has evaluated these arguments in two case studies of defensive agreements. The reactions to NAFTA, an agreement laden with discriminatory clauses against outsiders, provided the starting point.

Following NAFTA's entry into force, direct investment by European firms in Mexico began to grow rapidly, creating a strong incentive for these companies to support an EU–Mexico PTA. Volkswagen was the most important individual firm to lobby for a defensive agreement. The company's position resulted from a strategic shift from domestic market orientation towards the use of Mexico as an export platform. In adopting this strategy, Volkswagen was trailing the US auto firms by several years. Once the decision was made, however, the company's operation would have a faced an increased tariff burden because of NAFTA: firms from third countries that wanted to use Mexico as beachhead were the direct targets of rules of origin and bans on MFN rebates. Although VW did not own maquiladoras due to its domestic market orientation, it used related schemes to obtain duty rebates, soon to be phased out under NAFTA, and was particularly hurt by the combination of restrictive rules of origin and Mexican MFN tariffs. Since newer automobile models produced for the US and Canadian markets used higher non-NAFTA content, the differential phase-in of rules of origin requirements for incumbent firms did not benefit Volkswagen as much as the US Big Three automakers.

Volkswagen therefore supported an EU–Mexico PTA to lower the costs NAFTA imposed on its operations, as predicted in hypothesis 4. The company mobilized its rent chain of suppliers, many of which had followed its main customer and invested in Mexico, to support a bilateral trade agreement. Just as in the case of NAFTA, the interests of home and host governments converged on FDI. Given the prospect of increased investment by Volkswagen in Mexico in order to export cars to the United States and back to European markets, the Mexican government responded positively to these initiatives, in particular when supported by the Mexican car parts manufacturers. The contrast to the liberalization of finished goods is striking: manufacturers that sought market access for exports from Europe fared badly in the negotiations, obtaining only a slow expansion of quotas over several years.

At the outset of the talks between the EU and Mexico, the European services industry, especially Spanish banks, pushed strongly for liberalization of the Mexican investment environment to achieve parity with the United States and Canada. NAFTA only allowed access to the Mexican market for banks that were incorporated in one of the partner countries. These restrictions were lifted unilaterally by the Mexican government during the first phase of talks with the EU prior to the actual negotiations. European services firms therefore focused on locking in these commitments and remained supportive of the agreement until its successful conclusion.

Reflecting both smaller investment interests and greater domestic resistance, the Japanese defensive agreement came much later than in the case of the EU, confirming the expectations of hypotheses 3 and 4. Abolition of the maquiladora system was bound to affect Japanese firms in the electronics industry the most. These firms used Mexico as a back door for the US market, producing television sets and other consumer electronics goods in customs-bond factories. Once the Mexican government was barred from rebating its MFN tariff for the parts imports of these firms, they had to pay 15 to 30 percent import duty. Notably, Japanese firms exhausted all other means to avoid the impact of NAFTA on their Mexican operations, unsuccessfully lobbying the Mexican government to grant tariff reductions. These efforts contrast with Nissan's relative indifference to NAFTA in its early years. After the merger with Renault, however, the company followed in Volkswagen's footsteps and used Mexico as a production site to supply the US market. Just as in the case of Volkswagen, the sequence of decisions supports the hypotheses put forth in this study. Firms that established beachheads in a PTA lobbied for defensive agreements, with those firms most affected by rules of origin and bans on tariff rebates reacting the fastest.

Because of Japan's protected and inefficient agricultural sector, the negotiations with Mexico nearly ended in a stand-off between MAFF and its rural constituents on one side and Mexican exporters on the other. After a struggle over pork (literally and figuratively) and oranges, the negotiations could only be brought to a conclusion by excluding from tariff reductions products that Mexico produces efficiently.

In both negotiations, the Mexican government sought to offer its domestic steel producers and auto parts manufacturers some protection, a measure that Japan and the EU tried to resist. Both agreements therefore featured longer phase-out periods for these products. But, for the most part, the interests of multinational firms such as Volkswagen and Nissan, the Japanese electronics producers, and their suppliers dominated the talks because their interests were represented on both sides of the table.

Neither the EU nor Japan would have accorded a PTA with Mexico such high priority in the absence of the discriminatory effect of NAFTA on their investment. The EU first rejected a Mexican offer, then wavered for several years in its commitment to a bilateral initiative. Japan had to overcome ideological and material resistance in the domestic arena before it could sign any preferential trade agreements at all. Weaker investment links suffice to trigger defensive agreements, and competitive pressures can motivate PTAs that would otherwise not have been feasible.

Findings: comparative cases

NAFTA, the EU–Mexico association agreement and the Japan–Mexico FTA are the closest to the ideal types of offensive and defensive agreements. In other instances, cases will have elements of both, because governments are increasingly aware of the discriminatory effects of PTAs, and because firms and other interest groups have organized their lobbying activities better. This was particularly the case for "newcomers" to preferential trade negotiations such as Japan. The case studies compared two negotiations with the same partner country.

Chile's PTAs with the United States and the EU

The case study of the Chilean PTAs contrasted the negotiating aims of the European Union and the United States. For the EU, the deal with

Chile was primarily an offensive agreement that locked in the gains already made by European firms. For the United States, the negotiations had offensive and defensive elements.

Both agreements focused almost exclusively on the services sector, reflecting the interest of foreign investors in telecommunications, electricity, and banking. Manufacturing firms played only a minor role as part of the rent chain of service firms. The key players in these industries were a handful of firms mostly from Spain and the United States. In the competition between these firms, first-mover advantages emerged most clearly when the government granted European service firms concessions that allowed them to establish commanding positions in the market, as predicted in hypothesis 2a. For US firms, the negotiations over a trade agreement leveled the playing field to restore access. While European firms did not seek further liberalization because they did not want to invite competition, US firms made demands that reflected their relative position. For example, they demanded access to the Chilean market via cross-border supply in financial services when investment would have been costly because European firms had the greater share of the market, or requested technology neutrality to avoid favoring firms that use competing standards.

Although Chile originally wanted to join NAFTA, the domestic political situation in the United States prevented the deal from going forward. The European Commission had an easier time obtaining a negotiating mandate, although it also witnessed attempts by France to block the initiation of talks. Only after the EU had begun to negotiate with Chile in earnest did US firms lobby strongly for a deal. Concerns about the loss of competitiveness vis-à-vis European firms played a central role. While lobbyists had earlier stressed that the advantages of NAFTA accession would be limited to member country firms, they later emphasized that US firms needed a PTA to regain markets and to avoid being left behind. Contrasting the agreements with Mexico and Chile has also shown the first-mover advantage PTAs create in the field of standard-setting. While Mexico adopted mostly US standards after NAFTA, the dominant position of EU firms in Chile reversed this situation. Accordingly, the EU pressed unsuccessfully for common standards in the negotiations with Mexico, while the United States tried to attain technology neutrality in Chilean regulatory policy by means of the United States–Chile PTA, confirming the expectations in hypothesis 2b.

Chile made significant concessions in both agreements, among them the acceptance of the EU's system of geographic indications for wine and the opening of Chilean ports for European fishing vessels, hoping to see the primary benefit in the form of more foreign direct investment. The outcome of these agreements is parity between the EU and the United States in their access to the Chilean service sector. The case underscores the fact that the competitive effects of PTAs are equally important in services, enough to drive North–South PTAs even without the support of manufacturing industries and with very low MFN tariffs charged by Chile. The contrasting case of the Japan–Chile agreement shows that without such competitive pressures PTAs are much less urgent. Importantly, the agreements also show the benefits of liberalization efforts: with a level playing field, Chilean customers will have access to more choice in financial and other services.

Japan's PTAs with Thailand and Malaysia

The cases of the Japan–Thailand and Japan–Malaysia economic partnership agreements contrasted the influence of different host country policies, foreign firms, and host country policies on the liberalization outcomes in PTAs. Both agreements are also the direct result of the "conversion" of Japan's trade bureaucracy from multilateralism to preferential trade agreements in reaction to NAFTA.

Following the Asian financial crisis both Thailand and Malaysia have tried to attract more foreign direct investment into their manufacturing industries. Thailand, more affected by the crisis than Malaysia, took greater steps towards liberalization. Both countries also experienced an export boom: Malaysia's electronics industry saw rapid growth, while Thailand became a highly attractive export platform for the automobile industry. Japanese firms began to emulate their US counterparts by producing cars in an emerging market country for both home and third country markets. This new strategy departs from the traditional practice of directly investing in the host market, in particular the United States, to circumvent restrictions on exports.

Japanese firms had been strongly supportive of regional integration efforts among ASEAN members, as these measures allowed them to rationalize their production networks and achieve greater efficiency. Preferential agreements with individual ASEAN countries as a stepping stone to a broader ASEAN–Japan deal provide an important boost to these efforts. The agreements show the difference that host country policies can make. The Thai government sought to protect its domestic auto parts and steel industry, just as the Mexican government had done during the negotiations with the United States and Canada, the EU, and Japan. However, unlike in the NAFTA negotiations, where Mexican suppliers colluded with US firms to raise the rule of origin threshold, Thai auto parts firms allied with non-Japanese multinational firms and slowed down the tariff elimination that Japanese manufacturers had sought. This contrasts with the Malaysian government, which primarily sought to protect its domestic vehicle industry but was much more willing to open the market for auto parts to give the national manufacturers a technological boost.

Although the Japanese rule of origin template is less restrictive than the models that the United States and the EU promote in North–South negotiations, several industries stand out in the Japan–Thailand EPA as strongly protectionist, most importantly fisheries and textiles. Here again, where firms source their inputs determines the rent chain, as per hypotheses 1a and 1b.

Both agreements also again show the limits of liberalization in North–South PTAs. Thailand only managed to obtain a deal by excluding the agricultural products that it produces most efficiently: rice and sugar. Malaysia did not manage to make plywood exports part of the agreement. Ultimately, the liberalization converges on the tariffs on goods traded by multinational firms with investment in the developing countries. Finally, the reaction of the European Union and its announcement of a "new trade policy" that counters with its own negotiation the agreements with ASEAN provide further evidence of the competitive force exerted by these PTAs.

Investment vs. comparative advantage: excluding agriculture

One of the central points put forth in this study is that North–South PTAs are not primarily driven by conventional trade policy concerns such as tariffs on finished goods. The limited market access gains for agricultural exports from developing countries offer further evidence for this claim. In many cases the very concrete threat to import-competing agricultural producers triggers vigorous opposition to liberalization, as hypothesis 3 predicts. Table 8.2 provides an overview of key agricultural exports of the developing country partner that were

Table 8.2. *Exclusion of agricultural exports*

PTA	Major exclusions	Type of barrier	Notes
NAFTA (US–Mexico)	None	15-year tariff phase-out period; US export subsidies permitted	
EU–Mexico	Sugar, poultry, beef, pork	Tariff-rate quotas	Mutual concessions on geographical indications
Japan–Mexico	Pork, beef, chicken, oranges, orange juice	Tariff-rate quotas	
EU–Chile	Sugar, poultry, beef, pork	Tariff-rate quotas	Geographical indications require some relabeling of Chilean wines
US–Chile	None	15-year tariff phase-out periods; US export subsidies only permitted to match those of competitors in Chilean market	
Japan–Chile	Rice, wheat, barley, sugar, pork, beef	Tariff-rate quotas	Dairy products left for renegotiation
Japan–Thailand	Rice, wheat, barley, beef and pork (fresh, frozen, and chilled), most items of prepared beef and pork, raw cane and beet sugar, refined sugar, starches, canned pineapple, plywood	Tariff-rate quotas	Pineapple, cane sugar, and starches left for renegotiation
Japan–Malaysia	Identical to Japan–Thailand, but increased tariff-rate quota for bananas	Tariff-rate quotas	Plywood left for renegotiation

either completely or partially excluded from liberalization. The principal means of exclusion or limitation are tariff-rate quotas as required by
the Uruguay Round agreement on agriculture. The United States is a
partial exception, offering better access than Japan and the EU, but still
maintaining US export subsidies. The product list is virtually identical
with the products in which the developing country in the PTA has a
comparative – in fact, usually an absolute – advantage. If the gains from
trade, mutual specialization, and consumer welfare were relevant for
PTA formation, or at least featured prominently in governments' calculations of costs and benefits, we would hardly see these products
excluded. But the persistence of trade barriers is less surprising when
we consider well-established results of endogenous tariff theory:[1] large
potential gains from trade imply costly adjustment and, accordingly,
prompt the most vehement lobbying for protection. If, on the other
hand, FDI and investment-related trade are the principal objective of
PTAs, then the lobbying of import-competing and export-oriented
sectors is almost a nuisance for trade negotiators whose primary mandates lie elsewhere. Many North–South PTAs are not the product of
reciprocal bargaining or give-and-take between exporters and
importers.

Assessment and implications

Manufacturing and services FDI in emerging markets differ in their
objectives. While the former primarily seeks efficiency by turning
developing countries into export platforms, the latter is mostly market-
seeking. Such different circumstances, however, lead to similar outcomes, since preferential liberalization of the investment environment
and tariffs on intermediate goods discriminates against firms from third
countries. The proliferation of PTAs therefore becomes endogenous.

The focus on FDI and trade in intermediate goods also helps to
explain why previous studies have failed to show trade diversion.
Such a net reduction of imports of PTA members from the outside
world forms the causal link of the domino theory of preferential trade
agreements. It also provides insight into why PTAs are not expanding

---

[1] Alt *et al.* (1996) provide what is perhaps still the best non-mathematical overview.
Gawande and Hoekman (2006) provide an up-to-date test of the specific-factor
model in the context of US trade policy.

into broader regional agreements, but form a dense network of mostly bilateral treaties. The answer to both questions rests as much with political as with economic choices. Trade diversion often does not occur because multinational firms choose to absorb the costs of trade discrimination, at least temporarily, and lobby for defensive agreements, rather than switch to suppliers located within the PTA – in short, they at least initially choose "voice" over "exit." This may be because of long-standing contractual links with the producers of intermediate goods outside the PTA, or simply because no adequate supplier can be found in the member countries. Moreover, although some outside firms may choose to relocate in the PTA zone, others will try to benefit from trade liberalization and use the developing country as an export platform. In that case, we will observe that the member states trade more with the outside world than before they signed their trade agreement, even if it contains discriminatory clauses. Preferential, mostly bilateral, agreements can also be better tailored to the needs of multinational firms, the most important constituency in their favor, than broader regional initiatives. The role of services FDI in North–South PTAs shows even more complex dynamics, because the discriminatory nature of preferential trade agreements is even less transparent than in goods. Standards, regulations, and first-mover advantages created by economies of scale threaten to exclude firms from non-member countries.

In the absence of major activity by multinational firms, PTA formation is less likely to become endogenous. Earlier waves of preferential trade agreements reached their peak in an age when exports of finished goods were vastly more important than foreign direct investment, and when North–South trade was dominated by exports of raw materials from developing countries and manufactured products from the developed world. Although these agreements may have caused actual trade diversion, they did not trigger the defensive moves towards PTAs that we witness today.

The account in this study gives prime importance to NAFTA as the first North–South PTA. In NAFTA, US firms chose restrictive rules of origin to create costs for European and Japanese competitors. The reaction of the excluded firms in the form of the two defensive PTAs may not have been foreseeable at the time. By now, firms, lobbyists, and governments seem to be well aware of the competitive effects of PTAs, as the growing number of initiatives for trade agreements shows.

What, then, are the implications of the proliferation of North–South PTAs? The most direct effect is an increase in the complexity of trade rules. With every new agreement that creates rules of origin for manufactured goods, transaction costs increase. Complex tracing methods and origin certificates burden firms immensely. As a result, as Anson *et al.* (2003) have shown, these rules depress trade and undermine the liberalizing potential of PTAs. Moreover, since they often reflect the lobbying efforts of different interest groups, they inevitably differ between PTAs. So far, only the EU has started to harmonize its rules of origin across all its bilateral agreements, but the impact is still not uniform because of varying host country tariffs.

Seen in a favorable light, rules of origin are just a snapshot of manufacturing industry interests at the time of negotiation. For example, the strict NAFTA rules of origin for television sets have already become redundant as cathode-ray tubes are replaced by liquid crystal and plasma displays manufactured in South Korea and China. Alternatively, rules of origin might eventually become such a burden on trade that their cost outweighs their benefits. The NAFTA countries have taken the first tentative steps towards simplifying the existing rules of origin that guide their trade relations. However, the relatively technical nature of rules of origin suggests that such efforts will take a long time and are by no means guaranteed to succeed. Likewise, the WTO has begun to investigate the subject. It is a sad irony that the global drive to PTAs has put yet another item on the agenda of an already overburdened multilateral organization.

More critically, North–South PTAs are characterized by stark asymmetries between the parties. Whatever bargaining leverage developing countries might gain because major economic powers are vying for equal access is offset by the need to compete with other developing countries to attract foreign direct investment. Accordingly, as the case studies in this work have shown, the interests of a few industries or even a handful of firms frequently dominate in the negotiations. Liberalization often focuses on the goods of interest to these firms. PTAs do not perform much better than multilateral rounds when it comes to reducing barriers on exports of finished goods, and usually fail to make inroads into protected agricultural markets. The weak disciplines of GATT Article XXIV permit "dirty" PTAs in which less than 90 percent of trade between the partners is liberalized. Such violations of Article XXIV are likely to become more common in the future, since neither the United States nor the EU are in a position to cast the first stone and demand a WTO examination of PTAs. Yet because North–South PTAs primarily focus on investment and the attendant trade, they come dangerously close to sectoral liberalization.

Sectoral reduction of trade barriers threatens to undermine the multilateral trade regime. Negotiators have long valued package deals to facilitate the liberalization of the most stubbornly protected sectors. Preserving the potential for such "issue linkage" was one of the original rationales for disciplines on regional trade agreements. As Davis (2003: 364) warns, although sectoral liberalization may be easier to achieve, it also makes cross-sector linkages difficult. The gains from liberalizing the trade and investment undertaken by multinational firms may look like an easily attainable short-term benefit. But by reducing the potential for linking the issues in which the interests of developed and developing countries converge with those where they diverge, as in agriculture, they present a problem for negotiators.

This assessment aptly characterizes the dilemma of the WTO. While many observers blame the stalled WTO for the popularity of preferential agreements, the findings of this study suggest that the causal arrow may also run the other way. As North–South PTAs advance liberalization of trade and investment where the interests of developing and developed countries converge, the WTO may be left with the most intractable problems. Failure of multilateral rounds becomes a self-fulfilling prophecy if no package deals can be made. By implication, preferential deals undermine multilateral liberalization by satisfying only the constituencies that could balance protectionist agricultural interest groups.

Liberalization through preferential deals is likely to remain partial and incomplete. Although the negotiation of an individual agreement may be easier than a multilateral round, the sum of bilateral PTAs increases transaction costs. Moreover, as the case studies have shown, the succession of proactive and defensive PTAs means that developed countries end up with parity. The proliferation of bilateral PTAs could therefore be seen as a game along the lines of the prisoner's dilemma: once countries turn towards preferential agreements, multilateralism unravels. Although preferential trade may seem like a mere detour from the ultimate goal of global free trade, much of the efficiency gains of increased trade and investment are eaten up by the patchwork of complex rules.

Eventually, the burden of compliance with numerous agreements may lead countries to reconsider the advantages of multilateral liberalization, recognizing what theories of international cooperation have long predicted: multilateral international institutions can significantly reduce transactions costs. Moreover, by lowering MFN tariffs, multilateral liberalization can take away the protectionist force of rules of origin: if the United States did not impose any tariff on imported vehicles, it would not matter whether they were produced in Mexico, Slovakia, or South Korea. Such considerations are likely to become more important when the most attractive host countries have become FDI "hubs" – the centers of a dense network of "spokes" of preferential trade agreements. At that time it may also be possible for these host countries to drop their remaining MFN tariffs. For example, once the Mexican PTAs with the EU and Japan are in full effect, most of Mexican trade will be covered by preferential agreements. This will spur on the necessary adjustment of the domestic parts industry. Mexico will then be in a position to reduce tariffs on these goods. At this point, the country could follow Chile's example, matching preferential liberalization with equivalent unilateral or multilateral commitments. If this holds for enough countries, then the problems of the current wave of preferential trade agreements may be overcome.

This study has analyzed the interests of developed and developing countries in signing preferential trade agreements. It has stressed the importance of foreign direct investment in North–South relations, and offered a perspective for integrating FDI in the study of preferential trade agreements. The explanation advanced in this work can usefully be extended to many of these agreements, for example PTAs between emerging market countries with different factor endowments in which investment flows primarily in one direction. The PTA between South Korea and Chile is among the first such agreements. Such agreements are likely to become even more common in the future. Despite a stalled FTAA process, the western hemisphere will see an even greater expansion of its dense network of preferential trade agreements beyond the region. Finally, the Asia-Pacific region experiences an even more rapid proliferation of PTAs. Preferential agreements will remain the preoccupation of trade negotiators for years to come.

References

Aggarwal, Vinod K. 1985. *Liberal Protectionism: The International Politics of Organized Textile Trade*. Berkeley and Los Angeles: University of California Press.

1998. *Institutional Designs for a Complex World: Bargaining, Linkages, and Nesting*. Ithaca, NY: Cornell University Press.

Aggarwal, Vinod K., Robert O. Keohane, and David B. Yoffie. 1987. "Dynamics of negotiated protectionism," *American Political Science Review*, 81 (2), 345–66.

Aggarwal, Vinod K., and Shujiro Urata (eds.). 2006. *Bilateral Trade Arrangements in the Asia-Pacific: Origins, Evolution, and Implications*. London: Routledge.

Alt, James E., Jeffry A. Frieden, Michael Gilligan, Dani Rodrick, and Ronald Rogowski. 1996. "The political economy of international trade: Enduring puzzles and an agenda for inquiry," *Comparative Political Studies*, 29 (6), 689–717.

Alt, James E., and Michael J. Gilligan. 1994. "The political economy of trading states: Factor specificity, collective action problems and domestic political institutions," *Journal of Political Philosophy*, 2 (2), 165–92.

Andrews, Donald W. K. 1993. "Tests for parameter instability and structural change with unknown change point," *Econometrica*, 61 (4), 821–56.

Anson, Jose, Olivier Cadot, Antoni Estevadeordal, Jaime de Melo, Akiko Suwa-Eisenmann, and Bolormaa Tumurchudur. 2005. "Rules of origin in North–South preferential trading arrangements with an application to NAFTA," *Review of International Economics*, 13 (3), 501–17.

Anson, José, Olivier Cadot, Jaime de Melo, Antoni Estevadeordal, Akiko Suwa-Eisenmann, and Bolorma Tumurchudur. 2003. *Rules of Origin in North–South Preferential Trading Arrangements with an Application to NAFTA*, CEPR Discussion Paper No. 4166. London: Centre for Economic Policy Research.

Aoki, Masahiko, Hyung-ki Kim, and Masahiro Okuno-Fujiwara (eds.). 1996. *The Role of Government in East Asian Economic Development*. Oxford: Clarendon Press.

Arimura, Sadanori. 2002. "Ajia kiki go, zaitō ajia nikkei kigyō seizō to kenkyū kanpatsu ni kansuru chōsa hōkoku [Research report on the manufacturing and R&D of Japanese companies in East Asia after the Asian crisis]," *Tōa Keizai Kenkyū [East Asian Economic Research]*, 61 (3), 293–313.

Asociación Mexicana de la Industria Automotriz. 1993. *Balance de la industria automotriz*. Mexico City: Asociación Mexicana de la Industria Automotriz.

Athukorala, Prema-chandra. 2005. "Trade policy in Malaysia: Liberalization process, structure of protection, and reform agenda," *ASEAN Economic Bulletin*, 22 (1), 19–34.

Aussilloux, Vincent, and Michael Pajot. 2002. "L'ALENA est-il discriminatoire à l'encontre des exportations européennes au Méxique?" *Economie Internationale*, (89–90), 315–38.

Baier, Scott L., and Jeffrey H. Bergstrand. 2004. "Economic determinants of free trade agreements," *Journal of International Economics*, 64 (1), 29–63.

   2007. "Do free trade agreements actually increase members' international trade?" *Journal of International Economics*, 71 (1), 72–95.

Bailey, Michael A., Judith Goldstein, and Barry R. Weingast. 1997. "The institutional roots of American trade policy: Politics, coalitions, and international trade," *World Politics*, 49 (3), 309–38.

Baldwin, Richard E. 1996. "A domino theory of regionalism," in R. E. Baldwin, P. Haaparanta and J. Kiander (eds.), *Expanding Membership of the European Union*. Cambridge: Cambridge University Press, pp. 25–48.

Banco Bilbao Vizcaya. 1998. *Informe anual*, Bilbao.

Baron, David P. 1995. "The nonmarket strategy system," *Sloan Management Review*, 37 (1), 73–85.

   1999. "Integrated market and nonmarket strategies in client and interest group politics," *Business and Politics*, 1 (1), 7–34.

Barth, James R., Triphon Phumiwasana, and Glenn Yago. 2005. "The foreign conquest of Latin American banking: What's happening and why?" in F. E. Martín and P. Toral (eds.), *Latin America's Quest for Globalization: The Role of Spanish Firms*. Aldershot (UK): Ashgate, pp. 109–33.

Barton, John H., Judith L. Goldstein, Timothy E. Josling, and Richard H. Steinberg. 2006. *The Evolution of the Trade Regime: Politics, Law, and Economics of the GATT and the WTO*. Princeton, NJ: Princeton University Press.

Beeson, Mark and Kanishka Jayasuriya. 1998. "The political rationalities of regionalism: APEC and the EU in comparative perspective," *Pacific Review*, 11 (3), 311–36.

Bennett, Douglas C., and Kenneth E. Sharpe. 1985. *Transnational Corporations versus the State: The Political Economy of the Mexican Auto Industry*. Princeton, NJ: Princeton University Press.

Berger, Allen N., Asli Demirgüç-Kunt, Ross Levine, and Joseph G. Haubrich. 2004. "Bank concentration and competition: An evolution in the making," *Journal of Money, Credit, and Banking*, 36 (3), 433–51.

Berger, Mark T. 1999. "APEC and its enemies: The failure of the new regionalism in the Asia-Pacific," *Third World Quarterly*, 20 (5), 1013–30.

Bhagwati, Jagdish. 1991. *The World Trading System at Risk*, Princeton, NJ: Princeton University Press.

Bhagwati, Jagdish N., and Anne O. Krueger. 1995. *The Dangerous Drift to Preferential Trade Agreements*. Washington, DC: AEI Press.

Bhagwati, Jagdish, and Arvind Panagariya, 1996. *The Economics of Preferential Trade Agreements*. Washington, DC: AEI Press.

Blank, Stephen, and Jerry Haar. 1998. *Making NAFTA Work: US Firms and the New North American Business Environment*. Miami, FL: North–South Center Press.

BMW de Colombia. 2004. *Camino Exito*. Bogotá: BMW de Colombia.

Borrego, Rene. 1991. "One-stop service," *Business Mexico*, 1 (8), 10–12.

Borrus, Michael G. 1999. "Exploiting Asia to beat Japan: Production networks and the comeback of US electronics," in D. J. Encarnation (ed.), *Japanese Multinationals in Asia: Regional Operations in Comparative Perspective*. Oxford: Oxford University Press, pp. 213–37.

Brenton, Paul. 2003. "Integrating the least developed countries into the world trading system: The current impact of European Union preferences under 'Everything but arms'," *Journal of World Trade*, 37 (3), 623–46.

Brenton, Paul, and Takako Ikezuki. 2006. "Trade preferences for Africa and the impact of rules of origin," in O. Cadot, A. Estevadeordal, A. Suwa-Eisenmann, and T. Verdier (eds.), *The Origin of Goods: Rules of Origin in Regional Trade Agreements*. Oxford: Oxford University Press, pp. 295–314.

Brown, Drusilla K., Kozo Kiyota, and Robert M. Stern. 2006. "Computational analysis of the menu of US–Japan trade policies," *World Economy*, 29 (6), 805–55.

Bulmer-Thomas, Victor, Nikki Craske, and Mónica Serrano. 1994. *Mexico and the North American Free Trade Agreement: Who Will Benefit?* New York: St. Martin's Press.

Busch, Marc L., and Helen V. Milner. 1994. "The future of the international trading system: International firms, regionalism, and domestic politics," in R. Stubbs and G. R. D. Underhill (eds.), *Political Economy and the Changing Global Order*. Toronto: McClelland & Stewart, pp. 259–76.

Büthe, Tim. 2002. "Taking temporality seriously: Modeling history and the use of narratives as evidence," *American Political Science Review*, 96 (3), 481–93.

Büthe, Tim, and Helen V. Milner. 2004. "The politics of foreign direct investment into developing countries: Increasing FDI through policy commitment via trade agreements and investment treaties," paper presented at the Annual Meeting of the American Political Science Association, Chicago, IL, September 2–5.

Byrne, Eileen. 1994. "A yen for Mexico," *Business Mexico*, 4 (3), 46–47.

Cadot, Olivier, Antoni Estevadeordal, Akiko Suwa-Eisenmann, and Thierry Verdier. 2006. *The Origin of Goods: Rules of Origin in Regional Trade Agreements*. Oxford: Oxford University Press.

Calder, Kent E. 1988. "Japanese foreign economic policy formation: Explaining the reactive state," *World Politics*, 40 (4), 517–41.

Calderón, Alvaro, and Ramon Casilda. 1999. *Grupos financieros españoles en América Latina: Una estrategia audaz en un difícil y cambiante entorno europeo.* Santiago de Chile: Economic Commission for Latin America and the Caribbean.

2000. "La estrategia de los bancos españoles en América Latina," *Revista de la CEPAL*, 70, 71–89.

Calderón, Alvaro, Michael Mortimore, and Wilson Peres. 1995. *Mexico's Incorporation into the New Industrial Order: Foreign Investment as a Source of International Competitiveness*. Santiago de Chile: Economic Commission for Latin America and the Caribbean.

Cameron, Maxwell A. 1997. "North American trade negotiations: Liberalization games between asymmetric players," *European Journal of International Relations*, 3 (1), 105–39.

Cameron, Maxwell A., and Vinod K. Aggarwal. 1996. "Mexican meltdown: States, markets and post-NAFTA financial turmoil," *Third World Quarterly*, 17 (5), 975–87.

Cameron, Maxwell A., and Brian W. Tomlin. 2000. *The Making of NAFTA: How the Deal Was Done*. Ithaca, NY: Cornell University Press.

Cameron, Maxwell A., and Carol Wise. 2004. "The political impact of NAFTA on Mexico: Reflections on the political economy of democratization," *Canadian Journal of Political Science*, 37 (2), 301–23.

Carillo, Jorge. 2000. "The integration of the Mexican automobile industry to the USA: Between policies and corporate strategies," in GERPISA (ed.), *Actes du GERPISA*. Val d'Essonne, Groupe d'Étude de Recherche Permanent sur l'Industrie et les Salariés de l'Automobile (GERPISA), Université d'Evry, pp. 55–77.

Carlsen, Laura, and Donald McCarthy. 1991. "Trade talks to shape auto industry future," *Business Mexico*, 1 (7), 20–22.

Carr, David L., James R. Markusen, and Keith E. Maskus. 2001. "Estimating the knowledge-capital model of the multinational enterprise," *American Economic Review*, 91 (3), 693–708.

Caves, Richard E. 1996. *Multinational Enterprise and Economic Analysis.* Cambridge: Cambridge University Press.

Chant, John F. 1993. "The financial sector in NAFTA: Two plus one equals restructuring," in S. Globerman and M. Walker (eds.), *Assessing NAFTA: A Trinational Analysis.* Vancouver: The Fraser Institute, available at oldfraser.lexi.net/publications/books/assess_nafta/.

Chase, Kerry A. 2003. "Economic interests and regional trading arrangements: The case of NAFTA," *International Organization*, 57 (1), 137–74.

2004. "From protection to regionalism: Multinational firms and trade-related investment measures," *Business and Politics*, 6 (2), 1–36.

2005. *Trading Blocs: States, Firms, and Regions in the World Economy.* Ann Arbor, MI: University of Michigan Press.

2008. "Protecting free trade: The political economy of rules of origin," *International Organization*, 62 (3), 507–30.

Claessens, Stijn, Asli Demirgüç-Kunt, and Harry Huizinga. 2001. "How does foreign entry affect domestic banking markets?" *Journal of Banking & Finance*, 25 (5), 891–911.

Claessens, Stijn, and Luc Laeven, 2004. "What drives bank competition? Some international evidence," *Journal of Money, Credit and Banking*, 36 (3), 563–84.

2005. *Financial Dependence, Banking Sector Competition, and Economic Growth*, World Bank Policy Research Working Paper 3481. Washington, DC: World Bank.

Comisión Nacional Bancaria y de Valores (CNBV). 1998. *Boletín Estadístico.* Mexico City: Comisión Nacional Bancaria y de Valores.

2004. *Boletín Estadístico.* Mexico City: Comisión Nacional Bancaria y de Valores.

Commission of the European Communities (EC Commission). 1993. *Information note: North American Free Trade Agreement (NAFTA).* Brussels: European Commission.

1995. *Towards Closer Relations between the European Union and Mexico: Commission Communication to the Council and Parliament,* COM/95/0003. Brussels: European Commission.

2006. *Global Europe: Competing in the World,* COM (2006) 567 final. Brussels: European Commission.

Crystal, Jonathan. 1998. "A new kind of competition: How American producers respond to incoming foreign direct investment," *International Studies Quarterly*, 42 (3), 513–43.

Curtis, Gerald L. 1999. *The Logic of Japanese Politics: Leaders, Institutions, and the Limits of Change.* New York: Columbia University Press.

Dauvergne, Peter. 1997. *Shadows in the Forest: Japan and the Politics of Timber in Southeast Asia.* Cambridge, MA: MIT Press.

Davis, Christina L. 2003. *Food Fights over Free Trade: How International Institutions Promote Agricultural Trade Liberalization.* Princeton: Princeton University Press.

2004. "International institutions and issue linkage: Building support for agricultural trade liberalization," *American Political Science Review*, 98 (1), 153–69.

Delegation of the European Commission in Mexico. 1995. *Informe de evolución de las relaciones UE-México.* Mexico City: Delegation of the European Commission.

Dent, Christopher M. 2006. *New Free Trade Agreements in the Asia-Pacific.* Basingstoke: Palgrave Macmillan.

Depken, Craig A. II, and Jon M. Ford. 1999. "NAFTA as a means of raising rivals' costs," *Review of Industrial Organization*, 15 (2), 103–13.

Destler, I. M. 1986. *American Trade Politics: System under Stress.* Washington, DC: Institute for International Economics.

2006. "Rules of origin and US trade policy," in O. Cadot, A. Estevadeordal, and A. Suwa-Eisenmann (eds.), *The Origin of Goods: Rules of Origin in Regional Trade Agreements.* Oxford: Oxford University Press, pp. 173–87.

Destler, I. M., John S. Odell, and Kimberly Ann Elliott. 1987. *Anti-protection: Changing Forces in United States Trade Politics.* Washington, DC: Institute for International Economics.

Doner, Richard F. 1991. *Driving a Bargain: Automobile Industrialization and Japanese Firms in Southeast Asia*, Berkeley and Los Angeles: University of California Press.

1997. "Japan in East Asia: Institutions and regional leadership," in P. J. Katzenstein and T. Shiraishi (eds.), *Network Power: Japan and Asia.* Ithaca, NY: Cornell University Press, pp. 197–233.

Downs, Anthony. 1967. *Inside Bureaucracy.* Boston: Little, Brown.

Dunne, Michael J. 2001. "Free trade: Who wants it?" *Automotive News International*, February, 32–33.

Dunning, John H. 2002. *Theories and Paradigms of International Business Activity.* Cheltenham: Edward Elgar.

Dür, Andreas. 2007. "Foreign discrimination, protection for exporters, and US trade liberalization," *International Studies Quarterly*, 51 (2), 457–80.

Duttagupta, Rupa, and Arvind Panagariya. 2003. *Free Trade Areas and Rules of Origin: Economics and Politics*, IMF Working Paper 03/229. Washington, DC: International Monetary Fund.

Economic Commission for Latin America and the Caribbean (ECLAC) 2000. *Foreign Investment in Latin America and the Caribbean.* Santiago de Chile: Economic Commission for Latin America and the Caribbean.

2001. *Foreign Investment in Latin America and the Caribbean.* Santiago de Chile: Economic Commission for Latin America and the Caribbean.

2002. *Foreign Investment in Latin America and the Caribbean.* Santiago de Chile: Economic Commission for Latin America and the Caribbean.

Eden, Lorraine, and Maureen Appel Molot. 1992. *Fortress or Free Market? NAFTA and its Implications for the Pacific Rim*, Occasional Papers in International Trade Law and Policy. Ottawa: Centre for Trade Policy and Law, Carleton University.

1993. "Fortress or free market? NAFTA and its implications for the Pacific Rim," in R. Higgott, R. Leaver and J. Ravenhill (eds.), *Pacific Economic Relations in the 1990s: Cooperation or Conflict?* Boulder, CO: Lynne Rienner, pp. 201–22.

Edgington, David W., and W. Mark Fruin. 1994. "NAFTA and Japanese investment," in A. M. Rugman (ed.), *Foreign Investment and NAFTA.* Columbia, SC: University of South Carolina Press, pp. 253–75.

Edwards, Sebastian. 1999. "How effective are capital controls?" *Journal of Economic Perspectives*, 13 (4), 65–84.

Egger, Peter, and Valeria Merlo. 2007. "The impact of bilateral investment treaties on FDI dynamics," *World Economy*, 30 (10), 1536–49.

Eichengreen, Barry J., and Hui Tong. 2006. "How China is reorganizing the world economy," *Asian Economic Policy Review*, 1 (1), 73–97.

2007. "Is China's FDI coming at the expense of other countries?" *Journal of the Japanese and International Economies*, 21 (2), 153–72.

Ekholm, Karolina, Rikard Forslid, and James R. Markusen. 2003. *Export-Platform Foreign Direct Investment*, NBER Working Paper 9517. Cambridge, MA: National Bureau of Economic Research.

Elkins, Zachary, Andrew T. Guzman, and Beth Simmons. 2006. "Competing for capital: The diffusion of bilateral investment treaties," *International Organization*, 60 (4), 811–46.

English, H. Edward. 1999. "Asia–Pacific crossroads: Regime creation and the future of APEC," *Pacific Affairs*, 72 (4), 572–74.

Ernst, Dieter. 2000. "Evolutionary aspects: The Asian production networks of Japanese electronics firms," in M. G. Borrus, D. Ernst, and S. Haggard (eds.), *International Production Networks in Asia: Rivalry or Riches?* London: Routledge, pp. 80–109.

Estevadeordal, Antoni, and Kati Suominen. 2004. *Rules of Origin in FTAs in Europe and in the Americas: Issues and Implications for the EU–Mercosur Inter-regional Association Agreement*, INTAL-ITD Working Paper 15. Washington, DC: Inter-American Development Bank.

Estevez-Abe, Margarita. 2006. "Japan's shift toward a Westminster system: A structural analysis of the 2005 lower house election and its aftermath," *Asian Survey*, 46 (4), 632–51.

Ethier, Wilfred J. 1998a. "Regionalism in a multilateral world," *Journal of Political Economy*, 106 (6), 1214–45.

1998b. "The new regionalism," *Economic Journal*, 108 (449), 1149–61.

2001. "The new regionalism in the Americas: A theoretical framework," *North American Journal of Economics and Finance*, 12 (2), 159–72.

Evans, Peter. 1979. *Dependent Development: The Alliance of Multinational, State, and Local Capital in Brazil.* Princeton, NJ: Princeton University Press.

Evans, Peter B., Harold K. Jacobson, and Robert D. Putnam. 1993. *Double-Edged Diplomacy: International Bargaining and Domestic Politics.* Berkeley and Los Angeles: University of California Press.

Falvey, Rodney E. 1981. "Commercial policy and intra-industry trade," *Journal of International Economics*, 11, 495–511.

Falvey, Rodney E., and Geoff Reed. 2000. *Rules of Origin as Commercial Policy Instruments*, Research Paper 2000/18. Nottingham: Centre for Research on Globalisation and Labour Markets, University of Nottingham.

Feenstra, Robert C., and Gordon H. Hanson. 1996. "Foreign investment, outsourcing, and relative wages," in R. C. Feenstra, G. M. Grossman, and D. A. Irwin (eds.), *The Political Economy of Trade Policy: Papers in Honor of Jagdish Bhagwati.* Cambridge, MA: MIT Press.

Feenstra, Robert C., Gordon H. Hanson, and Deborah L. Swenson. 2000. "Offshore assembly from the United States: Production characteristics of the 9802 program," in R. C. Feenstra (ed.), *The Impact of International Trade on Wages.* Chicago: University of Chicago Press, pp. 85–122.

Fernández, Raquel, and Jonathan Portes. 1998. "Returns to regionalism: An analysis of nontraditional gains from regional trade agreements," *World Bank Economic Review*, 12 (2), 197–220.

Fink, Carsten, and Aaditya Mattoo. 2002. *Regional Agreements and Trade in Services: Policy Issues*, Policy Research Working Paper 2852. Washington, DC: World Bank.

Fiorentino, Roberto V., Luis Verdeja, and Christelle Toqueboeuf. 2006. *The Changing Landscape of Regional Trade Agreements: 2006 Update*, Discussion Paper 8. Geneva: WTO Secretariat, Regional Trade Agreements Section, Trade Policies Review Division.

Fontagné, Lionel, Michael Freudenberg, and Guillaume Gaulier. 2006. "A systematic decomposition of world trade into horizontal and vertical IIT," *Review of World Economics*, 142 (3), 459–75.

Frankel, Jeffrey A. 1997. *Regional Trading Blocs in the World Economic System.* Washington, DC: Institute for International Economics.

Frankel, Jeffrey A., Ernesto Stein, and Shang-jin Wei. 1995. "Trading blocs and the Americas: The natural, the unnatural, and the super-natural," *Journal of Development Economics*, 47 (1), 61–95.

Freeman, Harry L. 1998. "The role of constituents in US policy development towards trade in financial services," in A. V. Deardorff and R. M. Stern (eds.), *Constituent Interests and US Trade Policy*. Ann Arbor: University of Michigan Press, pp. 183–94.

Freund, Caroline. 2000. "Different paths to free trade: The gains from regionalism," *Quarterly Journal of Economics*, 115 (4), 1317–41.

Frieden, Jeffry A. 1991. *Debt, Development and Democracy: Modern Political Economy and Latin America, 1965–1985*. Princeton: Princeton University Press.

Frischkorn, Allen R. Jr. 1993. "Why NAFTA will benefit US telecommunication equipment manufacturers," *Telecommunications*, 27 (2), 17.

Gallant, Nicole, and Richard Stubbs. 1997. "APEC's dilemmas: Institution-building around the Pacific Rim," *Pacific Affairs*, 70 (2), 203–18.

Garay, Luis Jorge, and Rafael Cornejo. 2001. *Metodología para el análisis de regímenes de origen: Aplicación en el caso de las Américas*, INTAL-ITD-STA Working Paper 8. Washington, DC: Inter-American Development Bank.

Gawande, Kishore, and Bernard Hoekman. 2006. "Lobbying and agricultural trade policy in the United States," *International Organization*, 60 (03), 527–61.

George, Alexander L., and Andrew Bennett. 2005. *Case Studies and Theory Development in the Social Sciences*. Cambridge, MA: MIT Press.

Gilligan, Michael J. 1997a. "Lobbying as a private good with intra-industry trade," *International Studies Quarterly*, 41 (3), 455–74.

1997b. *Empowering Exporters: Reciprocity, Delegation, and Collective Action in American Trade Policy*. Ann Arbor: University of Michigan Press.

Gowa, Joanne, and Edward D. Mansfield. 1993. "Power-politics and international trade," *American Political Science Review*, 87 (2), 408–20.

Graham, Edward M. 1994. "NAFTA, foreign direct investment, and the United States," in A. M. Rugman (ed.), *Foreign Investment and NAFTA*. Columbia, SC: University of South Carolina Press, pp. 105–23.

Graham, Edward M., and Erika Wada. 2000. "Domestic reform, trade and investment liberalisation, financial crisis, and foreign direct investment into Mexico," *World Economy*, 23 (6), 777–97.

Greenaway, David. 1992. "Trade related investment measures and development strategy," *Kyklos*, 45 (2), 139–59.

Greenaway, David, Robert Hine, and Chris Milner. 1994. "Country-specific factors and the pattern of horizontal and vertical intra-industry trade in the UK," *Weltwirtschaftliches Archiv*, 130 (1), 77–100.

Grinspun, Ricardo, and Maxwell A. Cameron. 1993. *The Political Economy of North American Free Trade*. Montreal: McGill-Queen's University Press.

Grossman, Gene M., and Elhanan Helpman. 1994. "Protection for sale," *American Economic Review*, 84 (4), 833–50.

1995. "The politics of free-trade agreements," *American Economic Review*, 85 (4), 667–90.

Gruben, William C., John H. Welch, and Jeffery W. Gunther. 1993. *US Banks, Competition, and the Mexican Banking System: How Much Will NAFTA Matter?* Working Paper 94–10. Dallas: Federal Reserve Bank of Dallas.

Grugel, Jean, and Wil Hout (eds.). 1999. *Regionalism across the North–South Divide: State Strategies and Globalization*. London: Routledge.

Guerrieri, Paolo. 2000. "International competitiveness, regional integration, and corporate strategies in the east Asian electronics industry," in M. G. Borrus, D. Ernst and S. Haggard (eds.), *International Production Networks in Asia: Rivalry or Riches?* London: Routledge, pp. 32–56.

Hafner-Burton, Emily. 2005. "Trading human rights: How preferential trade agreements influence government repression," *International Organization*, 59 (3), 593–629.

Haggard, Stephan. 1995. *Developing Nations and the Politics of Global Integration*. Washington, DC: Brookings Institution.

1997. "Regionalism in Asia and the Americas," in E. D. Mansfield and H. V. Milner (eds.), *The Political Economy of Regionalism*. New York, Columbia University Press, pp. 20–49.

Hansen, Bruce E. 1992. "Tests for parameter instability in regressions with I(1) processes," *Journal of Business and Economic Statistics*, 10 (3), 321–35.

Harms, Philipp, Aaditya Mattoo, and Ludger Schuknecht. 2003. *Explaining Liberalization Commitments in Financial Services Trade*, Policy Research Working Paper 2999. Washington, DC: World Bank.

Hatakeyama, Noboru. 2003a. "Short history of Japan's movement to FTAs (Part 1)," *Journal of Japanese Trade and Industry*, 21 (6), 24–25.

2003b. "Nichiboku jiyū bōeki kōshō ketsuretsu ga shimesu keizai senryaku fuzai seiji ga kawaranai ka giri nihon botsuraku suru [The collapse of Japan–Mexico free trade negotiations shows: If the policy lacking an economic strategy does not change, it will be Japan's downfall]," *Chūō Kōron*, 118 (12), 50–55.

Hatch, Walter, and Kozo Yamamura. 1996. *Asia in Japan's Embrace: Building a Regional Production Alliance*. Cambridge: Cambridge University Press.

Hayes, John P. 1993. *Making Trade Policy in the European Community*. New York: St. Martin's Press.

Head, Keith, and John Ries. 2001. "Overseas investment and firm exports," *Review of International Economics*, 9 (1), 108–22.

Head, Keith, John Ries, and Barbara J. Spencer. 2004. "Vertical networks and US auto parts exports: Is Japan different?" *Journal of Economics, Management and Strategy*, 13 (1), 37–67.

Hideya, Taida (ed.). 2002. *Issues and Requests Relating to Trade and Investment in 2002*. Tokyo: Japan Business Council for Trade and Investment Facilitation.

2003. *Issues and Requests Relating to Trade and Investment in 2003*. Tokyo: Japan Business Council for Trade and Investment Facilitation.

Hirsch, Moshe. 2002. "International trade law, political economy, and rules of origin: A plea for the reform of the WTO regime on rules of origin," *Journal of World Trade*, 36 (2), 171–89.

Hirschman, Albert O. 1970. *Exit, Voice, and Loyalty: Responses to Decline in Firms, Organizations, and States*. Cambridge, MA: Harvard University Press.

Hoekman, Bernard, and Pierre Sauvé. 1994. "Regional and multilateral liberalization of service markets – complements or substitutes?" *Journal of Common Market Studies*, 32 (3), 283–317.

Hook, Glenn D., Julie Gilson, Christopher W. Hughes, and Hugo Dobson. 2002. "Japan and the east Asian financial crisis: Patterns, motivations and instrumentalisation of Japanese regional economic diplomacy," *European Journal of East Asian Studies*, 1 (2), 177–97.

Hornbeck, J. F. 2003. *The US-Chile Free Trade Agreement: Economic and Trade Policy Issues*, CRS Report for Congress RL31144. Washington, DC: Congressional Research Service.

Hsieh, Peggy, F.-M. Leong, and J. Rudloe. 2001. "Jellyfish as food," *Hydrobiologia*, 451 (1–3), 11–17.

Humphrey, John, and Antje Oeter. 2000. "Motor industry policy in emerging markets: Globalisation and the promotion of domestic industry," in J. Humphrey, Y. Lecler, and M. S. Salerno (eds.), *Global Strategies and Local Realities: The Auto Industry in Emerging Markets*, New York, St. Martin's Press, pp. 42–71.

Husan, Rumy. 1997. "The continuing importance of economies of scale in the automotive industry," *European Business Review*, 97 (1), 38.

Ioannou, Lori. 1994. "Better banking with NAFTA," *International Business*, 7 (1), 40–43.

Japan Bank for International Cooperation. 2003. "Wagakuni seizōgyō no kaigai jigyō tenkai ni kan suru chōsa hōkoku [Study report on the overseas activities of our country's manufacturing industry companies]," *Kaigai Tōyūshi [Overseas Finance and Investment]*, 10 (1), 10–18.

Japan External Trade Organization (JETRO). 1994. "NAFTA hirogaru takakuteki na eikyō [NAFTA expansion: The multilateral effect]," *JETRO Sensor*, 44 (12), 10–40.

2001. *Study Report on the Japan–Chile Free Trade Agreement*. Tokyo: JETRO.

2004. *Chūnanbei shinshutsu nikkei kigyō keiei jittai chōsa [Survey on Japanese firms in Latin America]*. Tokyo: JETRO.

Japan Institute for Overseas Investment (JOI). 1997. "Tokushū mekishiko no tōshi jōkyō: JOI chōsa kekka hōkō: Nikkei sangyō shinshutsu jōkyō oyobi tōshi kankyō hōka [Special issue on the Mexican investment environment: Report on the findings of Japanese Institute for Overseas Investment study: The current situation and investment environment of Japanese enterprises]," *Kaigai Yūshi*, 6 (4), 8–18.

Japan Machinery Center for Trade and Investment (JMCTI). 2001. "PROSEC ni kan suru yōbōsho wo mekishiko keizai daiji ni tei [Proposal for the requests regarding PROSEC to the Mexican minister of the economy]," *JMC Journal*, 49 (4), 5–6.

Japan–Mexico Joint Study Group on the Strengthening of Bilateral Economic Relations. 2002. *Final Report*. Tokyo and Mexico City: Ministry of Economy, Trade, and Industry (METI) and Secretaria de Comercio y Fomento Industrial (SECOFI).

Jensen-Moran, Jeri. 1996. "Choice at the crossroads: Regionalism and rules of origin," *Law and Policy in International Business*, 27 (4), 981–89.

Johnson, Chalmers A. 1982. *MITI and the Japanese Miracle: The Growth of Industrial Policy, 1925–1975*. Stanford, CA: Stanford University Press.

Johnson, Jon R. 1993. *What is a North American Good? The NAFTA Rules of Origin*. Toronto: C. D. Howe Institute.

Katada, Saori N. 2001. *Banking on Stability: Japan and the Cross-Pacific Dynamics of International Financial Crisis Management*. Ann Arbor, MI: University of Michigan Press.

2002. "Japan and Asian monetary regionalisation: Cultivating a new regional leadership after the Asian financial crisis," *Geopolitics*, 7 (1), 85–112.

Katada, Saori N., Mireya Solís, and Barbara Stallings (eds.). In press. *Competitive Regionalism: FTA Diffusion in the Pacific Rim*. London: Palgrave.

Keidanren. 1999. *Working Group on Japan–Mexico Bilateral Treaties*, Japan–Mexico Economic Committee, Final Report. Tokyo: Keidranren.

Kemp, Murray, and Henry Wan. 1976. "An elementary proposition concerning the formation of customs unions," *Journal of International Economics*, 6 (1), 95–97.

King, Gary, Robert O. Keohane, and Sidney Verba. 1994. *Designing Social Inquiry: Scientific Inference in Qualitative Research*. Princeton, NJ: Princeton University Press.

Kitamura, Kayoko. 2003. "Ajia ni okeru nikkei seizōkigyō no genjō to kadai: Susumu ajia jigyō senryaku no saikōchiku [The current conditions and tasks of Japanese manufacturing industry enterprises: A reconstruction of the Asian enterprise strategy]," *Kaigai Tōyūshi [Overseas Finance and Investment]*, 12 (1), 20–24.

Kiyota, Kozo. 2006. "Why countries are so eager to establish bilateral free trade agreements: A case study of Thailand," in V. K. Aggarwal and S. Urata (eds.), *Bilateral Trade Agreements in the Asia-Pacific: Origins, Evolution, and Implications*. London: Routledge, pp. 206–31.

Kobrin, Stephen J. 1987. "Testing the bargaining hypothesis in the manufacturing sector in developing countries," *International Organization*, 41 (4), 609–38.

Koido, Akihiro. 1991. "The color television industry: Japanese–US competition and Mexico's maquiladoras," in G. Székely (ed.), *Manufacturing across Borders and Oceans: Japan, the United States, and Mexico*. La Jolla, CA: Center for US–Mexican Studies, University of California San Diego, pp. 51–75.

Krauss, Ellis S., and Benjamin Nyblade. 2005. "In Japan? The prime minister, media and elections in Japan," *British Journal of Political Science*, 35 (2), 357–68.

Krishna, Kala, and Anne O. Krueger. 1995. "Implementing free trade areas: Rules of origin and hidden protection," in A. Deardorff, J. Levinsohn and R. Stern (eds.), *New Directions in Trade Theory*. Ann Arbor: University of Michigan Press, pp. 149–87.

Krishna, Pravin. 1998. "Regionalism and multilateralism: A political economy approach," *Quarterly Journal of Economics*, 113 (1), 227–51.

    2005. *Trade Blocs: Economics and Politics*. Cambridge and New York: Cambridge University Press.

Krueger, Anne O. 1993. *Free Trade Agreements as Protectionist Devices: Rules of Origin*, NBER Working Paper 4352. Cambridge, MA: National Bureau of Economic Research.

    1995a. *Trade Policies and Developing Nations*. Washington, DC: Brookings Institution.

    1995b. *American Trade Policy: A Tragedy in the Making*. Washington, DC: AEI Press.

    1999. *Trade Creation and Trade Diversion under NAFTA*, NBER Working Paper 7429. Cambridge, MA: National Bureau of Economic Research.

Krugman, Paul R. 1993. "Regionalism versus multilateralism: Analytical notes," in J. de Melo and A. Panagariya (eds.), *New Dimensions in Regional Integration*. Cambridge: Cambridge University Press.

Kucik, Jeffrey, and Eric Reinhardt. 2008. "Does flexibility promote cooperation? An application to the global trade regime," *International Organization*, 62 (3), 477–505.

Kume, Ikuo. 1998. *Disparaged Success: Labor Politics in Postwar Japan.* Ithaca, NY: Cornell University Press.

Kunimoto, Robert, and Gary Sawchuk. 2004. "Moving toward a customs union: A review of the evidence," *Horizons*, 7 (1), 23–31.

Lamy, Pascal. 2002. "Mexico and the EU: Married partners, lovers, or just good friends?" Speech by the EU Commissioner for Trade at the Institute of European Integration Studies, Instituto Tecnológico Autónomo de México (ITAM), Mexico City, April 29.

Lecler, Yveline. 2002. "The cluster role in the development of the Thai car industry," *International Journal of Urban & Regional Research*, 26 (4), 799–814.

Levy, Philip I. 1997. "A political–economic analysis of free-trade agreements," *American Economic Review*, 87 (4), 506–19.

Limao, Nuno, and Marcelo Olarreaga. 2006. "Trade preferences to small developing countries and the welfare costs of lost multilateral liberalization," *World Bank Economic Review*, 20 (2), 217–40.

Lipsey, R. G. 1957. "The theory of customs unions: Trade diversion and welfare," *Economica*, 24 (93), 40–46.

Lustig, Nora. 1998. *Mexico: The Remaking of an Economy.* Washington, DC: Brookings Institution Press.

McAlinden, Sean B. 1997. "What's the right size for an assembly plant?" *Automotive Manufacturing & Production*, 109 (10), 14–15.

McIntyre, John R., Rajneesh Narula, and Len J. Trevino. 1996. "The role of export processing zones for host countries and multinationals: A mutually beneficial relationship?" *International Trade Journal*, 10 (4), 435–66.

McKeown, Timothy J. 1999. "Case studies and the statistical worldview: Review of King, Keohane, and Verba's designing social inquiry," *International Organization*, 53 (1), 161–90.

McLaren, John. 2002. "A theory of insidious regionalism," *Quarterly Journal of Economics*, 117 (2), 571–608.

Magee, Christopher S. P. 2008. "New measures of trade creation and trade diversion," *Journal of International Economics*, 75 (2), 349–62.

Magee, Stephen P., William A. Brock, and Leslie Young. 1989. *Black Hole Tariffs and Endogenous Policy Theory: Political Economy in General Equilibrium.* Cambridge: Cambridge University Press.

Manger, Mark S. 2008. "International investment agreements and services markets: Locking in market failure?" *World Development*, 36 (11), 2456–69.

Mansfield, Edward D., and Marc L. Busch. 1995. "The political economy of nontariff barriers – a cross-national analysis," *International Organization*, 49 (4), 723–49.

Mansfield, Edward D., and Eric Reinhardt. 2003. "Multilateral determinants of regionalism: The effects of GATT/WTO on the formation of preferential trading arrangements," *International Organization*, 57 (4), 829–62.

Markusen, James R. 1995. "The boundaries of multinational enterprises and the theory of international trade," *Journal of Economic Perspectives*, 9 (2), 169–89.

Markusen, James R., Anthony J. Venables, Denise Eby Konan, and Kevin H. Zhang. 1996. *A Unified Treatment of Horizontal Direct Investment, Vertical Direct Investment, and the Pattern of Trade in Goods and Services*, NBER Working Paper 5696. Cambridge, MA: National Bureau of Economic Research.

Mattli, Walter, and Tim Büthe. 2003. "Setting international standards: Technological rationality or primacy of power?" *World Politics*, 56 (1), 1–42.

Maxfield, Sylvia, and Adam Shapiro. 1998. "Assessing the NAFTA negotiations: US–Mexican debate and compromise on tariff and nontariff issues," in C. Wise (ed.), *The Post-NAFTA Political Economy: Mexico and the Western Hemisphere*. University Park, PA: Pennsylvania State University Press, pp. 82–118.

Mayer, Frederick. 1998. *Interpreting NAFTA: The Science and Art of Political Analysis*. New York: Columbia University Press.

Meade, James E. 1955. *The Theory of Customs Unions*. Amsterdam: North-Holland.

Meller, Patricio. 1996. *Un siglo de economía política chilena*. Santiago de Chile: Editorial Andrés Bello.

Mendiola, Gerardo. 1999. *México: Empresas maquiladoras de exportación en los noventa*. Santiago de Chile: Economic Commission for Latin America and the Caribbean.

Messmer, Ellen. 1992. "Mexico may relax networking policies," *Network World*, 9 (49), 33–34.

Meunier, Sophie. 2005. *Trading Voices: The European Union in International Commercial Negotiation*. Princeton: Princeton University Press.

Meunier, Sophie, and Kalypso Nicolaïdis. 1999. "Who speaks for Europe? The delegation of trade authority in the EU," *Journal of Common Market Studies*, 37 (3), 477–501.

Mill, John Stuart. 1843. *A System of Logic, Ratiocinative and Inductive: Being a Connected View of the Principles of Evidence, and the Methods of Scientific Investigation*. London: J. W. Parker.

Milner, Helen V. 1988. *Resisting Protectionism: Global Industries and the Politics of International Trade*. Princeton: Princeton University Press.

1997. "Industries, governments, and the creation of regional trade blocs," in E. D. Mansfield and H. V. Milner (eds.), *The Political Economy of Regionalism*. New York: Columbia University Press, pp. 77–106.

1999. "The political economy of international trade," *Annual Review of Political Science*, 2 (1), 91–114.

Ministry of Economy, Trade and Industry (METI). 2001. *Tsūshō hakusho [White paper on international trade]*. Tokyo: Ministry of Economy, Trade and Industry.

Molot, Maureen Appel. 1993. *Driving Continentally: National Policies and the North American Auto Industry*. Ottawa: Carleton University Press.

Moravcsik, Andrew. 1993. "Preferences and power in the European Community: A liberal intergovernmentalist approach," *Journal of Common Market Studies*, 31 (4), 437–524.

1997. "Taking preferences seriously: A liberal theory of international politics," *International Organization*, 51 (4), 513–53.

1998. *The Choice for Europe: Social Purpose and State Power from Messina to Maastricht*. Ithaca, NY: Cornell University Press.

Moreno Brid, Juan C. 1994. *La competitividad de la industria automotriz en México*. Mexico City: Economic Commission for Latin America and the Caribbean.

1996. *Mexico's Auto Industry after NAFTA: A Successful Experience in Restructuring?* Working Paper 232. Notre Dame, IN: Kellogg Institute of International Studies, University of Notre Dame.

Motor and Equipment Manufacturers Association. 1991. *Discussion Paper: Rules of Origin for the US–Mexico–Canada Free Trade Agreement*. Washington, DC: Motor and Equipment Manufacturers Association.

Mulgan, Aurelia George. 1999. *The Politics of Agriculture in Japan*. New York: Routledge.

2003. "Japan's 'un-Westminster' system: Impediments to reform in a crisis economy," *Government and Opposition*, 38 (1), 73–91.

2005a. *Japan's Interventionist State: The Role of the MAFF*. New York: RoutledgeCurzon.

2005b. "Japan's interventionist state: Bringing agriculture back in," *Japanese Journal of Political Science*, 6 (1), 29–61.

2005c. "Where tradition meets change: Japan's agricultural politics in transition," *Journal of Japanese Studies*, 31 (2), 261–98.

Munakata, Naoko. 2001. *Evolution of Japan's Policy toward Economic Integration*. Washington, DC: Center for Northeast Asian Policy Studies (CNAPS), Brookings Institution.

Nagai, Fumio. 2003. "Thailand's FTA policy: Continuity and change between the Chuan and Thaksin governments," in J. Okamoto (ed.), *Whither Free Trade Agreements? Proliferation, Evaluation, and Multilateralization*.

Chiba: Institute of Developing Economies, Japan External Trade Organization, pp. 252–84.

Nelson, Douglas. 1988. "Endogenous tariff theory: A critical survey," *American Journal of Political Science*, 88 (3), 796–838.

Nesadurai, Helen E. S. 2000. "In defence of national economic autonomy? Malaysia's response to the financial crisis," *Pacific Review*, 13 (1), 73–113.

Neumayer, Eric, and Spess, Laura. 2005. "Do bilateral investment treaties increase foreign direct investment to developing countries?" *World Development*, 33 (10), 1567–85.

Noble, Gregory W. 2002. "On the road to Asia: Japanese automakers in ASEAN," in V. K. Aggarwal and S. Urata (eds.), *Winning in Asia, Japanese Style: Market and Nonmarket Strategies for Success*. New York: Palgrave MacMillan, pp. 123–56.

Ogita, Tatsushi. 2002. *An Approach towards Japan's FTA Policy*, Working Paper 01/02 No. 4. Chiba: APEC Study Center, Institute of Developing Economies, Japan External Trade Organization.

2003. "Japan as a late-coming FTA holder: Trade policy change for Asian orientation?," in J. Okamoto (ed.), *Whither Free Trade Agreements? Proliferation, Evaluation, and Multilateralization*. Chiba: Institute of Developing Economies, Japan External Trade Organization, pp. 216–51.

Okimoto, Daniel I. 1989. *Between MITI and the Market: Japanese Industrial Policy for High Technology*. Stanford, CA: Stanford University Press.

Oman, Charles. 1994. *Globalisation and Regionalisation: The Challenge for Developing Countries*. Paris: Development Centre of the Organisation for Economic Co-operation and Development.

Ostry, Sylvia. 1990. *Governments and Corporations in a Shrinking World: Trade and Innovation Policies in the United States, Europe and Japan*. New York: Council on Foreign Relations Press.

Panagariya, Arvind. 1999. "The regionalism debate: An overview," *World Economy*, 22 (4), 477–511.

2000. "Preferential trade liberalization: The traditional theory and new developments," *Journal of Economic Literature*, 38 (2), 287–331.

Panagariya, Arvind, and Ronald Findlay. 1996. "A political economy analysis of free trade areas and customs unions," in R. C. Feenstra, D. A. Irwin, and G. M. Grossman (eds.), *The Political Economy of Trade Reform: Essay in Honor of Jagdish Bhagwati*. Cambridge, MA: MIT Press, pp. 265–87.

Pastor, Manuel, and Carol Wise. 1994. "The origins and sustainability of Mexico free-trade policy," *International Organization*, 48 (3), 459–89.

Pempel, T. J. 2006. "The race to connect east Asia: An unending steeplechase," *Asian Economic Policy Review*, 1 (2), 239–54.

Pempel, T. J., and Keiichi Tsunekawa. 1979. "Corporatism without labor? The Japanese anomaly," in P. C. Schmitter and G. Lehmbruch (eds.), *Trends toward Corporatist Intermediation*. Beverly Hills and London: Sage Publications, pp. 231–70.

Peres Nuñez, Wilson. 1990. *Foreign Direct Investment and Industrial Development in Mexico*. Paris: Development Centre of the Organisation for Economic Co-operation and Development.

Pomfret, Richard. 2007. "Is regionalism an increasing feature of the world economy?" *World Economy*, 30 (6), 923–47.

Putnam, Robert D. 1988. "Diplomacy and domestic politics – the logic of two-level games," *International Organization*, 42 (3), 427–60.

Ramírez, Miguel D. 1989. *Mexico's Economic Crisis: Its Origins and Consequences*. New York: Praeger.

Ravenhill, John. 2000. "APEC adrift: Implications for economic regionalism in Asia and the Pacific," *Pacific Review*, 13 (2), 319–33.

2003. "The new bilateralism in the Asia Pacific," *Third World Quarterly*, 24 (2), 299–317.

2006. "The political economy of the new Asia-Pacific bilateralism: Benign, banal, or simply bad?" in V. K. Aggarwal and S. Urata (eds.), *Bilateral Trade Agreements in the Asia Pacific: Origins, Evolution, and Implications*. London: Routledge, pp. 27–49.

Richardson, J. David. 1991. *US Trade Policy in the 1980s: Turns – and Roads Not Taken*, NBER Working Paper 3725. Cambridge, MA: National Bureau of Economic Research.

Robert, Maryse. 2000. *Negotiating NAFTA: Explaining the Outcome in Culture, Textiles, Autos, and Pharmaceuticals*. Toronto: University of Toronto Press.

Rose-Ackerman, Susan, and Jennifer Tobin. 2005. *Foreign Direct Investment and the Business Environment in Developing Countries: The Impact of Bilateral Investment Treaties*, Yale Law & Economics Research Paper. New Haven, CT: Yale Law School.

Rozas Balbontín, Patricio. 2001. *La inversión europea en la industria energética de América Latina*. Santiago de Chile: Economic Commission for Latin America and the Caribbean.

Ruggie, John G. 1982. "International regimes, transactions, and change: Embedded liberalism in the postwar economic order," *International Organization*, 36 (2), 195–231.

1993. *Multilateralism Matters: The Theory and Praxis of an Institutional Form*. New York: Columbia University Press.

Russell, Joel. 1992. "Continental banking: Integration of financial services across the border," *Business Mexico*, 2 (5), 44–46.

Sáez, Raúl E. 2006. *Trade in Financial Services: The Case of Chile.* Washington, DC: World Bank, Finance, Private Sector and Infrastructure Department.

Sally, Razeen. 2007. "Thai trade policy: From non-discriminatory liberalisation to FTAs," *World Economy*, 30 (10), 1594–620.

Sally, Razeen, and Rahul Sen. 2005. "Whither trade policies in southeast Asia? The wider Asian and global context," *ASEAN Economic Bulletin*, 22 (1), 92–115.

Sanahuja, José Antonio. 2000. "Trade, politics, and democratization: The 1997 global agreement between the European Union and Mexico," *Journal of Interamerican Studies and World Affairs*, 42 (2), 35–64.

Santín Quiroz, Osvaldo. 2001. *The Political Economy of Mexico's Financial Reform.* Aldershot: Ashgate.

Sauvé, Pierre. 1995. "Assessing the General Agreement on Trade in Services – half-full or half-empty?" *Journal of World Trade*, 29 (4), 125–45.

2000. "Developing countries and the GATS 2000 round," *Journal of World Trade*, 34 (2), 85–92.

Schott, Jeffrey J. 1983. "The GATT Ministerial: A postmortem," *Challenge*, 26 (2), 40–45.

1989. *Free Trade Areas and US Trade Policy.* Washington, DC: Institute for International Economics.

Schulz, Heiner. 2006. "Foreign banks in Mexico: New conquistadors or agents of change?" unpublished manuscript, Department of Political Science, University of Pennsylvania.

Searight, Amy. 1999. "MITI and multilateralism: GATT and the evolution of Japanese trade policy," Ph.D. dissertation, Stanford University.

Secretaría General de la Comunidad Andina. 2003. *Analisis del tratado de libre comercio Chile–Estados Unidos.* Lima: Secretaría General de la Comunidad Andina.

Shadlen, Kenneth C. 2005. "Exchanging development for market access? Deep integration and industrial policy under multilateral and regional-bilateral trade agreements," *Review of International Political Economy*, 12 (5), 750–75.

Shimokawa, Koichi. 2004. "ASEAN: Developing a division of labour in a developing region," in J. Carillo, Y. Lung, and R. van Tulder (eds.), *Cars, Carriers of Regionalism?* Houndmills: Palgrave Macmillan, pp. 139–56.

Silverstein, Jeff. 1992. "Survival of a dinosaur: After NAFTA, will maquiladoras face extinction or prosperity?" *Business Mexico*, 2 (11), 4–6.

Simmons, Beth A., and Zachary Elkins. 2004. "The globalization of liberalization: Policy diffusion in the international political economy," *American Political Science Review*, 98 (1), 171–89.

Slaughter, Matthew J. 2000. "Production transfer within multinational enterprises and American wages," *Journal of International Economics*, 50, 449–72.

Solís, Mireya. 2003. "Japan's new regionalism: The politics of free trade with Mexico," *Journal of East Asian Studies*, 3 (3), 377–404.

2004. *Banking on Multinationals: Public Credit and the Export of Japanese Sunset Industries*. Stanford: Stanford University Press.

Solís, Mireya, and Saori N. Katada. 2007. "Competitive regionalism: strategic dynamics of FTA negotiation in Japanese trade diplomacy," paper presented at Annual Convention of the International Studies Association, Chicago, February 28–March 3.

Stephenson, Sherry M. 2000. "GATS and regional integration," in P. Sauvé and R. M. Stern (eds.), *GATS 2000: New Directions in Services Trade Liberalization*. Washington, DC: Brookings Institution, pp. 509–29.

2002. "Regional versus multilateral liberalization of services," *World Trade Review*, 1 (2), 187–209.

Stephenson, Sherry M., and Deunden Nikomborirak. 2002. "Regional liberalisation in services," in S. M. Stephenson and C. Findlay (eds.), *Services Trade Liberalisation and Facilitation*. Canberra: Asia Pacific Press, pp. 89–124.

Suominen, Kati. 2004. "Rules of origin in global commerce," Ph.D. dissertation, University of California, San Diego.

Suzuki, Sanae. 2003. "Linkage between Malaysia's FTA policy and ASEAN diplomacy," in J. Okamoto (ed.), *Whither Free Trade Agreements? Proliferation, Evolution, and Multilateralization*. Chiba: Institute of Developing Economies, Japan External Trade Organization, pp. 285–314.

Székely, Gabriel. 1991. "In search of globalization: Japanese manufacturing in Mexico and the United States," in G. Székely (ed.), *Manufacturing across Borders and Oceans: Japan, the United States, and Mexico*. La Jolla, CA: Center for US–Mexican Studies, University of California San Diego, pp. 1–24.

Szymanski, Marcela, and Michael E. Smith. 2005. "Coherence and conditionality in European foreign policy: Negotiating the EU–Mexico global agreements," *Journal of Common Market Studies*, 43 (1), 171–92.

Takeuchi, Junko. 1993. "Foreign direct investment in ASEAN by small- and medium-sized Japanese companies and its effects on local supporting industries," *RIM: Pacific Business and Industries*, 4 (22), 36–57.

Teichman, Judith A. 2001. *The Politics of Freeing Markets in Latin America: Chile, Argentina, and Mexico*. Chapel Hill, NC: University of North Carolina Press.

Terada, Takashi. 1998. "The origins of Japan's APEC policy: Foreign Minister Takeo Miki's Asia-Pacific policy and current implications," *Pacific Review*, 11 (3), 337–63.

Thompson, Aileen J. 1994. "Trade liberalization, comparative advantage, and scale economies – stock-market evidence from Canada," *Journal of International Economics*, 37 (1–2), 1–27.

Tiberghien, Yves. 2007. *Entrepreneurial States: Reforming Corporate Governance in France, Japan, and Korea*, Ithaca, NY: Cornell University Press.

Tirole, Jean. 1988. *The Theory of Industrial Organization*. Cambridge, MA: MIT Press.

Toral, Pablo. 2005. "The advantage of Spanish firms in Latin America, 1990–2002," in F. E. Martín and P. Toral (eds.), *Latin America's Quest for Globalization: The Role of Spanish Firms*. Aldershot: Ashgate, pp. 31–57.

Tōyō Keizai Shuppan. 2002. *Kaigai shinshutsu kigyō sōkan* [Overview of overseas activities of firms]. Tokyo: Tōyō Keizai Shinbunsha.

Ueda, Akira. 2001. "NAFTA to Mekishiko no makiradora kōgyō: Keizai tōgō to takoku sekikigyō [NAFTA and Mexico's maquiladora industry: Regional integration and multinational corporations]," *Dōshisha Shogaku*, 51 (3), 292–320.

United Nations Centre on Transnational Corporations (UNCTC). 1992. *Foreign Direct Investment and Industrial Restructuring in Mexico: Government Policy, Corporate Strategies and Regional Integration*. New York: United Nations.

United Nations Conference on Trade and Development (UNCTAD). 1998. *World Investment Report 1998: Trends and Determinants*. Geneva: United Nations Conference on Trade and Development.

2001. *Host Country Operational Measures*. Geneva: United Nations Conference on Trade and Development.

2004a. *World Investment Report: The Shift towards Services*. Geneva: United Nations Conference on Trade and Development.

2004b. *World Investment Directory: Latin America and the Caribbean 2004*. Geneva: United Nations Conference on Trade and Development.

2007. *Bilateral Investment Treaties 1995–2006: Trends in Investment Rulemaking*. Geneva: United Nations Conference on Trade and Development.

US Congress, House of Representatives, Committee on Ways and Means, Subcommittee on Trade. 1992. "North American Free Trade Agreement," Hearing before the Committee on Ways and Means, 102nd Congress, 2nd Session.

2001. "Free trade deals: Is the United States losing ground as its trading partners move ahead?" Hearing before the Committee on Ways and Means, 107th Congress, 1st Session.

2003. "Implementation of US bilateral free trade agreements with Chile and Singapore," Hearing before the Committee on Ways and Means, 108th Congress, 1st Session.

United States Department of Commerce. 1998. *Fourth Annual Report to Congress: Impact of the North American Free Trade Agreement on US Automotive Exports to Mexico (and on Imports from Mexico).* Washington, DC: Government Printing Office.

United States General Accounting Office (GAO). 2003. *International Trade: Mexico's Maquiladora Decline Affects US–Mexico Border Communities and Trade: Recovery Depends in Part on Mexico's Actions,* Report GAO-03-891. Washington, DC: GAO.

United States International Trade Commission (USITC). 1990. *Review of Trade and Investment Liberalization Measures by Mexico and Prospects for Future United States–Mexican Relations.* Washington, DC: US International Trade Commission.

1991a. *The Likely Impact on the United States of a Free Trade Agreement with Mexico.* Washington, DC: United States International Trade Commission.

1991b. *Rules of Origin Issues Related to NAFTA and the North American Automotive Industry: Report to the Committee on Ways and Means, US House of Representatives, on Investigation No. 332–314 under Section 332 of the Tariff Act of 1930.* Washington, DC: US International Trade Commission.

1993. *Potential Impact on the US Economy and Selected Industries of the North American Free-Trade Agreement: Report to the Committee on Ways and Means of the United States House of Representatives and the Committee on Finance of the United States Senate on Investigation No. 332–337 under Section 332 of the Tariff Act of 1930.* Washington, DC: US International Trade Commission.

Vandevelde, Kenneth J. 1993. "US bilateral investment treaties: The second wave," *Michigan Journal of International Law,* 14 (3), 621.

Vernon, Raymond. 1977. *Storm over the Multinationals: The Real Issues.* Cambridge, MA: Harvard University Press.

Viner, Jacob. 1950. *The Customs Union Issue.* New York: Carnegie Endowment for International Peace.

Wade, Robert. 1990. *Governing the Market: Economic Theory and the Role of Government in East Asian Industrialization.* Princeton: Princeton University Press.

Walter, Andrew. 2002. *The Political Economy of FDI Location: Why Don't Political Checks and Balances and Treaty Constraints Matter?* Singapore: Institute for Defence and Strategic Studies.

Walzer, Robert P. 1995. "Car makers speed up export production," *Business Mexico,* 5 (4): 32–34.

Warr, Peter G. 1989. "Export processing zones and trade policy," *Finance & Development,* 26 (2), 34.

1990. "Export processing zones," in C. Milner (ed.), *Export Promotion Strategies: Theory and Evidence from Developing Countries.* New York: New York University Press, pp. 130–61.

Weiss, Linda. 2000. "Developmental states in transition: Adapting, dismantling, innovating, not 'normalizing'," *Pacific Review*, 13 (1), 21–55.

Welch, John H., and William C. Gruben. 1993. "A brief modern history of the Mexican financial system," *Financial Industry Studies*, 1–11.

Whalley, John. 2008. "Recent regional agreements: Why so many, why so much variance in form, why coming so fast, and where are they headed?" *World Economy*, 31 (4), 517–32.

Williams, Barry. 2003. "Domestic and international determinants of bank profits: Foreign banks in Australia," *Journal of Banking & Finance*, 27 (6), 1185–210.

Wilson, Patricia Ann. 1992. *Exports and Local Development: Mexico's New Maquiladoras.* Austin: University of Texas Press.

Wise, Carol, and Isabel Studer (eds.). 2007. *Requiem or Revival? The Promise of North American Integration.* Washington, DC: Brookings Institution Press.

Womack, James P. 1991. "A positive sum solution: Free trade in the North American motor vehicle sector," in M.D. Baer and G.F. Erb (eds.), *Strategic Sectors in Mexican–US Free Trade.* Washington, DC: Center for Strategic and International Studies, pp. 31–65.

Wonnacott, Ronald J. 1993. *The NAFTA: Fortress North America?* Toronto: C. D. Howe Institute.

Woo-Cumings, Meredith (ed.). 1999. *The Developmental State.* Ithaca, NY: Cornell University Press.

Wunsch-Vincent, Sacha. 2003. "The digital trade agenda of the US: Parallel tracks of bilateral, regional and multilateral liberalization," *Aussenwirtschaft*, 58 (1), 7–46.

Xing, Yuqing, and Guanghua Wan. 2006. "Exchange rates and competition for FDI in Asia," *World Economy*, 29 (4), 419–34.

Yoshimatsu, Hidetaka. 1999. "The state, MNCs, and the car industry in ASEAN," *Journal of Contemporary Asia*, 29 (4), 495–516.

2002. "Preferences, interests, and regional integration: The development of the ASEAN industrial cooperation arrangement," *Review of International Political Economy*, 9 (1), 123–49.

2005. "Japan's *keidanren* and free trade agreements: Societal interests and trade policy," *Asian Survey*, 45 (2), 258–78.

Zeileis, Achim, Friedrich Leisch, Kurt Hornik, and Christian Kleiber. 2002. "Strucchange: An R package for testing for structural change in linear regression models," *Journal of Statistical Software*, 7 (2), 1–38.

Zlabudovsky, Jaime, and Sergio Gómez Lora. 2007. "Beyond the FTAA: Perspective for hemispheric integration," in C. Wise and I. Studer (eds.), *Requiem or Revival? The Promise of North American Integration*. Washington, DC: Brookings Institution Press, pp. 91–107.

Index

Italic numbers refer to index entries in illustrations.

102X104